YOU CAN TEACH YOUR CHILD INTELLIGENCE

YOU CAN TEACH YOUR CHILD INTELLIGENCE

by

DAVID LEWIS

SOUVENIR PRESS

ISBN 0 285 62479 2

Printed in Great Britain by
Bristol Typesetting Co. Ltd,
Barton Manor, St Philips, Bristol

This book is dedicated to the children of tomorrow in the hope that, through the wisdom of their parents, they may be wiser than the generation which bore them.

Acknowledgements

I would like to express my grateful thanks to my colleagues in the Mind Potential Study Group for their assistance and encouragement in developing this programme and especially to my associate James Greene for his valuable contribution to the research on which it is based. I would also like to express my thanks to the many parents and children in Europe and America who participated in the study during our initial trials of the programme; to the PreSchool Playgroups Association and the National Association for Gifted Children. The illustrations used in the assessments and elsewhere in this book are by Richard Armstrong.

Contents

Chapter One

GREATER INTELLIGENCE CAN BE TAUGHT

The idea that intelligence is something children learn and parents teach may strike you as surprising and rather remarkable. Certainly this is not the way we are used to thinking and talking about mental abilities. According to the popular view intellect is not an acquisition but a possession. The child's IQ level is regarded as being determined by a genetic blue-print which is passed down from the parents and cannot be significantly improved by experience. Put simply, the widely accepted notion has long been that each of us was born bright or dull and must stay that way from the womb to the tomb.

More than twenty years ago this assumption was being seriously challenged by many eminent psychologists, among them Professor John McVicker Hunt of Illinois University who wrote :

'It is reasonable to hope to find ways of raising the level of intellectual capacity in a majority of the population.'

Considered a vain and unlikely proposal at the time, this hope can now be realised by any parents sufficiently concerned and caring to want to increase their child's intellectual success.

In universities and research laboratories around the world, psychologists have developed many powerful new techniques for improving such crucial aspects of mental functioning as remembering and recalling; rapid learning; accurate understanding; creativity and problem solving efficiency. These detailed studies have not only provided us with exciting opportunities for giving every child a higher IQ, they have also confirmed what many perceptive parents and teachers must have long suspected. The old ideas about fixed levels of intelligence and predestined educational failure were disastrously wrong. Greater intelligence *can* be taught provided we know what lessons are needed and how, when and where they can best be given. It is to supply practical answers to these vital questions that this book has been written.

Perhaps the prospect of trying to teach your child intelligence seems a little daunting. If you have slightly unhappy memories of your own schooldays then the thought of trying to instruct your child in some formal lesson may bring to mind images of tedious periods behind a desk during which you vainly attempted to pay attention and stay awake! If this is how you see the role of the teacher and the fate of the pupil, I can well understand a reluctance to inflict such a dismal experience on either yourself or your unfortunate child.

But the sort of lessons and the kind of learning I shall be describing have nothing in common with classroom studies. Teaching your child greater intelligence may prove a challenge at times but it need never become a chore. There is nothing to be learned by heart, so you will not be asked to try your patience by attempting to spoon-feed facts into a bored and barely co-operative youngster. Nor are there any sessions of formal instruction. Much of the programme consists of procedures which can be conveyed in the form of a game which you play together, acquiring fresh insights and important understandings effortlessly and enjoyably as you do so. Much of the secret of success lies in developing new and more constructive attitudes towards intellectual growth and a better appreciation of what can go wrong and why.

You will not be teaching your child *what* to think but *how* to think. Not *what* to learn but *how* to learn. You are not going to make him remember things but give him the ability to remember things more effectively. You will not be setting problems for him to solve but showing him how to solve problems more easily. You will find out how to improve the poor scholar's attitude towards academic studies, to motivate the underachieving child and to enhance the self-image of the youngster who has come to doubt his own intellectual ability. These skills and attitudes form the very foundations on which a high IQ is constructed, yet you will never find them taught in schools and seldom even mentioned during debates about the nature of academic attainment.

Teaching this straightforward, relatively simple and entirely practical programme of IQ enhancement does not demand any special experience or qualifications on your part. Even if you were always bottom of the class you are still quite capable of helping your child to become top of the form. All that is necessary is a genuine desire to channel your love and ambitions for them into a programme designed to stimulate mental development, so that the tremendous intellectual potential that is the birthright of each youngster, and about which I shall have more to say in the next chapter, can be most fully realised. By following this approach you can become the active participant in your child's intellectual growth instead of being obliged, like the majority of parents, to be merely the passive and largely impotent spectators of this vital process. For the sorry truth is that, however concerned they may be about their children's progress, most mothers and fathers lack the knowledge to identify the underlying causes of school problems and never fully understand how best to help and guide the child towards academic success.

'Knowledge itself is power,' said Sir Francis Bacon.

Certainly where your child's mental development is concerned possessing the necessary knowledge does provide parents with the power to offer constructive assistance and practical advice during times of difficulty and to provide the most appropriate rewards and encouragement at moments of achievement.

For all these reasons and many more, which will become apparent as you start to put the procedures into pratice, teaching your child greater intelligence should prove a rewarding and enriching experience for the whole family. Above all I am sure you will find it fun. A pleasurable addition to the stimulation of parenthood that brings you closer to your child as you share their delight in discovery and enjoy the mutual fulfilment that comes from collaborating on an important and interesting endeavour.

Which Children Can Best Be Helped?

In my experience most of the procedures contained in this programme will prove of value to any child. Even youngsters who are doing well in school and show every sign of being clever and achieving can be guided more surely and successfully once their parents understand the true nature of intellectual ability. By appreciating the subtle interplay of psychological forces, that exert an influence over the expression of intelligence, it becomes possible to safeguard the child against set-backs, resolve many difficulties even before they occur and ensure that the desirably high level of academic performance is sustained.

There are, however, three types of children in special need of your help and guidance. Let me describe each of their problems in turn. Perhaps what I am going to say applies to your own family situation. If this is the case then a programme of intellectual enhancement is urgently needed and the procedures I describe in later chapters should prove of considerable benefit.

The Hare and Tortoise Child

There are certain youngsters who appear very intelligent before they start formal education and may continue to excel for the first couple of years in the classroom. Then, for no reason you can discover, they start to fall behind the others. Perhaps they started out with a lively curiosity and the ability to perform some intellectual task ahead of their brothers or sisters. Maybe they were early readers or showed an aptitude for numbers. You were confident they would take to school and do well. At first such optimism seemed fully justified. Then everything began to go wrong. The academic hare was transformed into a very unacademic tortoise. Marks began to drop. Their position in class declined. An early reader seemed to lose all interest in books. The child who enjoyed counting is baffled by the simplest sums. Lively interest is replaced by an apathetic rejection of anything connected with school subjects. Teachers express concern but seem unable to offer either an explanation or any solution to the problems. At the same time there may be psychological difficulties; bed wetting, nightmares, temper tantrums, periods of silent withdrawal, school refusal or truancy.

Given patience and understanding time may bring about an improvement in the situation. But time is usually just what the schoolchild does not have. Ground is easily lost and regained only with difficulty. The child who falls badly behind in the early years may never catch up. Unable to comprehend the basic skills needed for academic achievement. Unable to cope with the demands of more advanced subjects they obtain low marks, poor grades and discouraging reports. Failure becomes a firmly entrenched part of their school career. Parents, teachers and the child himself come to consider his abilities as meagre, his potential as negligible and his prospects as dismal. Under these circumstances it is hardly surprising that the youngster frequently develops a very negative attitude towards the value of academic studies. He will lose confidence, motivation declines and he may start to become either very apathetic or seriously disruptive. Reasons why children who fail in class should adopt these tactics will be explained in a moment.

With practical help and a proper understanding of what has gone wrong and how it can best be put right, an improvement in performance is possible at almost any time during the first twelve years of life. What needs to be done and the best way of bringing about these changes will be described in a later chapter. But rest assured that the set-backs need only be temporary. The hare did not turn into a tortoise from choice and the transformation need not prove permanent.

The False Starter

In my book *How To Be A Gifted Parent* (Souvenir Press) which dealt with the first five years of life, I commented that :

'Parents do not create giftedness in their children. That is neither possible nor necessary. Just as a seed contains all that is needed for successful growth, and requires only a rich soil and the right conditions in order to flourish, so does each infant arrive with a promise of genius just waiting to grow.'

I explained that youngsters who failed in school often did so because of what happened to them in the first sixty months of life. It is during this time that the infant can acquire habits of thinking and responding which drastically inhibit their inborn potential. Such failure was not usually due to deliberate neglect or disinterest on the part of their parents but arose from an unfortunate mismatch between the true needs of the child and the outlook of the adults.

Children who begin school with this sort of handicap are *false starters*. They have embarked on full-time education with important mental concepts still unlearned. Because of this deficit they may appear slow or even stupid to their teachers. The danger is that unless this perception is changed for the better, these youngsters may soon develop the kind of negative attitudes described above.

But the situation is not irreversible. By making use of the procedures described in this book the false starter can be helped to surge ahead again.

The Middle Classer

I use this term to describe a classroom strategy rather than the social standing of the child. Middle classing is an approach to school work adopted by youngsters whose ambition is to do neither especially badly nor particularly well. It is a tactic chosen in order to keep anxiety to a minimum and indicates a poorly motivated, underconfident child with a low opinion of his own abilities.

Why should children decide to stay around the middle of the class? We can best understand the value of such a strategy by looking at the sort of rewards and penalties likely to be involved. First take the youngster who is always at the bottom of the class. He is likely to be criticised by parents and teachers, to be looked down on by some of his classmates and, generally, to have a negative self-image when it comes to academic studies. The middle classer wants to avoid these problems, but sees a position close to the top of the form as presenting an equal number of difficulties. Such high standing in class brings with it considerable pressures and responsibilities. A poor exam result or a low mark leads to critical comments by adults. There is the constant strain of maintaining a high level of performance with humiliation the price paid for any defeat. I am not saying this is necessarily an accurate perception, but it is one believed to be true by the middle classer. They decide, although I am not suggesting that it is a conscious choice, that the maximum rewards and the minimum risk can be obtained by staying around the middle of the class. This benefits them in two ways. If they enjoy a success, adults are quick to praise them and acknowledge their achievements, usually in the hope that the effort will be sustained. Bright children are simply expected to do well and their attainments are often ignored although their failures are seldom overlooked. Any set-backs for the middle classer, however, tend to look less serious. The child who has come top of the form consistently would probably see a drop back to fourth place as amounting to a disastrous humiliation. But the child normally twelfth in a class of thirty appears to have done far less badly if he drops the same number of places to fifteenth position. This type of approach is called a *minimax* strategy because it serves to maximise gains while minimising losses. But while it may give the anxious child a sense of security it can never offer them any chance of real achievement. In order to attain better results such children must be helped to develop feelings of greater competence and self-confidence, provided with stronger motivation and given the skills needed to tackle school work more effectively. How such a desirable state of affairs may be brought about will be explained in later chapters.

Why You Should Teach Greater Intelligence
So far I have talked about greater intelligence mainly in terms of such academic attainments as higher marks and better examination grades. This is certainly a topic of major interest and concern to most parents and undeniably an important expression of intellectual ability. But IQ cannot be equated solely with classroom accomplishment and I would certainly not suggest that a child who fails in school is, by definition, stupid. Many clever youngsters do extremely poorly in class for reasons which have nothing to do with their levels of intelligence.

If greater intelligence meant no more than a few extra marks in an end-of-term test one might fairly question whether it was worth an investment of time, effort and energy. If the only outcome of a higher IQ was a smart alec youngster who, to paraphrase Oscar Wilde's famous definition of a cynic, knew the answer to everything and the truth about nothing, it would hardly rate as a goal worth working for. But intellectual ability is far more valuable than this. Indeed academic attainment should be seen as the by-product, rather than the end-product, of a greater than average intellect.

Intelligence gives the child choice. It provides a passport to further opportunity. The key that unlocks doors to new and more rewarding experiences. The bright youngster can, to a far greater extent than the dull child, exert control over his own destiny. He has the privilege of deciding, with more confidence and certainty than the unintelligent child, where he would like to go in life and how best to get there. We might liken the abilities of such a child to a millionaire's wealth. The rich man can choose to live in poverty if this seems to provide a more fulfilling life-style. But the pauper can never opt for a life of luxury. Circumstance and not personal preference dictates his prospects.

Similarly, a highly intelligent student might come to the conclusion that academic work was a waste of time. He might choose to fail examinations, leave school at the earliest possible moment and follow a mentally undemanding career. But that decision, however disappointing and inexplicable it appears to his parents, was one he could *choose* to make. Life did not force him to follow that particular road. He was a volunteer and not a conscript into the army of the unqualified.

The child whose mental development has been so restricted that learning and studying are beyond his abilities has no such options available. He will probably fail examinations even though he tries hard to pass them, be obliged to leave school although his desire is to stay on, and find himself forced into a routine occupation no matter what his ambitions might have been.

By teaching your child greater intelligence you are, essentially, offering him greater choice. You are providing the chance to exert control over his own destiny so that he can make important decisions and influence, to a far greater extent, the onrush of events.

It is this ability to exert such control over their lives which, some psychologists believe, explains the greater emotional stability and better physical health enjoyed by men and women of above average IQ's. For, contrary to popular belief, all the evidence indicates that gifted individuals are not unbalanced and miserable loners but are happier and better adjusted than most people. Such an assertion is supported by several important studies, but I will describe just one of them. One which is among the most detailed long term psychological investigations ever attempted. It is a piece of research which has done a great deal to demolish that widely held notion about genius and insanity being two sides of the same coin.

In 1921 an American psychologist named Lewis Terman embarked on a mammoth task. He decided to follow the lives and fortunes of 1,500 Californian boys and girls whose scores on IQ tests placed them among the top two per cent of the population. Professor Terman, who had pioneered intelligence testing in the United States, wanted to find out if early classroom promise predicted success in adult life. His findings were impressive.

More than 80 per cent of the children studied went on to achieve considerable eminence in their chosen professions and careers. Even by their early twenties this, relatively small, group had published more than ninety books and filed patents on a hundred new inventions. They had obtained jobs with higher status and pay than the average college graduates and were well regarded by their employers. Far from their high IQ's making them unhappy or unstable they were found to be better adjusted than many of their colleagues. They were socially successful as well, popular both at work and in their communities. In part their greater than average mental and physical health could be attributed to the high standards of living made possible by high salaried occupations. But that was not the whole explanation. An extremely significant factor was undoubtedly their ability to exercise a considerable amount of control over what happened to them in life. They were, to a far greater extent than most, masters of their own fate.

The need to exert such control is a powerful, basic human instinct which affects children no less than adults. Caught up in events which we feel unable to direct or influence we quickly become confused, disorientated and afraid. One of the first techniques used in brain washing is to induce this sense of helplessness in the victim. To make them believe that nothing they can say or do will have the slightest effect on the things which happen. Confronted by such a total loss of control the individual often breaks down and becomes receptive to any ideas one wishes to implant. The emotional responses to helplessness range from apathy and bewilderment to great fear or unpredictable aggression. Such behaviour, in a less intense form, is often found in children whose intellectual skills are unequal to the demands of school work. It is behaviour which reflects an inner sense of anxiety or frustration over an inability to influence events. An inappropriate attempt to control a situation, perhaps by changing it through disruptive, and even violent, conduct. Given a less assertive temperament another child may respond to the same emotional crisis by withdrawing himself from it entirely. He either withdraws in a physical sense, through school refusal or truancy, or else mentally by showing a minimum amount of interest in anything that happens and resisting all attempts to help him. Such children can be assisted towards a more productive attitude, and ways in which this may be achieved will be discussed in later chapters. But the usual methods, of punishment or bribery, seldom if ever produce the desired results and can make matters a good deal worse.

Let me illustrate what happens by drawing on the case histories of two eleven-year-old boys who seem destined for very different academic futures. Mark is bright and Billy is dull. Their behaviours in the classroom seem to have little in common, yet each can be seen to contain certain tactics aimed at controlling events.

Mark works quickly, grasps new ideas easily and tackles even unfamiliar problems with confidence. He influences what happens to him by using social and intellectual skills. Because he can achieve what he wants, in most cases, by means of intelligent responses he has no cause to resort to bullying, coercion or disruptive conduct.

Billy, lacking the other boy's mental ability, has dismissed school work as worthless and pays little attention in class. Inarticulate and deficient in social skills he bullies his companions in order to get his own way, behaviour which gives him short term gains but leads to his increasing isolation and unpopularity. He is disliked by the teachers as well for, unable to attract attention by achievement, he constantly disrupts lessons. This not only allows him to become the centre of interest but also brings to an end the frustration and misery of having to tackle questions to which he can find no solutions and problems for which he is quite incapable of supplying any answers. Not surprisingly Billy is often in trouble and frequently gets punished, usually by having to write out lines or stand outside the classroom door. These penalties do nothing to change his behaviour and simply waste precious time which should have been used to advance his studies. One can sympathise with the teachers for wanting to remove such an unhelpful student from their classes and easily see why Billy receives little help or encouragement from the staff. Yet without such help and encouragement his conduct can only get worse and his performance decline still further.

So I am not suggesting that children should be taught greater intelligence solely, or even primarily, as a means of achieving academic goals however important or desirable these appear at the time. No less valuable, and in the long term just as helpful, is the opportunity such teaching provides for increasing their range of options in life. By doing so you will enable them to confront challenges more capably and confidently so that decisions are realistic and judgements as rational and productive as possible. Your ultimate aim should be to give a child the greatest opportunity to become a stable, happy and integrated member of society. The possessor of that essential intellectual freedom on which true fulfilment depends – the ability to think and to act for oneself.

Perhaps you feel that while what I have suggested is doubtless desirable it is unreasonable to propose that such glittering prizes lie within the grasp of every youngster. You may believe that the destiny of children like Mark and Billy has been written even before they are born. Laid down, if not in their stars exactly, then on the genetic blue-print which I mentioned at the start of this chapter.

If these are your views then you must have shaken your head in disbelief when I talked about realising each child's inborn potential. All very well for the bright youngsters, you may have thought, but what about the naturally stupid child? How can he, or she, ever be helped towards greater intelligence? Surely, you will protest, it is a matter of irrefutable fact that considerable differences in intellectual ability exist. To assert otherwise runs contrary to commonsense and common observation. One need only go into any classroom in the country to see the gulf which exists between the clever student and the dim one.

Because the notions of innate and largely fixed levels of intelligence are so widely held and firmly entrenched, I have felt it desirable to consider them in some detail. This discussion occupies the next chapter and, if you are uninterested in what has become known as the nature v. nurture debate and only want to get started on the practical business of teaching your child greater intelligence, I suggest you skip to Chapter Three. If you still doubt that such teaching can really prove possible but would like to be convinced, please read on. We are going to explore one of the most damaging and invidious pieces of twentieth-century fiction. The myth of inborn inadequacy.

Chapter Two

YOUR GIFTED CHILD

Your child was born gifted. Gifted by nature with a brain of virtually unlimited intellectual potential. Endowed by millions of years of evolution with the ability to grasp complex ideas readily and solve intricate problems effortlessly. Such is the birthright of brilliance enjoyed by all infants, except those unfortunate few born with chronic brain damage. And I should add that even these children generally have a far greater capacity for intellectual growth and a far higher mental potential than most people are prepared to accept or allow them the chance to prove.

Whether or not that tremendous innate promise is fully realised, however, depends on the lessons learned during childhood. Intelligence is a skill that must be taught since children discover by experience not only *what* to think but *how* to think. It is the parents who have to do most of that essential teaching.

There is no way this process can be switched off or responsibility for providing the vital lessons avoided. Your child's busy brain acquires knowledge, and the ability to make use of that knowledge, during every waking moment and probably during sleep as well. He learns not only from what adults say and do but from all those things they refrain from saying and doing; from attitudes they keep to themselves just as much as from those openly expressed. The infant learns from indifference as well as affection. He learns when rejected as well as when deeply loved. He learns from neglect and he learns from devotion. To be sure *what* is learned by these kinds of upbringing will be very different, but the lessons are mastered no less efficiently.

The choice is never whether or not parents are willing to teach intelligence. It is only one between whether they do so efficiently or ineffectively. The more helpful and constructive the teaching the greater the likelihood that the child's inborn abilities will find expression in the thoughts he thinks, the knowledge he gains and the things he does. The more fully will he be able to make use of that astonishing biological thinking machine that is the human brain. The greater will be his intelligence.

By stating my position in these terms, I am expressing what has become known as the *nurturist* view of mental development. The belief that a child's ultimate level of intellect is a consequence of experience. The outcome of a powerful and continuous interaction with the environment.

I have already sketched in the opposing view, that of the *naturists*, which argues that genetically determined variations in IQ are the result of inheritance and that the differences in ability we see cannot be explained by environmental factors. Those who favour this approach would accept that intelligence can be diminished as a result of deprivation, for example starvation during the early months of infancy profoundly affects brain function, but refute the suggestion that it can be significantly enhanced.

It is not hard to see why their proposals should have found widespread popular support, for they offer much to parents, teachers, politicians, psychologists and even the children themselves.

When things go wrong our first response is to find somebody who can be blamed. We are never happy with the notion of pure chance and the unavoidable accident, preferring to attribute even a lightning strike to an act of God rather than a purely random natural event. The need for a scapegoat when things start to go wrong is well known to social psychologists who have noted, among other examples of scapegoating, that lynchings in the Southern states of America always increased during the years when there was a failure of the cotton crop; that racial prejudice against minorities becomes more open at times of economic crisis and that we would sooner regard crime as a reflection of individual wickedness rather than an expression of social inequity.

Where intellectual failure is concerned, and few could deny that it exists on a terrifying scale in the Western world, the search for scapegoats tends to take us round in a frustrating circle all the while we look for environmental causes. Parents may blame teachers, who say it is the fault of the pupils, or the politicians, or parents. This circular recrimination can be neatly side-stepped if a naturist argument is accepted. Then it becomes possible to attribute the blame to somebody, or rather something, outside ourselves. The villain, it transpires, was not really man but unfeeling mother nature. Mental ability now becomes a matter of racial roulette. A lucky pull on the chromosomal fruit machine and out tumbles intellect to give the child a brain as bright as his prospects. Another spin and this time the biological tumblers register a lemon. But there is little one can do in such a case except hope for better luck on the next occasion.

Students who fail in school can draw some comfort from the idea that their failure was predestined. Youngsters who spend their time at the bottom of the class often tell me:

'I do my best. I try as hard as I can. It isn't my fault I was born stupid.'

Parents and teachers can take a similar line. Intellectual inadequacy is not the fault of child rearing methods, professional skills or the system which society has obliged them to operate. Echoing the sentiments of many in the profession, one headmaster commented:

'We do the best with the raw materials provided. You know what they say about making a silk purse out of a sow's ear. That would be a cinch, believe me, compared with the task of teaching some of the pupils we are landed with.'

Teachers invariably fall back on this line of argument. They use it not only on parents but with their pupils as well, being only too eager to assure them that poor marks and low grades reflect the students' stupidity rather than their own incompetence. Here are a few comments made to pupils which, in my experience, find daily expression in almost every classroom in the world:

'If we could open your head we should not find any brain but only a lump of white fat.'

'Your brain is addled.'

'You are too stupid ever to amount to anything.'

The children so dismissed as born to fail were the English writer G. K. Chesterton, the American inventor Thomas Edison, and the German born physicist Albert Einstein.

Politicians frequently favour the naturist viewpoint since it provides an 'explanation' for the failure of whole social and ethnic groups that absolves them from any charges of prejudice or their own failure to provide equality of opportunity. No poli-

tical party or society can be expected to control the consequences
of inferior genes.

Finally I must confess that psychologists often have a tremendous intellectual investment – and sometimes a fairly substantial commercial interest as well – in advancing the naturist
argument. Once you have established your academic reputation
by advocating this viewpoint it becomes difficult, if not impossible, to change your mind without seriously harming your
professional standing. As for the financial incentive, nobody
would deny that IQ testing – whose whole basis is the concept
of an inborn and more or less stable intellectual ability – is other
than a major psychological growth industry. It provides considerable profit to those engaged in the construction, distribution and
administration of such assessments.

I must make it perfectly clear that I am not attributing
intellectual dishonesty to the many, very eminent, men and
women who argue on the naturist side of the debate. I am certainly not implying that they have been persuaded of the soundness of their views out of financial considerations. What I am
suggesting is that the argument is sustained by powerful pressures
which are not always either recognised or acknowledged by those
who propagate the myth of inborn inadequacy.

Let me give you an example of how these subtle pressures can
operate. One of the foremost supporters of the naturist proposals
was Sir Cyril Burt, a British psychologist who, until fairly
recently, enjoyed a considerable reputation in his profession.
Then it was revealed that some of the vital statistics used to
support his arguments had been invented. Not only that, but he
also appears to have invented a research assistant supposedly
responsible for gathering the data concerned !

When it was no longer possible to deny the truth of these
allegations – the first tactic his defenders resorted to – it was
then maintained that the data were not crucial and their fictitious
nature did nothing to weaken the naturist's position. You may
feel this is a classic example of having your intellectual cake and
eating it ! But, in my view, the main interest lies not in the fact
that a respected researcher should have faked some figures, but
what the justifications used tell us about the pressures within the
debate.

Had Cyril Burt been alive to answer his critics, I feel certain he would have adopted an approach similar to that used by his supporters. The argument that even though the statistics were false the picture they painted remained true :

'Had I really gathered the data,' he might have contended, 'they were bound to be more or less identical with those pulled out of the air.'

If you start from the position that you are right then anything which follows from that line of argument must, logically, also be correct. Similarly if you reject an opposing argument then any evidence in support of it has to be misleading, misguided or mistaken.

Lest it be thought that this is exactly what I am doing, where the naturist's theory is concerned, let me point out one important difference. You do not have to *believe* what I am saying. You can put it to the test. Karl Popper, the philosopher of science, has proposed a famous qualification for a true theory. It must, he says, be capable of falsification. This is necessary because, in science, one can never actually prove anything to be correct. Everything is a matter of probability. There is no certainty. Even if a theory is right a million times in a row the chance must exist that, on the millionth and first trial, it will be disproved. Unless this is a possibility you have not got a theory.

The proposal that greater intelligence can be taught is extremely easy to disprove. You just use the procedures and see what happens. The techniques either work or they do not work. To put the matter in very unscientific terms you only have to suck it and see !

Am I claiming, then, that biology plays no part in determining a child's level of intelligence? That the differences we see have no genetic basis? Without seeming to have it both ways, I must answer with a firm yes and no !

You see, I have no doubt that there are theoretical upper limits to mental ability, that there may exist considerable individual differences between these upper limits, and that these limits are set by the genetic blue-print. All behaviour is an expression of biological function and the capacity to perform any intellectual task at the highest levels of accomplishment must owe much to innately decided factors. While I am confident, for example, that any normal youngster could become a competent mathematician, an accomplished musician or a talented artist,

I am not claiming that within every cradle there lies a potential Einstein, Mozart or Monet.

But, that having been said, I would also argue that these biologically established variations have little practical significance because they are never, normally, reached. You might own a hundred acres of land while I possessed no more than twenty. But since we are never going to cultivate more than ten of them our very different holdings are unimportant.

All the intellectual skills necessary to succeed in education up to and even beyond graduate level are so relatively trivial – compared with the potential of every healthy human brain – that we should all be able to cope with the challenges almost effortlessly.

If you doubt this I invite you to consider the demands the developing brain must meet and the accomplishments which have to be won during the earliest weeks and months of life. Attainments without which the infant could not function at all.

To the newborn infant no distinction exists beween himself and other people. For some time after birth his mother remains the extension of his own body she was during the nine months within her womb. The discovery that he has a unique identity, although it seems obvious to us, is actually an intellect al concept in its own way as brilliant as anything we subsequently achieve. The child learns to control bodily functions, to regulate emotions so that they can be used appropriately rather than indiscriminately, to co-ordinate hand and eye movements, to understand the relationship between cause and effect.

Almost from the first a baby is precociously sociable, a fact which far too few parents appreciate. He wants and needs contact with other human beings. Given that opportunity he quickly realises that meaningful communication is possible and soon develops a large vocabulary of silent speech signals in order to make his wishes known and his feelings clear. Within a short space of time body language is augmented by the spoken word. The acquisition of verbal ability must rank as one of the most difficult tasks we ever have to accomplish – just think how hard it can be for an adult to master Chinese or Russian for instance – yet the infant brain achieves perfect fluency without apparent effort. It makes no difference which language the child is expected to become proficient in, nor is it much of a problem for him to master several at the same time provided there is sufficient exposure and adequate practice.

Even more complex, however, is the far earlier ability the child must perfect of making visual, auditory and tactile sense of the world about him. We are born only with the potential to attain such understanding, not with any ready made mental image of the way our surroundings look, sound and feel. All must be painstakingly learned as the brain constructs, from literally billions of nerve signals, a world of images and noises, touch and tastes. Consider, for example, the art of seeing. We take this for granted and find it almost impossible to imagine how one could be sighted and yet not make visual identification of objects in the environment. But this is just what happens to some adults who, blind from birth, have their eyesight restored by an operation. Their fully developed brains may never be capable of making sense of the signals coming from their eyes. Their world remains incomplete and inaccurate. A bizarre reflection in a mentally distorting mirror. A failure of the brain to learn rather than of the eyes to observe. The mind of the child can cope with the enormous challenge of imposing an order on the tumult of electrical signals from the retinas, those sensitive layers at the back of the eyes which transform light energy into nerve impulses. From the babble of information the infant's brain rapidly discovers how to construct a world of shapes and colours that is both consistent and meaningful.

It has been estimated that at no time during our lives do we make use of more than 20 per cent of the brain's total power. That there is always ample thinking capacity in reserve.

When one considers just how far mankind has advanced over the past few thousand years, such a claim seems both realistic and justified. In a space of time that counts for no more than a blink in the eye of evolution, the human race has moved from the era of cave dwelling to the age of Concorde. From being the users of primitive tools, fashioned from stone or crudely cast in metal, we have become the designers of high technology. The creators of computers whose logical ability and thinking potential is, in some ways, greater than our own.

Because all these changes have occurred in a relatively brief period of history there cannot have been significant genetic changes in the brain's structure or function. The minds inside the skulls of twentieth-century men cannot be different from those possessed by our Bronze Age forbears, yet there can be no comparison in terms of capability.

The brain is sometimes likened to a computer, a somewhat unflattering analogy since the human mind is far more sophisticated than any electronic device likely to be developed in the foreseeable future. But, staying with this comparison for a moment, let us consider the child's brain as a type of problem solving machine. We can then think about the factors likely to influence its efficiency and enhance its performance.

Clearly the machine's effectiveness will depend on the soundness of the design and construction and the usefulness of the program employed. By that I mean the way in which it is instructed to process information, make logical connections and identify the essential aspects of any task. Nature provides the design and construction. Short of major surgery or the implantation of some electronic gadget – both of which may become all too possible in the next few decades – we can do little to change either. But the program does lie entirely within our powers to manipulate since it is written by all that happens to the child in the first months and years of life. In altering the program we do, in effect, change important aspects of the brain's construction since, unlike the integrated circuits which make up a computer's thinking circuits, the human biocomputer is not 'hard wired' at birth. It develops interconnections between various parts as a result of learning. It has what biologists term *plasticity*, that is the capacity to respond to external circumstances in an adaptive and flexible manner. In this way the brain is able to match the demands of its environment and so ensure the best chance of survival. The brain of a child born and raised in a jungle will have a rather different program to that of a city born youngster because their needs are so different. As Dr William Mason of the Delta Regional Primate Research Centre in Louisiana has commented :

'Intelligence . . . is a way of bringing about a better fit between the vital needs of the organism and the inescapable requirements that the environment imposes.'

In other words, the brain gets more efficient the more efficiently it is used. The ability to solve problems correctly increases with every correctly solved problem. Memory works better the harder it is made to work. If this were not the case we would still be living in caves, hunting in tribes and having to eke out a meagre existence from bodily labour rather than enjoying the benefits of our superior intellects.

The horizons of the child's mind are almost limitless. It is life which raises barriers by restricting understanding, creating uncertainty and inhibiting creativity. It is experience and not genetic inheritance that constructs the mental prison behind whose bars the brain must serve out a life sentence. Most nurturists would argue that children start out stupid and learn to become bright. That their minds begin as a *blank tablet* on which the world writes their destiny. My view is quite the reverse. Infants start out highly intelligent and acquire the habit of stupidity. Dullness is a learned response. To teach greater intelligence we need only break down those barriers, abolish the restricting perceptions and equip the mind with the skills needed to handle particular kinds of problems.

To claim that the upper limits of human intellect are determined biologically, is reasonable and almost certainly correct. But to suggest that a child fails a third grade maths test or is incapable of taking an examination at the age of fifteen because the upper limits of intellect have been reached is absurd. Yet this is the explanation normally offered for educational failure. A siren song of inborn inadequacy, it has seduced generations of parents into accepting the notion of unavoidable intellectual incompetence and condemned generations of children to second class academic citizenship. It has resulted in the wholesale sacrifice of early promise to a self-fulfilling prophecy of mental imperfection and blinded us to the brain's true potential.

In many ways even more harmful has been the inevitable consequence that since intelligence is not seen as something that has to be learned no attempts have ever been made to teach it. At school children receive instruction in a wide range of subjects that demand the use of their minds yet never get any training in how best those minds should be used. Instead of teaching intelligence we go fishing for it, using IQ tests and examinations as the nets with which to trawl classrooms in search of academic ability. Those who do well are rewarded with the opportunity to do even better in the future. Those who do badly are frequently abandoned to their own devices. Left to cope as best they can in a world which is willing to offer them a certain amount of sympathy but does not believe it can provide them with any practical assistance.

If you doubt that this is a fair picture of what goes on in the classroom I suggest you look back on your own school experiences. You were certainly given many problems to solve, but did anybody ever teach you the best way of solving problems in general? I am sure you had to memorise many facts and figures, but I am equally certain nobody ever showed you the most effective ways of remembering and recalling information. I think it equally unlikely you were helped to feel motivated to learn more enthusiastically or given assistance in building greater self-confidence in yourself as a student.

Yet all these are essential if the brain is to be used most effectively :

In order to think successfully the child needs lessons in thinking.

In order to use his memory properly he needs lessons in remembering.

In order to solve problems efficiently he needs to learn problem solving skills.

In order to use his brain creatively he needs practice in intellectual creativity.

To do any of these things the child must be both motivated and sufficiently self-confident.

When we look at an intelligent youngster solving a problem effortlessly or involved in some highly original creative activity, we are not observing the expression of a single, inborn mental skill as is so often believed. What we actually see is the logical outcome of a complex interaction between certain attitudes, perceptions and abilities. All the components of this dynamic mosaic are essential to intellectual achievement. All have been acquired by experience.

Chapter Three

FOUR KEYS THAT UNLOCK INTELLIGENCE

In the first chapter, I talked about eleven-year-old Billy, the little boy who seems unlikely ever to shine in class or gain much from his years of full-time education. Most adults, when they talk to him about his school work, look at his hopelessly inadequate attempts to complete form projects or examine his grade averages, come to the conclusion that he is really a fairly unintelligent child. Everything about Billy seems to confirm this belief. His slow learning and inability to remember much of what has been taught. His meaningless answers to questions. His messy, written work and wildly inaccurate mathematical calculations.

But let's look at Billy a little more carefully. Listen to him tell us how he views studying and sees himself as a student. His teachers believe the boy is stupid. Billy thinks much the same of them and the lessons they try to teach him. He finds the subjects not only baffling but intensely boring. He has no real interest in what happens in the classroom, regarding it more as an arena in which he can display his disruptive talents than a place of learning. He admits he is careless and seldom gets a right answer, but blames those who teach him for not making his time at school more interesting.

All this might seem a more or less inevitable response from a child who cannot cope with the demands of education. The search for a scapegoat to explain away his own failings. But Billy acknowledges his own lack of ability even while he dismisses with contempt the subjects in which he fails. He despises himself, talks disparagingly about his intellect and mocks his memory.

Billy's attitude, towards school and towards himself, is extremely negative. He sees little good in either education or his intellect. His self-image is that of a child born to fail in school, who must grab his successes as and when he can. By attracting attention as the classroom clown. By ruining the lessons he so dislikes. By frustrating the attempts to teach him by adults he has come to see as his natural enemies. He has very little motivation to try and do better, since experience has taught him such efforts are almost always doomed to failure.

Because he pays such little attention and misses so many lessons, either through truancy or being sent out of the room, his ability to handle problems of any kind is extremely poor. He has never mastered basic strategies needed to tackle them effectively and is made very anxious by anything new or unfamiliar.

Billy is, in many ways, an extreme example of the failing child. But the difficulties he experiences can be found, in a less intense form, in the vast majority of children.

The factors which we have examined in his own school career – those of attitude, self-image, motivation and problem solving skills – are fundamental to the expression of intelligence. They are the key aspects of behaviour which can unlock the intellect or imprison it for ever. In order to teach your child to think more efficiently it is essential to understand how these factors arise, how they interact with each other and how they can be enhanced. We will start by examining each in a little more detail to see what is involved and how it exerts an influence on all the others.

* *Attitudes* : These include those of both the parents and the children. How adults and youngsters look on their ability, what the child feels about school work, academic ambitions and the value of classroom achievement. Attitudes are built up from experience. The child holds those which appear to be confirmed by what happens to him and discards any that seem to be disproved by events. He acquires attitudes by watching himself in action, observing how parents and teachers regard him and by comparing his successes and failures with those of his companions.

* *Self-image* : Attitudes affect and are affected by the way the child sees himself, the manner in which he defines his role in the world. Self-image arises from past performance and the child's predictions of further setbacks or achievements. It both influences and is profoundly influenced by . . .

* *Motivation* : Which can be defined as the energy a child invests in any activity, especially novel and unfamiliar tasks where the outcome is uncertain. Motivation plays a major part

in determining how effectively such tasks are tackled and how long the child is going to persevere in the face of setbacks and frustrations. Motivation stems from the child's desire to meet certain goals in life. It is determined by attitudes, self-image and his level of competence with . . .

* *Problem handling skills:* The final factor which makes up intelligent behaviour, this probably comes closest to what people usually believe intelligence is all about. Problem handling consists of both a mechanical and a creative ability. A child well versed in one is not, necessarily, going to be equally good at the other. Yet, for the fullest expression of mental abilities, it is essential to develop a high level of ability in both. The mechanical aspects of problem solving consist of applying the right sort of strategy to a particular question and then using it correctly in order to produce a desired answer. The more strategies the child learns and the better he is able to use them the greater the chance of coming up with the right solution in any problem where the question is clearly stated.

But intelligence consists of more than just being able to find the correct answer to a given problem. If that were not the case, then a cheap pocket calculator would have an IQ equal to the finest mathematicians. The difference between mechanical problem solving and true intelligence lies in the ability to realise that a problem exists even when none has been directly stated. It is primarily the ability to pose interesting questions, in situations where other people saw nothing out of the ordinary, that distinguishes the world's greatest thinkers. It is through creative problem seeing, just as much as by the finding of answers, that the giant leaps forward in human knowledge have been achieved.

My own definition of intelligence is, in fact, *the ability to see and solve problems.* Neither is of any real value without the other, although schools focus almost all their energies on trying to improve the child's *problem solving* skills, often to the detriment of creative *problem seeing.* I shall be showing you how to enhance both abilities to provide your child with greater intelligence in the fullest meaning of the word.

Problem handling skills are influenced by attitudes, self-image and motivation. How well the child deals with problems will affect all the other factors in turn. We can sum up the interplay of forces like this:

ATTITUDES

PROBLEM HANDLING
SKILLS

MOTIVATION

SELF–IMAGE

As you can see, there is a constant interaction between all four factors, with problem handling skills occupying the centre of the stage. The ability which a child shows in any intellectually demanding situation is the dynamic expression of this inter-relationship. Each connects with the other, influences it and is influenced in turn. One cannot alter any of the factors without also bringing about changes in all the rest.

This is a fact which few parents or teachers appear to appreciate. They try to help the underachieving child by improving one aspect of their performance without considering the likely effects on the other factors involved. For instance, they may seek to enhance motivation through bribes or encouragement, to improve attitudes in much the same way, or to help the child develop better problem handling skills through extra instruction.

Let me give you a typical example of what happens. A child is doing badly at some subject. I will use the instance of failure in mathematics since this is such a frequent source of difficulty. Parents and teachers decide to give him additional coaching after school. Schools maths consists almost entirely of learning how to apply the right problem solving strategies so this is the area on which the teacher will concentrate. The effects of extra work on attitudes, self-image and motivation are not considered by this approach which may fail to help the child as a result. Improvement in performance can only occur if the child's negative attitude towards maths is transformed, his low self-image enhanced and motivation increased. This *might* just happen simply by focusing on the problem solving factor but in my experience is not very likely to do so. The situation is made more complicated by the fact that adults bring to the task of helping children exactly the same interplay of factors.

The child is underachieving. That is the overall problem and to improve matters certain strategies must be adopted and put into effect. Whether or not they prove successful will depend on whether the problem has been correctly identified in the first place (creative problem seeing) and the soundness of the strategies developed and used (problem solving). In addition, success or failure will be determined by your feelings towards the child's abilities and the importance of academic success (attitudes), the confidence with which you regard your abilities as a teacher (self-image) and the strength of your desire to bring about change (motivation). You, and your partner, the child's brothers and sisters, relatives and friends, teachers and all who exert any influence over the child are drawn together in a seamless web of interrelationships. But your influence, because of the unique position of power which parents usually exert over their children, is inevitably going to prove the most lasting and profound.

The writer E. M. Forster had a maxim : 'Only connect . . .' In the 'sixties people spoke of 'getting it all together'. The message here is essentially the same and expresses the single most important concept to grasp before you can teach greater intelligence. Everything connects. Everything is part of a whole.

How Things Can Go Wrong
Let me explain how the interplay of forces can prove damaging to the child's mental development by looking at a fairly typical case history from our files. Michael was ten years old and consistently bottom of his form. He fooled around a great deal in class, getting the attention he craved by acting the clown. Good

at games, he was far happier on the sports field than in the class-room. He approached most school work with a resigned certainty of failure. His standing on the key factors of intellectual ability was as follows:

Attitude: Towards his own ability and school work – *negative*.

Self-image: As a student – *poor*.

Motivation: To try and do better in school – *very low*.

Problem handling skills: Due to lack of attention in class, low motivation to persist when confronted by setbacks – *poor*.

Both his parents were university graduates. They had one other child, a daughter three years older than Michael who was hardworking and academically successful. The father, a college lecturer, blamed the boy for his lack of achievement and frequently punished him for low marks and poor grades. He compared him unfavourably with his sister, showed no interest in his son's ability at sports and made his disappointment in the boy only too obvious. His position on the four factors was as follows:

Attitude: Towards Michael and his abilities – *very negative*.

Self-image: Regarded himself as an intelligent man who placed a high value on academic success and would not tolerate fools gladly.

Motivation: To make Michael get better results in school – *strong*.

Problem handling skills: *excellent*.

Michael's father was powerfully motivated to help improve the boy's schoolwork and, in terms of skills at his disposal, was seemingly in a good position to do so. But his approach was quite wrong because it concentrated mainly on problem handling abilities, seeking to change the child's attitudes only through threats and to improve his motivation only via punishments. This simply made Michael more negative and less motivated, since he now equated school subjects not only with failure in class but with painful humiliations at home. Because the father was so expert at problem solving, and used to teaching young adults rather than children, he was unable to appreciate the ten-year-old's difficulties. He was impatient and regarded every mistake as further confirmation of his belief in the child's innate lack of intelligence.

The starting point for teaching greater intelligence – instead of greater stupidity – was for the father to realise just why his approach was so unhelpful. He was then able to develop a constructive programme for improvement which took into account the influence of all the factors involved. As the boy's attitude and self-image improved so did his motivation to learn. He paid more attention in class and was successfully coached by his father who, using patience and understanding, helped him make up lost ground. Better problem handling resulted in higher marks, encouraging reports and a further improvement in his self-image. The damaging downward spiral of cause and effect had been broken and replaced by a chain-reaction of positive family interactions which led to a substantial and lasting improvement in the boy's intellectual performance.

How This Programme Will Work For You

From what I have said so far, three points will – I hope – have clearly emerged. The first is that intelligence must be seen as a skill which depends on the child's relationships within the family. Your role is just as important as his when it comes to establishing attitudes, self-image and motivation. Unless these are positive it is unlikely that the fourth component, of problem seeing and problem solving, will be mastered successfully.

So we will not be looking at the child in isolation and making him the passive recipient of a teaching process, but the active participant in a programme of constructive change which requires an involvement by the entire family.

The second point is that, in order to bring about any changes that may be necessary, it is essential to identify existing difficulties as objectively as possible. Once again, because we are dealing with the outcome of a family interaction, we must consider not just the child but the parents as well. In the following chapters you will find a series of assessments designed to pinpoint any problems that may be tending to restrict successful mental growth. There is one set of assessments for the parents, and it would be most helpful if both of you could carry them out, and another for the child. By completing these quite simple, quick, tests you will be able to score yourself and the child. These scores are then transferred to what is called a Check Sheet, a box divided into nine separate oblongs. Although this may look slightly daunting at first glance, you will find it quite easy to understand and use. By taking your own score and that of the child you will automatically be directed to one of the nine boxes and this, in turn, will identify the kind of situation which is most likely to exist in your own family at the present time. In this way you can create a teaching programme most closely tailored to your unique, individual family needs. Only in this way has it been possible to provide procedures sufficiently flexible to take into account the very different requirements of a particular child/parent interaction. Without the ability to analyse your current position and then select techniques best suited to meet any difficulties that have been identified, the teaching programme would be too stereotyped to be truly effective. Some parents would find much of what was suggested helpful, others that a great deal of the material was irrelevant to their problems.

In a moment I want to tell you how best to administer these assessments, but before doing so, let's consider the third point of importance. From an understanding of intelligence as the outcome of everything the child has learned and experienced, and the objective identification of any difficulties which may be restricting mental growth, comes the obvious need to bring about positive change where necessary. You can do this by employing the appropriate teaching procedures under the family situation to which the Check Sheet will have directed you. Our experience has been that such teaching is most effective if you bear in mind the following considerations :

* Create the sort of relaxed atmosphere in which the teaching becomes a pleasure to look forward to rather than an anxiety producing ordeal. Be patient, understanding and supportive.

* You will obviously find this easier to achieve if you can remain relaxed yourself. Stop the session immediately if you start to become irritable or impatient. Keep each teaching period short and try to make the lessons part of your family's whole life-style rather than something special and separate. Never attempt the teaching if you are tired, depressed, frustrated or under exceptional stress.

* Always bear in mind that the four factors of attitudes, motivation, self-image and problem handling skills are in constant, dynamic interaction. You cannot expect to resolve difficulties with any one of them by tackling it in isolation.

* Involve your child as fully as possible right from the start.

If he is old enough to understand this type of book, and interested enough to want to read it, why not let him do so and make his own suggestions about what would be helpful? Encourage a full and active participation, listen to comments and criticisms. Modify your approach in the light of his views whenever this seems appropriate. Allow the child to develop at his own pace and always respect his rights as an individual.

Now let's look at the way in which these assessments should be given if they are to produce the kind of honest, objective responses needed for an accurate identification of the family situation.

How To Give The Assessments

1. As with the whole teaching programme, the keynote for success is to maintain a relaxed friendly atmosphere. The questions in the child's assessments have been made as interesting as possible and most can be given as a game. If you administer them in this way, rather than as an intrusion into the home of school type tests, most youngsters are only too keen to try their hands at them. But never turn the game into a competition between members of the family or you are bound to undermine the confidence and motivation of the less successful child.

2. Avoid suggesting which answers you would like or expect, either by what you say or by anything in your tone or expression. This is an especially important point to watch when reading the assessment statements aloud to younger children. You can all too easily bias their replies and so make the assessment invalid.

3. Never pass a comment on the child's choice of response. Even if you are pleased with their answer it is essential to keep your expression and tone neutral. This is necessary because one can give the assessments on a number of occasions, after a suitable period of time has elapsed, in order to keep a constant watch on their attitudes, motivations and self-image. If you have previously praised or criticised a response the child is more likely to remember it and either repeat or avoid that answer in the future.

4. Make certain that the child, especially the younger child, fully understands the questions. Read through them yourself first so that you do not make any mistakes when presenting them. Even with an older child, who is capable of working

through the tests alone, be on hand to explain anything that confuses him and to keep the score accurately.

5. When reading the questions to younger children it may, occasionally, be helpful to modify the wording slightly to make it easier for them to grasp what is wanted. Do so by all means, but be sure to keep the sense of the question the same.

6. Because older children, especially the more intelligent children, sometimes find a few of the questions trivial it may be necessary to involve them as fully as possible in the programme. Do not simply inflict it on them but work through it with them. Get them to take an active part at all stages. Let them mark your assessments as well as their own. Discuss the points raised as fully as possible. This, in itself, will prove a useful addition to the schedule.

7. Never ask a child to complete the assessments when tired, irritable, if playing an interesting game or watching a favourite TV show. The resentment created and the desire to complete the tests as quickly as possible will make an accurate result hard to obtain.

8. Space out the tests. Giving one every few days helps prevent boredom with them. Follow the same timetable yourself.

Carry out the assessments only when asked to do so in the text. Some of them must be completed before you read the information in a particular section in order to avoid biased responses. None of them is very time consuming and most can be completed in less than five minutes.

Once you have created and taught a particular set of procedures this is not the end of the book's usefulness. Changing family circumstances and those unavoidable periods of transition in a child's life, for instance when starting at a new school, may create different problems in the future. These can be monitored by using the assessments and a fresh programme developed to meet the new conditions. I consider an interval of at least four months necessary between carrying out the same assessments, otherwise the child is likely to repeat the original answers even if the situation has actually changed quite drastically. But if you have used the procedures correctly it is extremely unlikely any fresh difficulties will be encountered during this period so long as the family situation remains stable.

In the research study from which this teaching programme was

developed, I and my colleagues have used the procedures successfully with children aged up to twelve, although there is no
reason why – in most instances – it should not prove equally
satisfactory with boys and girls in their early 'teens. For children
younger than six, I suggest that you refer to my earlier book
How To Be A Gifted Parent which deals specifically with the
difficulties and challenges of the first five years of life.

Before ending this chapter and embarking on the teaching
programme proper, I would like to add a note of sincere apology
to parents of daughters! As you will have seen there is a constant
use of the male gender which persists throughout the book. I
have used it with great reluctance, fully aware of the implications
of such a sexist presentation. But really there is no alternative.
If you try and write he/she and his/her on every occasion the
text becomes far more confused and difficult to read, while con-
fining myself solely to *she* and *her* throughout seems no more
satisfactory a solution. I am sensitive to the risks of such sexual
stereotyping, especially when writing about children, and do
not see this as a trivial point.

Please be assured that although I refer to he and him, I am
not implying that girls may not be taught greater intelligence
just as effectively as boys. Indeed our experience has been that
they are frequently more receptive – and I fear often more in
need of help. Because they are brought up in a society which
has consistently, if not always overtly, stressed the academic
and intellectual superiority of males we find that the attitudes
and self-images of many young girls is damagingly and quite
unnecessarily negative.

I need hardly say that merely *reading* a book designed to
provide practical techniques and guidance will not bring about
the changes you desire. Learning the procedures does not demand
anything very difficult or arduous, but it does mean *working*
with your child in the way I describe. Now we are ready to
begin. In the next chapter I will explain the importance of the
first of our four keys that unlock intelligence : the role played in
mental growth by the attitudes you and your child have acquired.

Chapter Four

WHY ATTITUDES MATTER SO MUCH

'When it comes to intelligence,' a wise teacher once told me, 'seeing is achieving.'

What she meant was the way adults, especially parents and teachers, regard a child exerts a powerful influence on the way the youngster comes to look on himself and his abilities.

Adult attitudes are vitally important because they provide much of the raw material from which the child constructs his own feelings about life. If children are held to be of above average intelligence then attitudes are likely to be positive and the world will be viewed with optimistic confidence. They see themselves as expected to achieve intellectual success and that, very often, is exactly what happens. But when children are considered unintelligent the unfavourable adult opinions exert an equally potent but restricting effect on performance and perceptions. They can easily and quickly create a self-fulfilling prophecy of unavoidable failure.

Few adults ever consider their attitudes in this way. They see them as the consequence rather than the cause of a child's level of intellectual ability.

'My views are formed by watching the children perform in class,' a teacher told me rather indignantly. 'I do not start the term with preconceived notions about their abilities. My opinions of a child are based on objective observation, not prejudgement or prejudice.'

Many parents and teachers will probably echo these sentiments. Their own attitudes, they feel are a fair and reasonable reflection of the child's ability as shown by everything he says and does, by all the things he achieves as well as by his failures.

To some extent it is a chicken and egg situation. One can never be certain which comes first, the attitude or the level of attainment. But the relationship between them is certainly far more intricate than most people realise. This intimate interplay is well illustrated by the disturbing findings of two American psychologists, Dr Philip Zelazo and Dr Richard Kearsly, co-directors of the Centre for Behavioural Paediatrics and Infant Development in New England. They assessed the *actual* intelligence of young children who, on the basis of tests carried out soon after birth, had been diagnosed as mentally retarded. Their results were surprising.

Although all the youngsters behaved as if they were backward, many had perfectly normal mental abilities. The original diagnosis had been wildly inaccurate, yet they had grown up to fulfil that false prediction. Philip Zelazo and Richard Kearsly showed that the children had done poorly on the initial tests only from a lack of interest. They were intelligent infants who could not be bothered to play what they must have considered a rather silly adult game. Their terrible punishment was to be labelled as retarded and treated as if they were subnormal during their vital, formative years. The victims of the attitudes of parents, teachers, doctors, psychologists and social workers, these unfortunate youngsters had grown up slow and dim-witted.

The discovery led to all the children being reassessed and those incorrectly diagnosed given intensive help in the hope of repairing some of the enormous intellectual damage done. That any recovery was possible at all is a tribute to the remarkable recuperative capacity of the young mind. If the mistake had not been detected until adulthood it is doubtful whether any improvement in their condition could have been achieved.

In collaboration with Professor Jerome Kagan of Harvard University, the doctors developed a new series of tests for infants designed to take a lack of interest into account. Thanks to their investigations a major cause of mistaken adult attitudes had been removed, although others remain and I shall be looking at them later in this chapter.

Apart from apparently 'objective' psychological tests, what else is likely to influence adult attitudes? What sort of clues do we look for when making up our mind about a child's intelligence and how much trust should we place in them? As research suggests that parents and teachers sum up the child's ability on the basis of rather different performance factors, we can most usefully look at them separately.

How Parents' Attitudes Are Formed

The kind of abilities which strike parents as particularly impressive vary to some extent on their own interests and skills. A father who is a keen chess player, for instance, may place great emphasis on his son's ability to learn the game at an early age. But a survey which I carried out, involving more than two thousand families in Europe and America, indicated three abilities which the majority of parents regard as revealing above average IQ's.

1. If the child asks what they consider to be intelligent questions and seems to understand the answers.

2. When the child is able to learn a new skill quickly and perform well after only a little practice.

3. When the child reads, writes and does sums at an earlier age than expected. Parents who notice any of these, especially in the younger child, are usually delighted and consider that the child is intellectually advanced for his age. They are certainly favourable signs which show that inborn mental potential is being realised. But their *absence* should not be regarded as indicating the opposite state of affairs. It does not mean, as parents sometimes believe, that such a child is less intelligent than a more inquisitive or competent brother or sister. Rather it suggests the child is facing certain problems which will need to be overcome so that progress can be made. Let me illustrate a few of the things which can go wrong by describing some case histories from our files.

Billy – An Over-anxious Child

Billy, aged seven, hated anything new. As a baby he had been extremely fearful and easily aroused. He was happiest in a familiar routine. When he went to school for the first time he suffered from some emotional problems, went through a period of bed wetting and nightmares, became withdrawn and tearful. But he seemed to settle down after a time, although his teachers reported a marked lack of interest in school work. His approach to problem solving was very inflexible. Even though it was quite clear some strategy was all wrong for that particular task he would persist in trying to use it, much to the irritation of his teachers. He made few friends and refused invitations to parties. In class he never volunteered answers and became upset if pressed to reply. His end-of-term test results were poor and his reports spoke of a negative attitude and lack of ability in most subjects.

Billy was assessed as being of below average intelligence, a fact which seemed to be confirmed by a low IQ score. His parents soon adopted the attitude that he was nowhere as bright as his older, twin, brothers. They let him go much his own way and never pressed him to do anything which might prove upsetting.

There are a great many children like Billy who do badly in school and whose parents believe them to be rather dull. In fact their problems usually have nothing to do with brain power at all. Their difficulties stem from an over-anxious attitude towards life.

Because of the ways in which their nervous systems work, it takes very little to make them highly aroused. They may respond to even commonplace situations the way most children react to extreme danger. They are invariably fearful of anything unfamiliar, whether the novelty lies in an object, a person or a task they are expected to perform. Because of this anxiety it takes them much longer to focus their minds on anything new. If you have been in a blind panic you will better understand how they feel in virtually every strange situation. Their minds become confused, they may feel physically ill, and are quite unable to concentrate. Given sufficient time to settle down and get used to things the anxiety will pass. They can then absorb information and answer questions quite as efficiently as the child who never suffers from such crippling initial fear. But this breathing space is normally denied them. Adults, seeing nothing the least anxiety arousing in the activity, usually respond with impatience, telling the child to 'pull yourself together' or 'stop wasting time'. Such remarks, and the frequently stern or mocking tone used, only increase the child's anxiety. They respond by doing their best to avoid the unknown entirely. They reject new ways of solving problems because the old ways – even if inappropriate – produce less anxiety and never ask questions or volunteer answers because this would be to venture into an unfamiliar situation.

Parents and teachers soon realise that the easiest way of dealing with the Billys of this world is by giving them what they apparently need. An absence of stimulation or exposure – so far as possible – to anything new. They no longer urge the child to be curious about the world, they cease to provide the opportunities and encouragement for that active exploration so essential to proper mental growth. After years of this treatment the initial judgement that the child was unintelligent generally comes to be justified.

Mary – A Slow To Warm Up Child

While Billy's problems might be said to be due to a nervous system with the volume control turned up too high, Mary suffered from exactly the opposite difficulty. She was a type of child sometimes described as *slow to warm up*. In simple terms, the lines of communication between her brain and the outside world worked rather inefficiently. Messages had to be sent loud and long before she became aware of what was happening. This was no defect of intelligence on her part. Given time she was just as capable of solving problems and answering questions as anybody else. But such children seldom get sufficient thinking time in school. At the age of ten Mary was considered stupid by her parents who compared her unfavourably with her older brother John:

'He was always quick and bright, even as a baby,' her mother told me. 'But she took ages to get interested in anything. It was the same then as it is now. She is slow and not very bright.'

Her parents' attitudes had been formed both from observations of the way the two children performed various tasks in the family and on the basis of school reports. In both situations Mary suffered more failures than she enjoyed successes. This was almost inevitable given unflattering comparisons with her livelier brother at home and the relentless pressures of a busy classroom. Teachers were either unwilling, or more usually unable, to give her enough time to think. Tests and examinations are always completed against the clock and when a question is asked it is those children who put their hands up first who get a chance to answer and prove themselves bright pupils. Like the overly anxious child, youngsters who are *slow to warm up* often avoid the unfamiliar. Not because the situation itself makes them fearful, but because they are anxious about their ability to respond effectively. They have known so much failure in the past, and found it so distressing, they seek to prevent future misery by withdrawing from the contest. They sit quietly in the back of the class, never venturing an opinion or even listening to what is said. Given the right sort of help they might do just as well as any other child because their brains are no less capable. But their parents' attitudes soon become as negative as their own. In time their mental growth may well be so restricted they really do deserve their reputations for stupidity.

Brian – Too Bright For His Own Good

Perhaps the saddest and most ironic situation of all occurs when a child is considered unintelligent by parents and teachers because he is just *too bright for his own good*. This is what happened to nine-year-old Brian, a little boy with severe behavioural problems. He was destructive and disruptive. His school work was an appalling mess and his school reports rated him one of the least capable children in the class. The real truth was that Brian was so highly intelligent none of the work handed out to boys his age presented the slightest challenge. He could do it all so easily he refused to do it at all. It was beneath him even to make an attempt. Bored and frustrated by the lack of stimulation for his alert and active brain, Brian resorted to all kinds of anti-social behaviour. The solution was to give him harder problems to solve and tougher challenges for his intellect. But the first step was to change his parents' attitudes so that this was possible. After all, to suggest that a child who is bottom of his form be given even more difficult school work seems almost like pouring water on a drowning man.

'Brian needs easier subjects,' his father protested, 'not more advanced work. He can barely cope with what he does now.'

But when the boy's mind was stimulated by actually having to work hard the behaviour problems declined and finally disappeared for good.

These are just three of the ways in which problems which have nothing to do with low intelligence can cause parents to think their children are dunces and develop their attitudes in line with this belief. There are other kinds of difficulties as well, and I shall be looking at some of them later in this book. There are, for instance, many impulsive children in our schoolrooms. They blurt out answers so quickly their brains are never given the chance to work on a problem for long enough. The complete opposite of slow to warm up youngsters like Mary they still suffer from poor marks, bad grades and negative parental attitudes about their abilities. Then there are children whose lack of muscular co-ordination or speed of thoughts makes it difficult for them to be neat. As I shall explain in a moment, neatness in presentation of work, especially when it comes to handwriting, is a powerful factor in influencing the attitudes of teachers. But it also affects the parents' views of a child's abilities, especially if the parents themselves are especially tidy and have a strong psychological need for order in their lives.

These problems will all be dealt with later when I shall be giving you practical advice on how to help the underachieving children develop a more positive set of attitudes both in their own minds and in the minds of their parents. Now let us consider some of the ways in which teachers form attitudes towards children in their charge and see how this may affect the outcome of school careers.

How Teachers' Attitudes Are Formed

It is sometimes assumed parents and teachers share the same view about what they mean by a bright child. That there is agreement over the kind of mental abilities which make up intelligent behaviour. My research suggests this is far from the case.

The attitudes of parents are coloured by hopes, expectations and ambitions for their child. Teachers, whose careers will span many generations of children, are more influenced by personal needs and professional aspirations. Because their perspectives are so different so too are their perceptions of the children in their classes.

To become an effective teacher you must have a desire to communicate ideas, to stimulate and broaden developing minds and to inspire if not a love for your particular subject, at least enough enthusiasm for the students to take their work seriously and do reasonably well in examinations. For it is on those results that a teacher's professional competence and worth will be judged by superiors. Under these circumstances it is hardly surprising that teachers favour children who will either get them the good passes they desire or else not actively hinder this process.

Bright children who are also neat, obedient, polite and docile are, therefore, most highly valued in the classroom.

When looking at parental attitudes I listed the three abilities which were seen as suggesting a high level of intelligence. Teachers gave very different responses. Their first three choices were :

1. Neatness in written work and accuracy when doing calculations.

2. A willingness to follow instructions and the ability to solve problems according to the methods taught.

3. The ability to adapt standard strategies, as necessary, to solve new kinds of problems.

The emphasis, as you can see, is on an orderly, methodical and confident approach to school work. This is most noticeable in replies from teachers whose subjects – mathematics, science and languages – are sometimes considered to demand the greatest levels of intelligence. Faced with such qualification to be considered especially bright, what kind of child is likely to do badly? The list looks rather daunting. It must include . . .

The over-anxious child who fears anything new.

The slow to warm up child who cannot keep pace with the others.

The impulsive child who acts without thinking.

The over-passive child who does not get enough done.

The poorly co-ordinated child whose handwriting and general neatness leave a lot to be desired.

The exceptionally advanced child who gets bored and distracted too readily.

The under-confident child who never answers although he knows the answers.

The insufficiently motivated child who cannot bother to do the work properly.

The list is by no means complete, for there are other difficulties which hold children back and cause adults to regard them as unintelligent. Some of these will be described later in the book.

Whatever the reasons, the results are very similar. The child receives poor school reports, produces indifferent work, obtains low marks in tests and often fails examinations. Such children, whatever their other qualities, are unlikely to be so highly valued by teachers as the clever, achieving child who reflects such credit on them.

Does it matter? Many people would argue that how you get on in school is really quite unimportant. In support of this view they will point to the many famous men and women who boast of having been classroom dunces. Although this may bring some comfort to parents whose children are doing badly, such cases are actually rare and tell us very little about the fate of most school failures. Few would seriously doubt that, in the modern world, qualifications *are* important. Increasingly, interesting and stimulating careers are closed to youngsters lacking the appropriate degree or diploma. To achieve these the child must do reasonably well throughout most of his school life and, for the more exacting professions, perform at a consistently high level.

Being well thought of by teachers is not merely useful because it gives the child an easier time in class. Research shows that it also plays a large part in determining the extent of academic achievement. There is also good evidence to suggest that teachers form their views about children early on and, once established, these attitudes tend to be self-perpetuating and hard to change.

Placing American kindergarten life under the magnifying glass, psychologist Dr R. C. Rist discovered just how far early judgements come to dominate the child's school career. In the kindergarten which he studied the head teacher sat children at one of three dinner tables according to her expectations for their future academic success. Her brightest hopes ate at one table, those she ranked as moderately intelligent at another while the ones she considered almost certain failures had their meals at a third. She picked children for each table on the basis of family background, the way they were dressed and how well they got on with staff. Despite the fact that IQ tests showed there was no real difference between the abilities of children at the three tables these groupings remained virtually unchanged during the next two years. The teacher saw little reason to promote any child from the 'failure' table or to demote any of those at the 'success' table.

As the years passed, however, changes in abilities between the groups became increasingly apparent. Children who had eaten with the success group did well while those who had dined with 'failures' did badly. Was she a highly perceptive teacher or could it be that those initial assessments set the course for the children's future progress through school? On the basis of other evidence the most likely explanation is that the attitudes of the kindergarten staff, conveyed to primary school teachers in the pupils' reports, which would then have gone with them to their secondary schools, established a pattern of prejudgement which played an important role in how each child was perceived. As Dr Rist commented, the head teacher's original predictions 'came to be justified not in terms of teacher expectations, but in apparently "objective" records of previous school working, including, by the beginning of the second grade, reading test performance'.

In a study of the effect which a teacher's belief in the pupil's IQ has on attainment, Dr J. Michael Palardy of University of Georgia at Athens, Georgia, discovered that the brighter a child was assumed to be, the better the results the teacher obtained in class. Groups of boys, aged between six and seven, were matched in ability on the basis of intelligence tests. They were then taught reading in separate classes, by teachers with identical qualifications using exactly the same methods. The only difference was that some of the teachers were told their particular group consisted of boys with above average ability who should prove faster and more able readers. There was, of course, not a grain of truth in this statement. But when the boys were tested at the end of the training period the teacher's false belief had been transformed into classroom reality. Those boys falsely credited with better reading ability *could* now read faster and more fluently than those in other groups.

A rather similar piece of research carried out by the American psychologist Dr B. Pigeon, revealed that this beneficial effect can extend to a whole group of children even when only a few of them have a greater ability than average. In primary schools where the classes were arranged by age, the older boys showed better than usual reading skills at the end of their junior year. The superior performances were due to the fact that, because some of the older boys in the class were able readers, the teachers were encouraged to have greater expectations for the whole group. And the children lived up to these expectations.

Work by Dr J. Burstall, another American education specialist, has shown that this explanation is more than mere speculation. He found that in a school where the head teacher believed all children could learn to speak French, no matter what their apparent aptitude for the language, every pupil did reasonably well and managed to pass end of term tests in the subject. In a second school, where the principal's attitude was that only children with a special aptitude for languages could be expected to understand French, some pupils did well but many failed dismally. In a separate study Dr Burstall examined the effect which the head's attitudes had on underachieving pupils. He found that in those schools where the principal believed that pupils who were bottom of the form still had a contribution to make they did surprisingly well and disproved the early, gloomier predictions. But if the head teacher had no interest in such youngsters and thought it a waste of time to offer much encouragement their performance was consistently poor.

The message from such studies is crystal clear. What teachers believe their students achieve. Classroom ability mirrors the attitudes of those who take the classes and run the schools.

Chapter Five

HOW WE MAKE UP OUR MINDS ABOUT IQ

As I have already explained, parents and teachers seem to attach importance to rather different kinds of mental ability. A talent which goes down well at home may mean a black mark in the classroom. A skill which receives warm approval at school can pass almost unnoticed, and quite unremarked, by even a concerned mother or father.

But although the evidence on which IQ judgements are formed varies in this way, the means by which it is gathered remains the same. When it comes to making up our minds about a child's level of intelligence, we have to rely on information obtained in three ways. In this chapter I want to examine each of them to see how much reliance they can safely be given. In particular I want to consider the value and reliability of IQ tests since these are now widely used as a means of producing a 'scientific' estimate of intellect.

Personal Observations

This is the most obvious source of information and one we use all the time. We all have a personal idea of what constitutes mental precocity, whether this is rapid learning or early reading, just as we have an opinion about the kind of inabilities which suggest a lower than average intelligence. These usually include being slow to learn new tasks or later than normal reading proficiency.

Other People's Views

These range from professional assessments carried out by teachers, doctors or psychologists, to the informal judgements of one's marriage partner, relatives – especially your own parents – close friends and even casual acquaintances.

Their views, like personal observations, tend to be highly subjective even when based on such seemingly *objective* information as reading ability, speed of learning or mathematical skill. Bias due to preconceptions and misconceptions can all too easily distort both the observations themselves and the conclusions drawn from them. This is especially true when attempting to assess the intelligence of a youngster you believe to be of below average IQ. The problem usually arises because an initial judgement is made very early on in the child's life – sometimes while he is still in the cradle – and this shapes subsequent attitudes in advance of any real indication of abilities. Let me give you two examples of what I mean. Philip was an early reader. By the time he was four his mother and father had given him his own set of junior encyclopaedias, so delighted were they with his skill. He also became good at manipulating numbers so that – by the time he went to school a year early – he was well ahead of other children in the three R's. That sounds like a highly objective form of assessment. There was no doubt that Philip could do all these basic educational tasks much better than most children of his age. Indeed I put his ability as equal to that of an eight-year-old.

To understand where subjective bias creeps in we have to go back in Philip's family history to the time when he was just a few months old.

'We always knew he was a bright baby,' his mother told me. 'He took such an interest in the world around him. He explored everything as soon as he could crawl.'

So the parents' *initial attitude* was a positive one. Philip's response to life was such that it matched his parents' belief in what a clever baby should be doing.

'When he was two I noticed him looking at the headlines in the newspapers,' his mother explained. 'I helped him by reading out the words and pointing to the letters. I thought then that he might be an early reader.'

So the expectation was there and Philip was given encouragement to start reading. But things might have been very different had his parents not adopted that attitude in the first months.

Another difference which many adults regard as important is speed of response. Clever children are usually regarded as those who can do things quickly, learn new skills with a minimum of practice, grasp ideas swiftly, and seldom need to be told the same thing twice. Parents will often say that this ability was clearly present in the cradle or when the infant first began to explore his surroundings.

'She always was very sharp for her age,' says the mother of a bright three-year-old. 'Picked up everything she was told. Her brother is just the opposite. He is very slow.'

This was true, but by the time the girl was three and her brother was two these differences were actually quite slight. On some of the problem solving tasks I gave them it amounted to only a few seconds. Sufficient for the parents to notice but not enough to matter much in practice. Two years later, however, when the children were tested again, the boy had become far slower and much more cautious while the girl had speeded up. Here again we were presented with apparently objective data about their differences in mental ability. It could actually be measured in terms of time taken to learn new tasks or solve unfamiliar problems. Yet the seeds of this variation in responsiveness were a subjective set of impressions on the part of the parents rather than a difference of any significance.

IQ Tests

This is the final source of information about children and one which parents and teachers usually set great store by. To them it sometimes seems the fairest and most objective method yet devised for separating the intelligent from the dull. Indeed IQ tests were designed with that express purpose in mind.

Because they are such a widely used and highly regarded (by some) form of assessment I would like to explain a little about their origins, their strengths and their weaknesses.

The first IQ test was developed by the French psychologist Alfred Binet in 1905 to help teachers sort their pupils into different levels of ability. His original set of questions was revised by the American psychologist Lewis Terman and published in the United States in 1916. Because the country was at war soon afterwards, and the army needed a method of selecting bright recruits for officer training, it became widely used. The test was popular because it was easy to administer and produced a seemingly straightforward result, the famous IQ or Intelligence Quotient. You needed no training in psychology to realise that somebody with an IQ of 130 was brighter than a person with an IQ of 100.

But how was the vital figure obtained? The test was, and is, rather like an intellectual obstacle race with the hurdles getting higher and higher. It continues until the subject fails to clear a particular hurdle and this sets the individual's mental age. If a nine-year-old boy managed to clear intellectual hurdles designed for an eleven-year-old then his mental age would be eleven. To obtain the IQ the tester simply divided the mental age by the child's physical age and multiplied by 100. In this case the child would have an IQ of 122. (ie $\frac{11}{9}$ x 100)

Today the calculation method has been replaced by a set of standardised tables and the term IQ, now inappropriate, is retained only because it has become so popular!

The idea of mental 'hurdles' has a logical appeal to it. After all, if you wanted to find out how high somebody could jump, you would start with a low bar and continue to make them jump over it at different heights. When they consistently knocked the bar down, you would know their limit had been reached. If you found a bar level which the majority of people, at a certain age, were able to clear, and somebody failed to jump over it, then you could reasonably say they were less good at jumping than most other people of their age. Binet set his hurdles by devising questions which 60 per cent of children at the intended age level were able to answer.

But there is clearly a big difference between making a fairly simple assessment of physical ability and trying to measure something as complex as intelligence.

There are many things which can affect the outcome none of which has anything to do with intelligence. For example the test, being constructed by white, middle-class psychologists, may contain biases that favour white, middle-class children at the expense of other social and ethnic groups. It has been found, for instance, that children sometimes do badly simply because they do not understand the questions. In one IQ test pupils were asked to decide which of the following was the 'odd' musical instrument: 'Harp, drum, cello, guitar and violin.' The tester meant the answer to be drum, but many youngsters selected *cello* because they had never heard the word and had no idea what it meant!

Even if the biases are eliminated the test will still not be equally fair to every child taking it. All those with the problems I listed earlier in this chapter, for instance, are likely to do badly despite being as intelligent as their fellow students.

Some will become so anxious they cannot concentrate or use their brains effectively. Bright youngsters may become bored and stop even attempting to find the answers. Children who are slow to warm up may not work fast enough to complete the test in the time allowed. Those who respond badly to novelty will be more adversely affected by the strange nature of the problems than more adaptable children. The impulsive child may never settle for long enough to give himself a reasonable chance of success.

There is no way of knowing how often this happens, but it seems likely that failure to achieve a good test result is more often due to temperamental difficulties than intellectual failings. This is certainly the judgement of psychologists who have investigated the effect of emotional states on IQ scores. In one study, kindergarten children were tested on entry to the school, and again six months later, when a considerable improvement in IQ levels was noticed. The researchers concluded that the change had been due to shyness during the original test. Once the children had settled into their classes, and learned how to get on with groups and with adults, they were able to tackle the tests much more confidently. Other research has shown that practice in solving problems similar to those contained in an IQ test can make a big difference to the results. This suggests that it is the strangeness of the problems which suddenly confront them which throws some children off balance. Especially confused by the type of questions included in many tests may be children from educationally deprived backgrounds, who lack not only the experience of handling those particular problems, but have never had the chance to think about the world in the way which these tests require.

Exploring this problem psychologists gave the same test to a group of four- and five-year-old children on two separate occasions one week apart. Some of the children came from impoverished homes, the rest from affluent ones. The IQ scores for children living in poverty rose by 10 points between the first and second test, while the IQ's for the advantaged children increased by only three points.

The danger is that these sources of bias and potential error are seldom appreciated either by the parents or by teachers. As a result the outcome is accepted at face value as a fair indication of the child's intelligence and decisions are then made on the basis of that result.

'We were delighted with John's IQ test,' a mother will tell me proudly. 'It came out at 120 points. Apparently that's well above average. It means he is more than usually intelligent.'

'It's come as a complete shock to us,' says the despondent mother of a child who did 'much worse' than expected. 'We always thought she was such an alert and intelligent child. But her IQ is only 105. That makes her very average, doesn't it?'

The IQ score has come to achieve an almost mystic significance in some schools and families where its validity is seldom doubted or the verdict pronounced by those fatal figures seriously questioned. Many adults regard the numbers as having equal weight with other statistics of infant growth. They will say:

'Anne is aged five. She is 44 inches tall. She weighs 42 lbs. Her IQ is 115.' This implies that all the measures are equally objective, all the numbers carry a similar reliability, and that the tests by which they were obtained are comparable. Vision is measured by eye tests, hearing by auditory tests, blood by blood tests, and intelligence by intelligence tests!

I am not saying that tests of mental ability have no value and should never be used. They are of considerable help to educational and clinical psychologists as *one* component in their assessment of a child's potential. The fact that they can be badly misused, and often are, is the fault of those who abuse them rather than a built-in failing of the tests themselves.

They are at their most dangerous when used by parents as the primary yardstick of intelligence, or by teachers to explain away failure in the classroom.

'What's the point in encouraging him to study,' the IQ dominated parent may say. 'He's only got average mental ability, the tests proved that. Why expose him to inevitable failures?'

'You can't expect me to make a good scholar out of him,' says the bad teacher, who used IQ tests as an excuse for incompetence. 'He only scored a few points above average on the test and these are the kind of results you must expect.'

Do not be blinded by the pseudo-science so often involved in intelligence testing. Just because the IQ figure seems specific and easy to understand, do not accept it as holy writ.

As the American psychologist K. B. Clark commented:

'Educators, parents and others really concerned with the human aspects of public education should look the IQ squarely in the eye, and reject it or relegate it to the place where it belongs. The IQ cannot be considered sacred or even relevant in decisions about the future of the child.'

How Attitudes Speak Louder Than Words

'We never told him we were disappointed in his results,' protested a mother when I suggested that parental attitudes had influenced their son's failure in school. 'We gave him every encouragement and never said a word in criticism.'

I believed her. But when it comes to communicating feelings to a child, attitudes speak louder than words. We convey our real views in scores of unspoken signals, many of them so subtle that they exert their powerful effect below the level of awareness. In a study carried out in America a twelve-year-old boy was given instruction by a number of teachers each of whom was given a different impression of the child's abilities. Some were informed he was highly intelligent, others that he was average, while the third group was told the boy was backward. Their teaching sessions were videotaped and the silent speech of their body language analysed.

It was found that when teachers believed the boy was exceptionally bright they sent much warmer and more positive nonverbal messages. They stood or sat closer to him, smiled more and gave greater eye contact. In those cases where he was thought of as backward the unspoken signals conveyed a much colder, more distant and less emphatic response.

Investigations into the responses teachers gave to different children in a class have shown that if the pupil is considered bright then tiny, unintentional messages of encouragement and support will be sent out when he attempts to answer a question. Small movements of the eyebrows, lips, and forehead indicate whether the child is on the right track and should continue or should pause and rethink the reply. Changes in posture and proximity are also used, without the teacher being aware of the fact, to guide the bright student to a correct answer. None of this is done deliberately and the teachers are unaware that they are sending out these unspoken clues. But children, who are generally very sensitive to adult body language, find little difficulty in reading their teachers like books. Good students, it has been found, are especially responsive to such silent guidance. When a pupil considered less capable attempts an answer, however, the teacher's body language is usually found to be at best neutral and at worst actively discouraging.

Psychologists term this type of non-verbal communication 'leakage' and regard it as a reflection of a person's true inner feelings. Without special training it is virtually impossible for us to prevent the 'leaking' of information about our attitudes and emotions, and even then we are likely to give ourselves away at moments of stress. Parents, as well as teachers, convey attitudes to children in this way, usually without being aware of the fact. They also reveal themselves in the tone of voice used, even when apparently praising or reassuring the child. Almost imperceptible variations in stress, changes in timbre and pitch are sufficient to convey the adult's true impressions about the child.

I must stress that 'leakage' is very different from deliberate attempts to conceal emotions. A teacher might imagine she is smiling encouragingly as a slow student fumbles for the right answer. But other signals will be telling a very different story. For example direct eye contact, accompanied by a warm smile and interested expression, encourages a child to continue and tells him he is on the right lines with a reply. But if the eye contact is maintained a fraction longer than expected, or the surrounding features change only slightly, then message could convey a threat, a criticism or a lack of interest.

During such a silent dialogue neither adult nor child may realise the exact nature of the communication between them. The teacher is certain he was understanding and patient, while the youngster is unable to explain the anxiety, distrust or dislike which he feels towards that particular master or the subject he teaches.

If you hold an attitude about a child you will convey those feelings to the child no matter how hard you try to conceal them.

That attitude is likely to have been formed on very subjective evidence, and even the apparently objective assessments provided by IQ tests need to be regarded with caution.

How you, the influential adults in the child's life, see that child will exert a powerful effect on the level of ability which develops. This performance, and your attitudes, will – in turn – influence the child's attitudes towards himself and his abilities. And so the circle of cause and effect continues to turn. Change those attitudes and you are very likely to change the child's achievements as well.

Before leaving this crucial topic let me describe just one more classic study which clearly shows the tremendous impact on a child's abilities of their teacher's perceptions.

Two American psychologists R. Rosenthal and L. Jacobsen decided to find out what would happen if teachers believed some children in their class were much more intelligent than they had previously realised. They administered an IQ test which, they explained, was especially designed to identify late academic developers. It would allow them to discover those students who, although they had not shown any real promise in the past, could be expected to achieve a much improved performance in the immediate future. The test was, of course, a fake and the children were chosen at random from among the less successful pupils in the class. A follow up study twelve months later showed that these youngsters had indeed done much better than previously anticipated, gaining much higher marks, better grades and more optimistic reports. Their level of intelligence had risen in accordance with adult expectations and perceptions. But their brains had not suddenly started to work better for any reason other than this crucial change in attitudes.

When making up your mind about a child's intellectual ability you can avoid serious errors of judgement by bearing in mind six golden rules for child assessment :

* Remember that every child responds to life in an individual manner. Although these differences may appear to owe more to emotions than intelligence they are, in fact, the foundations on which mental ability is constructed. Be understanding about these needs, even when they conflict with your own way of looking at things and try to satisfy them as fully as possible.

* Never forget that *all* assessments are subjective. Judgements are as much an outcome of attitudes as of observation. When we think a child is dull we tend to pay far greater attention to all the stupid things he says or does. Try seeing the

child as bright and focus on any original or intelligent achievements. These may be outweighed by rather silly behaviour at first, but by attending to them and being encouraging you will be more likely to increase their number.

* Avoid being swayed too strongly by teachers or other child 'experts'. Remember that their assessments, however seemingly objective, are also the product of professional needs and personal biases.

* Do not place too much faith in IQ tests. Although they appear the most objective of all assessment methods they are, as I have explained, prone to many errors. They are difficult to administer properly and even harder to interpret correctly. Above all, pay no attention to the kind of pop IQ tests published in magazines or newspapers. You might as well rely on the astrology page to guide you!

* Try not to impose your own attitudes and ideas on what activities are worthwhile and indications of high intelligence. Children need to be able to sample life as widely as possible if they are to make sense of the world. Many activities, which parents dismiss as requiring no mental ability, do in fact require considerable concentration and skill.

* Finally, believe me when I assure you there is no such thing as an innately stupid child. Except where brain damage is diagnosed, all children have an inheritance of potential brilliance. If they do something which seems to you very unintelligent, try looking at it through their eyes. Search for explanations other than stupidity. What failure of understanding has led to that seemingly unintelligent response? Could it have occurred through an inability to handle problems correctly? This is often at the root cause of such behaviour and, later in the book, I will tell you how considerable improvement in problem-handling skills can be brought about.

If you follow these half-dozen points in mind it will be much easier to avoid the kind of damaging, subjective judgement that can so harm a child's prospects. How easy it is for you to adopt my suggestions will depend, to a great extent, on your current attitudes towards the whole subject of intellectual endeavour. It is these attitudes that we are going to take a closer look at in the next chapter.

Chapter Six

ASSESSING YOUR OWN ATTITUDES

The starting point for developing the most helpful and positive attitudes towards intellectual attainment on the part of your child, must be an assessment of your own feelings on the subject. The value and importance you place on such things as school work, academic achievement, examination results, formal qualifications and intellectual pursuits in general will have already exerted a powerful influence.

It would be most helpful if both you and your partner could complete the short assessment below, since the child's outlook is likely to reflect all the attitudes within the family. If there are any substantial disagreements between you and your partner over the importance of educational attainment, this conflict of opinion may have affected the child's own attitudes in a number of significant ways. The assessment will enable you to find out whether such a divergence of views exists – if these are not already apparent – and in the next chapter you will be able to discover what effect this may have had on your child's outlook.

When choosing your responses to the twelve statements in the assessment it is essential to be completely honest. Do not attempt what psychologists term 'faking good' in order to produce a socially desirable answer. Nobody need see your replies and only if they are a true reflection of your feelings can the assessment hope to be accurate. The same comment does, of course, apply to each of the assessments contained in this book. Always record your answers on a separate sheet of paper to avoid marking the book. As I have already explained these assessments can be carried out on a number of occasions provided they remain unmarked.

In order to make the attitude assessment you should simply make a note of the response to each statement that comes closest to expressing your own point-of-view. You must only select one response in each instance.

1. Children should leave school as soon as they are allowed in order to gain a practical skill and start earning a living.
Strongly Agree   Agree   Disagree   Strongly Disagree

2. History shows us that scientific discoveries are, on the whole, more harmful than helpful to mankind.
Strongly Agree   Agree   Disagree   Strongly Disagree

3. Children of above average intelligence tend not to get on with other people.
Strongly Agree   Agree   Disagree   Strongly Disagree

4. Genius and insanity are often two sides to the same coin.
Strongly Agree   Agree   Disagree   Strongly Disagree

5. Children who are bright at lessons are usually dunces on the sports field.
Strongly Agree   Agree   Disagree   Strongly Disagree

6. Emotions are a better guide than logic when deciding what action to take.
Strongly Agree   Agree   Disagree   Strongly Disagree

7. Intelligent children often suffer from bad eye-sight or poor health.
Strongly Agree   Agree   Disagree   Strongly Disagree

8. Too much reading is bad for you.
Strongly Agree   Agree   Disagree   Strongly Disagree

9. Children with greater than average intelligence are often very miserable.
Strongly Agree   Agree   Disagree   Strongly Disagree

10. Intelligent children tend to miss a lot of the simple joys of childhood.
Strongly Agree   Agree   Disagree   Strongly Disagree

11. IQ tests are a reliable guide to a child's intelligence.
Strongly Agree   Agree   Disagree   Strongly Disagree

12. Neat handwriting is usually a clear sign of high intelligence.

Strongly Agree   Agree   Disagree   Strongly Disagree

How to Score The Assessment

For every statement with which you *strongly* agreed write down two B's. If you simply *agreed* with the statement this is worth one B.

A *disagreement* is awarded a single A, while a *strong disagreement* receives two A's.

Total all the A's and B's and make a note of them. You could have obtained a maximum score of either 24 A's or 24 B's, but most people find they have a mixture of both.

In the next chapter I will show you how to assess the attitudes of your child. By using the two scores it will then be possible to find out how your views interact and whether the outcome is favourable or unfavourable to mental growth. You will be able to identify possible difficulties and, by taking the practical steps I shall describe to overcome them, provide the first lessons in teaching your child greater intelligence.

Chapter Seven

ASSESSING YOUR CHILD'S ATTITUDES

Attitudes are mirrors of the mind, reflecting inner feelings about life. If expressed honestly and openly they can tell us a great deal about the child's views of the world. Often, however, children try to conceal or disguise their true attitudes for fear they will conflict with those of adults. Sometimes they hide them so well that parents are given a quite false impression of how the child really feels.

'It came as a bombshell when Peter told us he hated school,' the father of one unhappy ten-year-old told me. 'We had always thought he enjoyed it. He never seemed the least bit upset. I loved my time at school and believed he did too.'

'I couldn't believe it when my eight-year-old daughter told me she actually enjoyed maths,' admitted a mother. 'I loathed it at school and thought all children did. It doesn't seem like a very feminine subject to me. I would have preferred her to take up dancing or art.'

Adults ought not to be too surprised to discover their children have kept quiet about attitudes which clash with their own. Most youngsters prefer peace and quiet and dislike family rows, so they stay silent rather than press their own viewpoints, especially when they are still very young. Also, children tend to be conformists, hating to stand out from the crowd, whether in the family or the classroom. Only when forced to make a choice between what they regard as their true needs and the views of others are they likely to express attitudes openly.

But there are ways in which you can assess these submerged feelings indirectly. By doing so it is possible to gain a far sharper picture of the way your child sees life, and to discover what goals are likely to prove important to him.

The assessment below makes use of a variety of techniques to gain insight into the child's thinking and to establish the sort of attitudes he holds. It can be completed by one or more child in a family but each should answer separately to avoid being influenced by another's replies. With children younger than seven, or if an older child does not seem to grasp what is wanted in a particular question, please explain the instructions in your own words.

If you have not read my comments about administering the assessments, which appeared in Chapter Three, please do so now. When helping younger children note down the responses as they are made. Make sure the older child also records his, or her, responses at the time. Be careful not to suggest which answer you prefer by your comments, expression or tone of voice.

1. Look at the drawings and say which of the four children you would most like to have for a friend.

Bob   Mary

David   Anne

2. Which of the presents shown in the drawings would you most like to be given on your birthday?

Pop Record   Chemistry Set

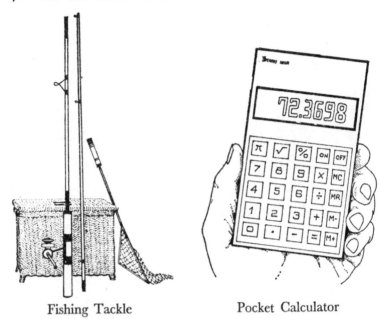

Fishing Tackle   Pocket Calculator

3. Which of the books shown here do you think would be most interesting to read?

How Motor Cars Work

How to go
Camping

How to Play
Sports

How to Play Chess

4. Imagine that you had to choose just two school subjects to do all day. Which of the following would you most enjoy?
Reading
Games
Dancing
Science
Making Things
Maths
Art

5. Which job do you think is the most interesting?

Scientist   Engineer

Farmer   Sportsman

6. Which sort of teacher do you like best?
One who helps you with the work and keeps good order in class.
One who is fun to listen to and keeps you amused.

7. The drawing below shows a classroom with sixteen desks. Where would you like to sit if it was your own class?

8. When you have free time what do you really enjoy doing? Pick two from those shown in the pictures.

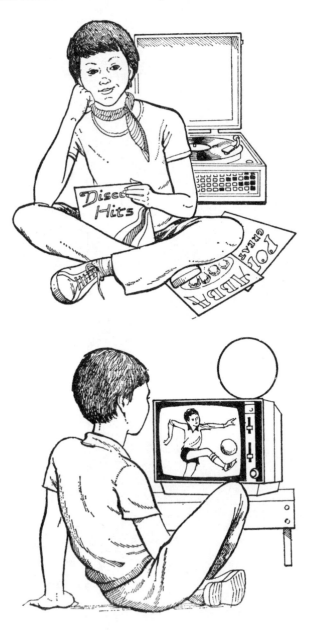

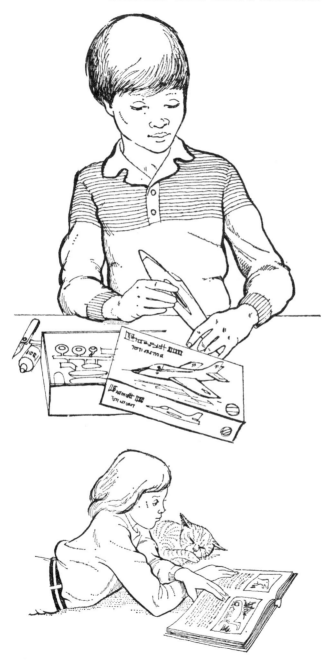

9. If you were asked to write a story, which subject would you most like to describe?

A journey through space and fights with alien monsters.

A visit to some famous place which you have seen recently.

A description of your favourite show on TV.

A description of how something works.

10. Here are descriptions of two children. Which one would you most like to play with?

1) Very lively, good at inventing games, always comes near top of class.

2) Fun to be with, can think up interesting things to do, likes to play all the time.

How to score the Assessment

Award A's or B's as shown below.

1. David or Anne score A.
   Bob or Mary score B.
2. Chemistry set or pocket calculator: Score A.
   Pop record or fishing tackle: Score B.
3. How Motor Cars Work or How to Play Chess: Score A.
   The other two do not score at all.
4. Reading, maths, science: Score A.
   Art, games, dancing, making things: Score B.
5. Scientist/Engineer: Score A.
   Sportsman/Farmer: Score B.
6. The first teacher scores A. The second teacher scores B.
7. Front row AA; second row A; third row B; fourth row BB.
8. Making something or reading scores an A.
   Watching TV, listening to pop music scores a B.
9. For the first and last subjects score an A. For the middle two score a B.
10. If the choice is child number one score an A; a B if the second child is chosen.

Now I want you to total up all the A's and all the B's. It is possible for the child to have scored a maximum of eleven A's or eleven B's. But in most instances you will find they have obtained a mixture of A's and B's.

How To Use The Assessments

By carrying out these short assessments you have a score for your own attitudes, and possibly one for your partner as well, and a score for each of the children in the family. These can be used together, by means of the Check Sheet which I described in Chapter Three, to explore the interplay of attitudes between you and your child. Remember that it is this *interaction* which determines each of the key factors that make up intellectual ability. Where your attitudes complement one another the result is more likely to prove favourable to mental development than in those instances where there is a clash of views. Even if your assessment identifies this type of difficulty, however, it is still possible to improve matters greatly by making use of the procedures most appropriate to the current family situation. In order to identify this situation, and so discover which techniques should be chosen, I am now going to ask you to compare your own score with your child's.

If you look at the Check Sheet on p. 79 you will see that the parents' score on the attitude test is noted along the top. Your child's score is recorded down the left side of the box.

The important element in both scores is how many more A's there were than B's. If yours had three or more A's than B's, then you will look at the first group of three boxes within the chart. If you obtained an approximately equal number of A's and B's you would go to the middle row of boxes while if you scored three or more B's than A's you would look at the end row.

Similarly with the child. Three or more A's than B's takes you to the first box on the left side of the chart. An approximately equal number of A's and B's to the middle box and three or more B's than A's to the last box.

First identify these two positions. Now locate the situation indicated by the meeting point of these scores. For example, suppose that both you and your child scored an approximately equal number of A's and B's. This would place both scores in the middle boxes and so direct you to Situation 5. Similarly if you scored three or more B's than A's (end box on the parents' score) while your child scored three or more A's than B's (first box on the child's score) you would be directed to Situation 7.

You might find this system a little confusing at first but once you have mastered the Check Sheet you will find it is the quickest, easiest and most direct method for identifying the correct family situation that can be devised.

It may well happen that you and your partner obtain different scores and so start at different positions on the Check Sheet. Equally, where a number of children in the same family have taken the assessment there is no reason to suppose they will all obtain the same score. This will mean that several situations are identified and a number of procedures suggested. Use all those indicated in order to create a programme which takes into account the individual needs of each child and the attitudes of both you and your partner.

	What the Parents Scored on the Attitude Assessment		
What the Child scored on the Attitude Assessment	Three or More A's than B's	Approximately Equal Number of A's than B's	Three or More B's than A's
Three or More A's than B's	Positive Child/Positive Parent. Please read my comments under Situation 1	Positive Child/Neutral Parent. Please read my comments under Situation 4	Positive Child/Negative Parent. Please read my comments under Situation 7
Approximately Equal Number of A's than B's	Neutral Child/Positive Parent. Please read my comments under Situation 2	Neutral Child/Neutral Parent. Please read my comments under Situation 5	Neutral Child/Negative Parent. Please read my comments under Situation 8
Three or More B's than A's	Negative Child/Positive Parent. Please read my comments under Situation 3	Negative Child/Neutral Parent. Please read my comments under Situation 6	Negative Child/Negative Parent. Please read my comments under Situation 9

Chapter Eight

HOW TO BUILD ACHIEVING ATTITUDES

The starting point for teaching greater intelligence must be the building of strong, positive attitudes towards the value of intellectual pursuits within the home. As I am sure you now appreciate, any changes which may be needed can only be brought about provided you are prepared to take into account all the major influences at work on the child. Attempts to improve his attitude in isolation are doomed to failure.

The Check Sheet has allowed you to identify the situation, or situations, which currently exist within the family. By putting into practice the procedures described under the appropriate situation heading, you will be able gradually to eliminate any barriers to mental growth and intellectual development which unhelpful, antagonistic attitudes may have been responsible for creating.

There is no need to read through all the nine situations described below, unless you are interested in understanding the various types of interaction that occur. To obtain the most rapid advice and guidance it is only necessary to turn to those situations indicated as a result of the assessments.

Situation One – Positive Child – Positive Parents

The results of the assessments suggest that both you and your child have positive attitudes towards intellectual pursuits. If your own A score was very high you should be careful not to place undue emphasis on academic work at the expense of other activities, such as uninhibited play, that provides the child with a chance to relax and let off steam. Parents are inclined to see childhood through rose tinted spectacles as a period in life when there are few real stresses or strains. In fact research has shown that a child under examination pressure at school can be just as stressed as the two-ulcer company executive. This applies to children who are consistently top of the form just as much as those who do badly in class.

If both you and your child scored highly on A's it indicates that the family's attention is narrowly, perhaps too narrowly, focused on school achievement. This could mean that equally important aspects of childhood are sometimes neglected. Of course school work is important and paper qualifications, as I stressed in the first chapter, are a vital passport to the more interesting and stimulating occupations. But for full emotional and social development the child must use the mind as a plaything as well as a thinking machine. Children with a high A score are unlikely to complain about pressures of work or press their parents for the chance to play uninhibitedly in a completely childish manner. Yet it is essential for children to enjoy themselves without the restraints, which may be imposed from the outside, by parental disapproval of anything other than actual studying or 'constructive' hobbies, or by the child himself by feelings that everything except serious pursuits are somehow worthless time wasters. The child who misses out on the carefree joys of being young may well develop resentments against those who imposed restraints and the activities which robbed him of childhood freedoms. In the late 'teens such anger can suddenly erupt and direct itself against both the parental attitudes towards academic study and school work itself. Just at the time when the most critical exams are about to be taken such children become rebels against anything connected with intellectual activities.

No less important than this potential danger is the fact that the child who spends too much time studying may be unable to learn the social skills essential to getting on with companions of the same age. It is the absence of these skills, rather than some innate unsociability, that causes some highly intelligent children to become isolated and friendless.

If your score was far higher than the child's, be careful not to push him too hard. Young children usually have a strong need to please their parents and win their approval. This means it is very easy for you to exert a powerful influence over their thinking. To win the reward of your praise and pleasure the child may well work far too hard for his own good. Apart from the obvious risks to emotional and physical health, excessive work can cause problems of motivation, self-image and anxiety.

In even the medium term, pressures to meet unreasonably high standards of excellence are likely to prove self-defeating. A quite probable outcome is for the child to lose confidence and become so worried about school work that he begins to avoid any kind of challenging mental activity. Difficulties of this kind should be identified by the assessments which I will provide in later chapters, where I will also tell you how best to deal with such problems. But your help will only prove effective if you also change your attitudes. I remember one child in tears because he had dropped from first to second place in a half-term test :

'My father will be so disappointed,' he told me. 'I'll be a failure in his eyes now.'

Assist the child towards a relaxed approach to achievement by showing him ways of using his brain more efficiently. In the chapters on problem handling I shall be providing advice about how to do just that.

If both you and your partner carried out the assessments you may well find that your scores are much the same. However, it could be that one of you scored high on A's while the other scored higher on B's. In this case the assessments will have directed you both to this situation and Situation Seven. I hope that the information which these contain will provide the basis for discussions between you on the best way to resolve any conflicts over the importance of developing mental potential as fully as possible. As you can see, I am advocating an approach which sacrifices neither the natural rights of the child to be a child, nor the need to acquire those intellectual skills necessary to become a successful and fulfilled adult.

If there are several children in the family you may well find that while one or two of them score high on A's, and so direct you to this situation, another child has a higher B score. In this case you will be directed to Situation Three. Read the suggestions which this contains carefully and try to implement them as fully as possible. In doing so attempt to maintain an even handed approach to the whole family.

Where one or both parents are strongly academically orientated, it is only natural for them to feel slightly more warmth and empathy towards the child, or children, who most closely match their desire for intellectual achievement. As a result they may undervalue a child whose talents lie in other directions.

Although you may try hard not to show favouritism this is often difficult to avoid. As I explained in an earlier chapter children are so sensitive to the most subtle aspects of communication, the tone of voice, the inflexion with which certain comments are spoken and the silent speech of body language which accompanies the spoken word, that it is very hard to conceal one's true feelings.

If one child is lagging behind the others no doubt you will be interested in helping him towards a greater intellectual success. Perhaps you purchased this book with that objective in mind. In this case please read the suggestions in Situation Three carefully. Take special note of my plea not to utilise this teaching as a form of punishment, or to present it in such a way that an under-confident child's already precarious self-image is further damaged. Most particularly do not use the child you consider to be brighter as a 'shining example' to the other. Such a tactic will be worse than self-defeating. Not only will you be unlikely to help the less successful child but it is quite probable you will also cause emotional damage to the brighter child.

Situation Two – Neutral Child – Positive Parent

The assessment suggests that, while you are very interested in academic success and intellectual activities, your child is a good deal less enthusiastic. This is a perfectly normal situation. It is healthy for the young child to want a world unbounded by the disciplines of the school time-table. Achievement should be seen in terms of *everything* at which the child succeeds, whether this is playing sports, making friends or just indulging in enjoyable games. It must not only be thought of as relating to attainment in classroom subjects.

However, if you are more strongly orientated towards success in school subjects and place an especially high value on activities which might be termed 'intellectual' then you may pressure the child to adopt the same attitude towards life. Because young children are usually so eager to win the love and regard of their parents, such a tactic is likely to enjoy at least some short-term success. But in the longer term you are liable to do more harm than good by attempting to exert so much control over their lives.

Children should *enjoy* the business of growing-up, which means being allowed a rounded experience of life. This inevitably results in their making mistakes, following some dead-end activities, expending time and energy on pursuits which may strike you as foolish.

While it is essential to give the child opportunities for as full and rich a life-style as possible, including the chance to follow activities which you value most highly, it is dangerous and damaging to try and force an interest in any of them by a withdrawal of love or the threat of more direct punishments.

Children who are being pushed too hard in a direction which seems unattractive to them may show signs of emotional problems. They may become anxious and withdrawn, sullen, or destructive. They may appear rude, off-hand, uncaring, ungrateful and uncooperative. All this is behaviour very likely to irritate and anger adults. The usual response, even with parents who have tried to be understanding and patient, is to return rudeness with rudeness and aggression with aggression. As a result there is an escalation of the difficulties, a disruption of family relationships and the creation of an atmosphere in which it may prove hard—or even impossible—to foster a more constructive approach in life. Where such acute conflicts have arisen it is essential to introduce a cooling off period, to execute a tactical withdrawal, to reconsider your own position and to look for possible reasons why the situation may have got so far out of control.

In later chapters I will explain how it is possible to persuade children to adopt a positive attitude towards increasing their intellectual abilities; by changing motivation and self-image; by teaching problem handling skills, and by reducing emotional blocks which are causing a crisis of temperament.

If both you and your partner undertook the assessment it is likely your scores were quite close. However it might be that your partner is much less positive in his/her attitude towards academic achievement than you are. In this case another situation will have been indicated by the assessment. Read the suggestions which it contains and ask your partner to consider these comments. When one member of the family has a rather negative attitude towards intellectual attainment while the other has a highly positive orientation, clashes and conflicts over the child's future are inevitable. These will lead to confusion and ambivalence on the part of the child and a lack of clear direction. Such an atmosphere is never conducive to the realisation of mental abilities on the part of the child.

Situation Three – Negative Child – Positive Parent

The result of the assessments suggest that while you are strongly motivated towards academic success and interested in intellectual pursuits, your child has a rather negative attitude. It is likely he or she is far more interested in non-academic activities than in school work. In the younger child such an attitude may not be especially important, although you should take steps to improve matters before these unhelpful perceptions become too well established. If an older child is involved it is essential to bring about changes in attitude as soon as possible. As work at school becomes more difficult and intellectually demanding, children who already look on studying as unattractive, are likely to become even more convinced that such activities are boring and unnecessary.

This produces a change in self-image and a decline in motivation which is often associated with increasing anxiety over anything requiring intelligence. These factors decrease ability and performance, making the child even less successful in school. The result is further and stronger rejection of any tasks demanding mental effort. In this way a downward spiral is generated, each failure leading to a greater rejection which, in turn, produces further failures.

The fact that the child has a strong dislike, or at best a lack of interest, in activities which you strongly favour can easily lead to family rows. The more you stress the importance of school studies and the need for intellectual effort, however, the more negative the child's attitude is liable to become. This is especially likely if the child does make an attempt to improve but fails.

The American psychologist Leon Festinger developed a theory called *cognitive dissonance* to explain what happens when a conflict arises between behaviour and attitudes. In a classic experiment he had students perform a very boring task, then they were asked to try and persuade others to do the same job by telling them how interesting it really was! Some of the students were paid a small sum to lie, others a large sum. Later, when their attitudes were explored, it was found that the students who had been given high payment still rightly regarded the tasks as stupendously boring. But the others felt they really were quite interesting after all! Festinger's theory explains the change of outlook like this. Where the payment for lying was large the students were able to tell themselves: 'I am only doing this because of the money!' But the low paid people could not make sense of their behaviour in this way. So they came to see the task as being more intrinsically rewarding than it had been.

In everyday life the same sort of thing happens when a heavy smoker is exposed to information about the health risks he runs. This produces conflict which, because it is emotionally distressing, must be resolved. He can achieve this in one of two ways. By changing the behaviour, that is giving up smoking, or by changing his attitude towards the risks involved. If he is unable to break the habit he will have to reject arguments which create dissonance. He may do this by telling himself:

'I know there is a health risk, but all life involves some sort of risks,' or he might think: 'My grandfather smoked fifty cigarettes a day and lived to be over eighty, so it can't be that risky!'

What he cannot do, according to Festinger, is live with the psychological conflict of both smoking and accepting it will harm his health. How does this help explain negative attitudes in the child? Well, when children are unable to do something which grown-ups tell them is important and which, in order to gain their parents' love and esteem they dearly long to accomplish, a similar kind of conflict is created.

Like the smokers, they have to get rid of the dissonance by changing either their behaviour or their feelings about the activities involved.

The child tries to improve at school, to get higher marks and better reports, to please his parents through greater successes. If these goals are attained the conflict will disappear. But if, like the chain smoker stuck with the habit, he is unable to alter his behaviour then he is likely to adopt an increasingly negative approach to intellectually demanding tasks. He will begin to reject all those activities which adults consider important but which, for various reasons, he cannot accomplish.

The degree of distrust or dislike with which certain tasks are regarded by such children is usually directly proportional to the value parents place on them. If they set a great store by neatness and care their child goes out of his way to make mistakes and produce thoughtless work. Parents who emphasise the need for a thoughtful, quiet approach to life may find the child grows rowdy and impulsive. If they stress the need for examination results good enough to lead to higher education their child may respond with failing grades and the decision to leave school as soon as possible.

An interesting effect of dissonance is that it makes us far more aware of anything which supports our attitudes. At the same time information which would contradict this viewpoint is overlooked or ignored, usually without our even being aware of the fact. The smoker, for example, will be attracted to stories about heavy smokers who lived to a ripe old age but fail to see articles, perhaps in the same newspaper, detailing the health hazards of cigarettes. It is just the same where the child is concerned. Anything which lends credibility to their views that intellectual activities and school subjects are a waste of time immediately captures attention.

In an experiment which I carried out not long ago, groups of children were shown, very briefly, slides of different newspaper stories. Some dealt with people like pop stars and footballers who had become millionaires overnight, others described the rewards offered by careers in science or industry. The children were then asked to write a list of the headlines they had seen. As anticipated those who had little interest in school work tended to have a much better recollection of articles which emphasised how fortunes could be made in non-academic pursuits. Because you have such a positive attitude towards intellectual activities you will tend to notice more readily and attach greater significance to, information which supports this view. Your child is likely to see the world rather differently. Although you share the same environment your minds will be focused on quite different aspects of it to support your very different ideas about what is most likely to lead to happiness and fulfilment.

It *is* important for children to develop their minds successfully. They need intellectual skills of a high order if they are to make sense of an increasingly complex world and to survive in a society which will place greater and greater emphasis on intelligence.

The attitudes created by dissonance *must* be changed if this growth is to occur. But the methods which parents normally use tend to be counter-productive, if not immediately, then in the long term.

You will never convince the child who has a firmly established negative attitude that he, or she, is wrong to dismiss learning and intelligence so readily. The most likely outcome is for him to produce counter arguments of the kind I have described. The result will be increasing anger and distrust on all sides. With such different views of the world discussion alone cannot be expected to bring about change. As the 18th-century writer Dr Samuel Johnson once remarked on seeing two housewives shouting at one another across a narrow street :

'I fear those ladies will never reach agreement since they are arguing from different premises!'

If 'discussion' produces nothing more than raised blood pressure on your part and resentment from the child, bribes, threats or punishments are going to prove equally unhelpful. They may bring about short-term changes in outward behaviour. The child may *pretend* an interest in order to win a reward or avoid a punishment. But their attitudes will not have altered and neither will their basic inability to perform adequately which led to those attitudes developing in the first place.

How then can change be brought about? Experience shows that the best approach is one which looks at the second component of conflict, the child's inability to perform effectively. Since their negative attitudes were generated by failure, and it is not possible to produce success by insisting on a more positive attitude, the only answer is to help the child become more successful. As performance improves, attitudes will then change automatically.

Many parents have found a practical starting point is to focus on all those positive aspects of the child's behaviour related to any kind of mentally challenging pursuit. By that I do not necessarily mean formal school subjects, but any activities which require a certain amount of intellectual input. These can often be developed and expanded until they include an increasingly wide range of mental skills. For example, the father of a nine-year-old, whose attitude towards school work was extremely negative, told me that his son was very interested in stamp collecting. In the past he had used the *promise* of new stamps in attempts to bribe the child towards greater effort and involvement in school subjects. Now a fresh approach was suggested. Instead of having to complete a certain piece of school work properly in order to win another stamp, the child had to produce a short essay about the country where the stamp came from or the historical event with which it was associated. Because this seemed to have nothing to do with school the child was quite happy to look up reference books and discover fresh facts about the background of a particular stamp. After a time he was doing this spontaneously. The essays improved his written English, and his knowledge of history and geography. This led to more favourable teachers' reports, better grades and an increasingly positive evaluation of him by the school staff, which resulted in a general improvement in all his subjects.

Another example comes from the case file of a very bright twelve-year-old boy who had taken an intense dislike to school. So great was his loathing that he frequently played truant or went down with some mysterious illness which kept him at home. The parents discovered that his main problem was mathematics and technical drawing. As the boy had an ambition to work in electronics the father tried to use this as a threat:

'Unless you get better results in your maths classes,' he often warned, 'you'll never be able to do that sort of job.'

The result was disastrous! Not only did the boy's maths deteriorate still further, and with it his desire to attend school, but he abandoned any interest in working in electronics.

A different approach was then suggested, based on the boy's natural liking for the practical aspects of electronic engineering. For his tenth birthday he was given a sophisticated teach-yourself electronics kit which enabled him to carry out many experiments and to build a large number of interesting items. The kit was deliberately selected as being just slightly *ahead* of the abilities to be expected from a child of that age.

With a little help from his father the first experiments were carried out successfully. The course required a certain amount of maths, which increased as the experiments became more complex. Gradually the father withdrew assistance until the boy was working entirely alone and having to perform quite complicated calculations all by himself. This led to a greater confidence in his ability to manipulate figures, an increase in his knowledge and a change in his feelings about the mathematics. Instead of seeing it as a dull and mysterious theoretical subject he now realised it was an intensely practical method for making things work properly. There was a marked improvement not only in his ability in that subject but, perhaps because he was now attending school regularly, in all other areas of academic work.

If you decide to try this approach be careful not to associate those activities which the child enjoys with schoolwork. Avoid remarks like:

'If you play this game you will get better marks in maths . . .' or 'this will help you write better history essays as well.'

The most likely result of such comments is to *reduce* interest in the activity so that it can no longer be used to bring about changes in school work. Produce the improvements you desire slowly, allowing an increase in ability in one area to spread gradually to a wider range of tasks. Be tolerant of mistakes at first. Any new skill is learned through a series of near misses; errors from which experience is gained. If you insist on perfection all at once the child may become bored, anxious or frustrated. As adults we are able to perform, with ease, many tasks which children find difficult and complex. If we could cast our minds back the same problems probably arose when we were trying to acquire the ability. But because early failures are usually forgotten, we expect the child to manage things as competently as we now do and often become irritable or impatient at lack of quick success.

Regard each attempt, however far short of total achievement it appears, as a step in the right direction. If you try to make the child progress too rapidly he is likely to suffer a decrease in self-image and motivation while becoming more anxious about the task. While *any* progress forward is being made reward the child. If setbacks are encountered find out why, do not be content to blame it on stupidity.

Situation Four – Positive Child – Neutral Parent

The result of the assessments suggests that while your child is interested in school subjects and feels positive about intellectual activities, you are rather less attracted to them. Despite this somewhat neutral attitude you may still feel that you give your child sufficient encouragement.

This could well be true. But you would be unwise to take it for granted. Even though you offer praise, show an interest and provide practical help, you might still be undermining the child's attitudes. The crucial point is the *honesty* with which those opinions are expressed and the real feelings you have about devoting your time and energy to them.

When parents tell the child something which is untrue they almost always betray the lie in some way. Perhaps by the tone used or by the silent signals of body language which accompany the words. This clash between what is being said on the surface and what the child understands the parents to mean, can lead to distress and conflict within the youngster. As a result their interest in a particular pursuit may decline even though they are, apparently, being helped and encouraged by their parents.

A good example of this was a nine-year-old girl, in my study, who loved playing the piano. Her teacher was so impressed by the child's enthusiasm and ability that she offered to give her extra lessons at the weekends. The parents would have to drive the child two miles to the teacher's home and collect her again an hour later. They agreed to do this and raised no objection to finding the fee.

'We weren't interested in music, and sparing money for the lessons was difficult at times,' the mother told me. 'But we never mentioned it to her. We never complained about wasting our time driving her backwards and forwards.'

After a while the girl lost her interest in piano playing and became much less competent. The lessons ceased and the child was blamed for not showing more persistence. Were the parents right in thinking it was her fault? Certainly the girl saw their true attitudes towards the lessons far more clearly than they realised :

'Daddy was always glancing at his watch while he drove me to my lessons,' she told me. 'Mummy was always saying how much shopping there was to do and would I be certain to be ready when she arrived.' So far as the money was concerned. 'Daddy was always making jokes about him being put in the poor house by me. Mummy would say I must be good and work hard because it was costing so much money.'

Is it any wonder that, with the assistance presented in this rather punishing way, the child should decide that her lessons were too much of a strain on her parents, or that her interest should decline so abruptly.

I am entirely sympathetic with parents whose time is at a premium and whose finances may be strained by out of school activities. But to present help in a grudging manner, to convey the impression that it is a serious burden, and to use it as a means of increasing the child's anxiety and guilt, however unintentionally, is worse than useless. It would be better not to provide any assistance at all than to do so in this punishing way.

The main danger about having a neutral attitude towards academic pursuits is that if the child's initially high level of interest starts to decline, as it frequently does during the early years of secondary education, the change may not be noticed in time to remedy matters. Difficulties associated with puberty and the growing desire for independence, make formal studying and the restrictions of school rules increasingly intolerable to many adolescents. They may well rebel by almost deliberately behaving in ways which reduce their effectiveness and lower their level of attainments. When this happens, it requires a perceptive, sympathetic and understanding approach to put matters right. The earlier such a reversal of attitudes is detected the easier it will be to restore their motivation, confidence and interest.

Situation Five – Neutral Child – Neutral Parent

The result of the assessments suggest, that neither you nor your child have any real interest in intellectual activities. This does not mean you dislike or despise them, but they do not appear especially important in your lives.

There is nothing particularly wrong about this and no problems need be created when you start to teach your child greater intelligence. This is especially true if the child is aged six to seven and so has only a short experience of school. With an older child there is a slight risk that more or less neutral attitudes towards studying and intellectual tasks may become more negative in the future, as the desire for independence increases during early puberty.

In order to help your child effectively it will be necessary for you, and your partner, to develop a rather more positive approach to the importance of intellectual achievements. The fact that you have been sufficiently interested to read this book and complete the assessment suggests that such a shift of focus will not present any major problems for you.

At the same time it will be worthwhile considering whether any special aspect of school studies, either intellectual or emotional, are causing difficulties and leading to the build-up of unfavourable feelings indicated by a high B score. The exact nature of these problems will be explored by the assessments in later chapters and I shall be explaining how best to overcome them at that time.

A useful source of information about your child's attitudes towards school can be the termly reports. Study them carefully and try to read between the lines to find out what the teacher was really trying to say. Very often, in an attempt to be tactful, teachers use general phrases to disguise specific problems they have encountered with the child. For example 'could try harder'; 'must apply himself more'; 'not sufficient concentration to give her best in this subject' are typical comments on a child lacking motivation or interest. Do not accept such remarks at face value. Try to find out more through sympathetic and gentle questioning of the child or by an informal discussion with the teacher.

This kind of comment usually depresses parents and makes them feel that the child is lazy, rebellious or being deliberately uncooperative. They may respond with threats, warnings, punishment or bribes depending on their personal views about child rearing. None of these approaches tackles the root cause of the difficulties and so is unlikely to do much to resolve the problems.

The only constructive method is to look far more carefully at where, why and how things are going wrong. Thought should be given to each of the factors controlling the expression of intelligence. You should explore self-image, motivation, problem solving skills and the effect of your own neutral attitudes on performance. Successful changes can only be brought about in partnership with the child. They cannot be imposed by means of your superior powers. If you attempt to do so the short-term obedience which results may lead to far more serious difficulties later in the school career. An important point to bear in mind about neutral attitudes is that they can move equally easily in either a positive or a negative direction. As the child grows older some shift is almost certain to occur. Which way the out-look changes is going to depend to a great extent on your feel-ings about the value of intellectual pursuits and school success.

Situation Six – Negative Child – Neutral Parent

The assessments suggest that while you have a fairly neutral attitude towards intellectual activities and academic studies, your child is more negative and tends towards interests which do not make great demands on his mental abilities. Children who, at an early age, develop a hostile attitude to school subjects in particular and the concept of intellectual pursuits in general, are placing considerable restrictions on their mental development. A lack of interest during this period of life is likely to result in a poor self-image, in relation to tasks requiring intellectual skills, a lack of motivation to pursue any kind of academic career, and rising levels of anxiety associated with school subjects. A down-ward spiral may be created in which hostility leads to poor performance, the lack of success to feelings of inadequacy and the sense of incompetence to further hostility towards all activi-ties seen as responsible for such unpleasant emotions.

One starting point for change is to re-examine your own feel-ings to try and discover why you have a more or less neutral attitude towards intellectual activities. Perhaps you hated school and try to avoid anything which revives those unhappy mem-ories. Maybe you feel that teaching is a job for the school and parents ought to leave everything to the professionals. It seems unlikely that this is the reason in your case, however, since you were sufficiently interested and motivated to read this book. You clearly have a positive desire to improve your child's perform-ance in class and to make them show a greater interest in mental activities.

I suggest you start by reading my comments for Situation Three, where I explained why children often adopt a negative attitude towards school subjects. This should help you under-stand the sort of problems you are facing and, hopefully, give you some practical methods of changing the child's attitudes.

The next step is to examine the attitudes of the child's brothers or sisters. If all the children have carried out the assessments, as I suggested, you will have discovered whether anybody else in the family shares the same negative outlook. If this is the case then the child could be getting support and encouragement in his, or her, outlook from within the family. This is most likely to occur, in my experience, when there is an older brother or sister who, having become disenchanted with school, exerts a powerful influence on impressionable youngsters. Work with the family as a whole. It will not be easy to bring about changes in one child while the others remain either indifferent or hostile to intellectual activities.

It might equally be that one or more of the other children is extremely positive about school studies and successful when it comes to mental challenges. In situations like this other children may simply stop trying to compete on the assumptions they will never achieve the same high standards and constantly suffer by being second best.

When using the approach I suggest in Situation Three, be careful not to make unfavourable comparisons between the under-achieving child and brighter brothers or sisters. Comments such as: 'Why can't you do as well as so-and-so' or 'You'd get on so much better if you followed so-and-so's example' will only serve to worsen negative attitudes. They may also begin to undermine the outlook of the successful child.

Situation Seven – Positive Child – Negative Parent

The assessments suggest that while your child has a positive attitude towards school work and intellectually demanding tasks, your own view is rather more negative.

Perhaps you fear that too great an emphasis on academic subjects will harm the child emotionally or maybe you are simply not very interested in what goes on in school. Equally if you are a very practical individual or one whose interests are more active, you may regard formal studying and book work as neither especially useful nor important.

While nobody would dispute your right to such opinions, it is necessary to provide the growing child with a constructive and encouraging atmosphere in which to develop mental skills. At its most basic, such an approach requires that you do not actively discourage intellectual pursuits, talk about them in dismissive terms, or suggest that because the child has interests contrary to your own you are disappointed in him.

However, in order to ensure successful mental development a

rather more active involvement in intellectual activities is highly desirable. This means *positively* encouraging the child in tasks which make demands on intelligence. Although you may not feel personally attracted by such pursuits you can still offer help and encouragement while making your own attitude plain. Do not feign either a knowledge or an interest in something which either baffles or bores you, but use neutral comments when providing what assistance is possible.

For example, one twelve-year-old boy in our study was fascinated by natural history. He kept worms in a large glass tank in his bedroom and obtained sheep's eyes from the local butcher in order to dissect them. The mother found his discussions about the structure of the eye, or the feeding habits of the worms, quite incomprehensible. While making no effort to disguise her own feelings, or lack of knowledge, she went out of her way to encourage and assist her son. This is the ideal approach, combining honesty with the offering of resources the child might otherwise have been denied. Her view as expressed to the child was:

'I find worms horrible things, but it's your room and you can do what you like in there.' Her lack of knowledge was stated in terms such as 'Honestly, Mike, I don't understand what you're saying, but it does sound very interesting.'

Compare this attitude with that of the father of a nine-year-old who had become interested in mushrooms and toadstools. He read many books on the subject, made a comprehensive collection from the woods and fields near his home, and even developed a card reference system which let him find all the details about any specimen within a few seconds.

'Why a boy should want to waste his time with disgusting looking things like that is beyond me,' his father said.

And he was constantly making the same comments to his son. These views were not expressed as his own opinions – to which, of course, he was perfectly entitled – but as unquestionable facts of life. When the boy tried to talk to either parent about his hobby the reaction was coldly dismissive:

'You don't know anything about them that's worth knowing,' his mother told him in my hearing. 'How can a little boy understand things like this?'

Eventually the father decided that the time had come to 'change' his son's interests. One morning he went into the room and threw the entire collection including the cards into the bonfire. He then bought the boy a football and told him to go and play 'proper' children's games with his friends. The result was a sullen, uncooperative child who developed emotional problems serious enough to need professional help to sort out. What an opportunity lost! How easily the child's interest could have been expanded to generate a desire to explore many other areas of study, chemistry and biology, ecology and geography, English and drawing. A chance for the child to expand his mind and his range of abilities in an enjoyable way had been destroyed perhaps for ever.

Do not try to impose your own views too powerfully on the child. It is reasonable to hope that they will be interested in the things which you find interesting but use tact and patience when putting over these views – especially if they tend to diminish the value of intellectual pursuits.

Situation Eight – Neutral Child – Negative Parent

The assessments suggest that while your child is uncertain about the right attitude to adopt towards school studies and intellectual pursuits, your own outlook is rather negative. Perhaps you consider that such interests are less worthwhile for the growing child than physical skills. Maybe you feel the child is too young to become seriously involved in academic work and should be allowed to play games and sports in order to build up good health.

Many parents who are rather uncertain about the importance of mental tasks see the intelligent child in stereotyped terms as the unpopular school swot, the weedy youngster with glasses who has no interest in games and spends his life among dusty books. Such children are also held to be socially inadequate, anxious, unhappy and emotionally disturbed. With such a mental image of the 'intelligent' youngster it is no wonder that parents do not want to encourage their own children to become over bright!

As I explained in an earlier chapter numerous studies have shown that children whose minds have been allowed to develop successfully are often above average in physical and social skills as well. Their health is usually superior, they are happier, more sociable and better balanced emotionally. On the sportsfield their physical prowess is matched by a high level of intelligence which allows them to plan winning strategies and then carry them through with confidence.

By helping the child to expand his, or her, mental abilities you will not be turning them into some kind of freak, unable or unwilling to relate well to others. On the contrary you are most likely to increase these social skills, make them more popular and better able to achieve a good measure of success in whatever they attempt. It is important for parents to adopt strong and positive attitudes towards the importance of intellectual activities in cases where the child seems uncertain which approach to choose. A neutral attitude can just as easily become negative as positive, and the direction of the shift will be determined very largely by your own outlook.

Situation Nine – Negative Child – Negative Parent

The assessments indicate that both you and your child have a fairly negative attitude towards academic activities and the importance of intellectual pursuits. This probably means that you see eye-to-eye on most things in life, and there is likely to be far less conflict over school work in your household than in those where the parents' attitude is much more positive than that of the child! But, clearly, unless something is done fairly soon the child is not going to feel sufficiently interested to gain academic qualifications. The fact you decided to read my book suggests you are interested in helping him become more intellectually successful even though you may not have realised that attitudes had anything to do with intelligence!

The child's current outlook is very likely a reflection of your own views. It is also probable that his friends are chosen from children who share an equally negative attitude towards school work. Such friendships provide encouragement for underachieving children and, if brothers or sisters share the same views, this support also extends into the family.

It may be that the very negative viewpoint has developed from a belief that intelligent children are unhappy, unhealthy and emotionally unbalanced. If you are rather extrovert and mostly interested in outdoor activities the notion that your child might develop in such a way could be extremely distressing.

It is essential to develop a strong, positive attitude towards intellectual challenges if your child is going to have freedom to increase his, or her, mental abilities. Even if you attempt to conceal your true feelings and to provide encouragement and support, the underlying attitudes are bound to become apparent through a whole range of small, subtle but unmistakable signals. These include the choice of particular comments, the tone in which praise is expressed, and the amount of interest shown as well as a whole range of body language signs. The barely suppressed frown of boredom or irritation as the child recounts some story about school, the forced and artificial smile of encouragement and praise for an academic success and the degree of tension in your body when involved in an intellectual activity will all serve to betray your true feelings to your child. As I explained in Chapter Three, attitudes are affected by all the other factors that combine to unlock intelligent behaviour. In turn they influence each of them to good or bad effect. Nowhere is their potency greater than when it comes to helping create the second key component of cleverness, the child's image of himself.

In the next chapter I will explain what makes self-image so vital, how children develop a view of their abilities and their worth and why, unless this image is bright, the child will never show his true brilliance.

Chapter Nine

DOES YOUR CHILD THINK HIMSELF STUPID?

Mark learns quickly, gets high marks in exams and is thought of as an intelligent child by parents and teachers. Martin learns slowly, does poorly in exams and is regarded as unintelligent by the adults who know him. What is even more important than the opinions of grown-ups, however, are the views those boys take of their own abilities. Mark sees himself as clever. Martin believes himself to be a dunce.

In this chapter I want to explore the role of self-image in intelligence, for research has shown that whether a child appears bright or dull to others depends to a great extent on how he appears to himself. As Dr Kaoru Yamamoto of Arizona State University, one of America's foremost experts on the influence of self-image, has remarked:

'The child's concept of his ability may be as crucial to his success as ability itself.'

In other words, children often seem unintelligent because they think themselves stupid!

The relationship between self-image and achievement has been investigated by two researchers at Wayne State University, Michigan. When they began their study, Dr William Wattenburg and Dr Claire Clifford knew that self-image was closely linked to academic success. What they wanted to discover was which came first. Did a good performance create a positive image of self or was it the other way around? To find out, they assessed children in their first term at kindergarten on tests designed to measure both self-image and general intelligence. Three years later they saw the children again, in their primary schools, and tested both their IQ and their reading ability. The results were conclusive. Children whose self-image had been strong when they started kindergarten – long before any classroom successes could have exerted an influence – were more fluent readers and had a higher IQ than children whose self-image had been poor.

But if school does not give the child a particular image of himself what does? Like so much else in life, this concept is now seen as resulting from what happens during the earliest months of life. A time when the parents exert their most powerful influence over the child's destiny.

How Your Child's Self-Image Is Created

An American psychologist who has done more than most to emphasise the importance of self-image in controlling the direction of life, is Dr Carl Rogers. The creator of Rogerian Therapy, he regards self-image as evolving from two basic human needs; the desire to be loved and accepted by people who really matter to us in life, especially parents, brothers and sisters and intimate friends. These, Dr Rogers believes, are the most powerful feelings we ever experience, stronger than physical desire and more potent even than the instinct for survival.

Gaining love and acceptance from his parents is probably the first lesson a baby learns. He quickly grasps the fact that smiles, wriggles, gurgles and leg kicks will produce a cuddle or a caress, an interlude of entertaining play, warm words and tender expressions; all messages assuring him that he is cared for and wanted by other people. As he grows older he comes to realise that more complicated responses are necessary to gain the same amount of affectionate attention. A smile alone is not enough. It must be made at the right time. Gurgling sounds have to be transformed into words, then phrases and finally intelligible sentences before parents accept them with any enthusiasm. It is not enough just to reach out blindly, movements have to be precise and associated with the right expression.

Gradually the child's behaviour changes to satisfy the demands of his parents. He perceives that the price of love and attention is being able to do certain things in a specific way. He also learns that other activities, which may seem just as interesting, produce a withdrawal of love and a rejection by the parents. In this way the child comes to understand ways of controlling situations. From this knowledge and ability, or lack of it, arise the two basic components of self-image; a sense of *competence* and a feeling of *personal worth*.

Competence is formed from the views of others, parents, teachers, brothers and sisters, as well as on the outcome of formal assessments such as examinations, term grades and IQ tests. How much importance is attached to these opinions and results will depend on how significant the adult appears to the child and how much value is placed on school studies. A child who fails in the classroom and is thought badly of by teachers may still have a strong sense of competence created by some other talent or skill, being good at sports, playing chess well, acting, dancing or singing for example.

Self-worth is usually assessed by the children themselves either in terms of their popularity with others or by evaluating the merits of their behaviour. Although the opinions of adults are important, when it comes to deciding whether some activity is 'good' or 'bad', even young children are capable of forming accurate judgements for themselves. In a recent study, I asked six-year-olds to write stories about imaginary animal characters who had fantastic adventures on a magic planet. I then talked to the children about the things their heroes had done. The idea was to create situations far removed from anything the child could have experienced, to see if they were able to apply rules of behaviour to abstract situations. The results showed that, even at this early age, most of the children were capable of assessing actions in terms of complex and – by adult standards – morally acceptable conduct. At birth a baby has no concept of *self* let alone any self-image. He sees everything in the world simply as parts of his own body. It is only very gradually that he comes to realise that certain objects, such as his hands and feet, belong to him while other equally important things – like the face of his mother – are outside his direct control. As he grows so does his self-image. Just as an oil painting is created from thousands of separate brushstrokes, all blending into a single impression, so too is the self-portrait the child forms made up of thousand upon thousands of individual experiences of the world. Some are big enough to stay in the memory for ever. A humiliating punishment or an unexpected reward, for example, may remain fresh throughout his life. If you think back to your own childhood I am sure half-a-dozen such incidents will almost immediately come to mind.

But the majority of image building events are so brief, slight and subtle they are barely even noticed although their effect may prove lasting and profound. A mother's fleeting smile, a flicker of anxiety or a flash of anger, on the face of a parent, a nod of brief encouragement or a quick frown of disapproval. All so rapid and apparently trivial that they are barely perceived and almost instantly forgotten. All of them, however, capable of adding one more brush stroke to that internal self-portrait.

In fact, they serve to create not just one image of self in the child's mind but two distinct portraits. These may be very similar or completely different. When they are identical emotional harmony reigns but when they differ the outcome is almost inevitably conflict and distress.

Your Child's Ideal-Image v. Your Child's Real-Image

Your child's ideal-image represents the sort of person he would dearly like to be. It will probably incorporate most of those qualities which you, the parent, admire. If you place a great emphasis on honesty, truthfulness, hard-work and success, then these are very likely to become part of the ideal-image of self.

The real-self is a portrait drawn not from ideals but from life itself. From everything which the child sees himself saying, doing and achieving. Very often the child does not much like this image and may deny that it is a genuine likeness. When this happens you can be certain there is very little similarity between the two portraits. The result is psychological conflict so disturbing it has to be resolved as rapidly as possible.

Such conflicts arise either through a lack of competence or a decline in self-worth. Usually one follows fast on the heels of the other. Consider, for instance, what happens to a child who starts secondary education confident of his ability to learn a foreign language. In his primary school he found no real difficulty and so has a positive sense of competence in the subject. But, when the lessons become harder, he begins to get confused and fall behind. Failure replaces success. He doubts his competence. If languages are important to him his self-worth will also be affected. Previously his ideal-image (as somebody who can learn languages) and his real-image (as somebody who does well when learning languages) were in agreement. Now the images no longer match and this leads to distress. He can restore the emotional harmony in one of two ways. By improving his performance or by changing his self-perceptions. He may attempt to do the former by working harder, asking for extra help and so on. If this succeeds in improving his ability then the two images will once again match. But if he fails, then ideal-image must be adjusted to take this inability into account. He may come to see himself as a child who is unable to learn languages, who despises them and can see no good purpose in wasting his time with such tedious nonsense! I am not saying that he *thinks* through the situation in this way, or is even aware of the reasons for his change of attitude. Like so much else concerned with the creation of self-image it all takes place below the level of everyday awareness.

I have chosen an example involving only one subject to illustrate the kind of changes which come about when conflicts arise between ideal-image and real-image. In practice the effects are usually far wider, covering many, or most, subjects and building a self-image in relation to school as a whole rather than any particular aspect of academic work. Even though it may start with dislike for a certain subject the decline in feelings of competence and self-worth which result usually spread their influence over the child's whole approach to life.

Initial failures can be due to many causes which are not a direct reflection of the child's mental abilities. Perhaps they were ill, missed classes and dropped behind the others as a result. Maybe there were initial confusions in the child's mind which he was too anxious or timid to admit to the teachers. It sometimes happens that a child is frightened of or dislikes a particular teacher and either misses as many of those lessons as possible or is too worried to concentrate. It can also be the result of an inborn difficulty that makes the child incapable of doing what is required.

This was the cause of the problems facing Jimmy, an eight-year-old who was brought to see me not long ago. In his first term at school he had done quite well. But success proved short-lived. In the second term he dropped to the bottom of the class and stayed there. At home he became, by turn, aggressive and rude or sullen and apathetic.

The impression made by his parents at our first meeting was interesting. They were carefully groomed, arrived exactly on time and handed me detailed notes describing their son's behaviour. It was clear they took a pride in careful, ordered and considered actions. There was an emphasis on neatness and precision in all they said and did. Unfortunately, it was equally apparent that Jimmy – partly because of the way his nervous system worked – was an extremely active, impulsive and poorly co-ordinated child. He had almost a gift for knocking things over, breaking anything he played with and generally creating chaos out of order. In the presence of his parents he became excessively anxious and this only made matters worse. Anybody who has experienced moments of complete panic will understand how much harder Jimmy's fears made it for him to do things right. His parents were made equally anxious by disorder and responded by criticising their son as a way of relieving their own embarrassment and distress.

Jimmy had been brought up with an ideal-image that included care, precision and order. His real-image was very different. He just could not meet his parents' unrealistic standards of excellence. It is doubtful that any child could have been as perfect as they expected, but with his inborn lack of co-ordination it was quite out of the question for Jimmy to do so. While he was still at home it had not been too bad. But school demonstrated to Jimmy just how 'incompetent' he really was. His handwriting was less tidy than the others, his numbers were poorly formed, in art classes he produced messes rather than masterpieces. As Jimmy became increasingly confused and anxious his performance took a sharp decline. Parents and teachers were critical. His drop in feelings of self-competence and self-worth led to an increasing separation between what he felt he *should* be capable of doing and what he could *actually* achieve. It was not a situation that could be tolerated emotionally so Jimmy set about resolving the distressing conflict between the two in the only way he knew how. He started to change his ideal-self to match the real-self. He embarked on a *deliberate* policy of not being able to do things. In this he found the 'achievements' he needed. He was extremely good at doing things badly! Adults scolded and punished him but other children, those who like himself could not cope in class, provided praise. They confirmed his opinion that his way of behaving was sensible; that school was a 'dumb place' to be, and that messing around made one a hero. So Jimmy went right on proving his ability to be the school's most successful failure.

Chapter Ten

TWELVE COMMENTS THAT SHATTER SELF-IMAGE

There can hardly be a parent who has not, at one time or another, scolded and reprimanded their children. But the way in which this anger is expressed varies greatly between families. To some extent, appropriate forms of punishment are determined by what is socially acceptable to a particular culture or society. In Victorian England, for example, children were regularly the victims of violent physical assaults in the home and at school. Then such punishments caused little comment. Today the same treatment would, quite rightly, land the parent or teacher in court.

But, within certain limits, parents are free to control children in any manner they see fit. The methods they choose will depend very largely to how they, themselves, were brought up. If they were beaten, then it is more likely they will strike their children. In cases of battering it is often found that the violent parent came from a home where such violence was regular and commonplace. In some instances blows may be the only comment on their behaviour children receive. I remember watching one young mother constantly slapping her small son although the child appeared to be playing blamelessly and received no explanation for the blows. When I asked her what he had done wrong she snapped :

'He knows . . .'

I doubt that the boy was any wiser than myself. Certainly his mother's frequent assaults did nothing to change his behaviour which continued just as before.

Curiously, many parents who hold up their hands in horror at the idea of physically ill-treating their children show little reluctance over abusing them just as violently with words. These psychological assaults include bitterly sarcastic remarks, guilt arousing complaints, critical comments about their appearance or behaviour, humiliating scoldings in front of others and personal attacks full of cruel invective. The more educated and articulate the parents the more likely it is they will resort to verbal rather than physical punishment. They may believe that a tongue-lashing does far less emotional harm than any other kind of lashing. That such attacks can readily be shaken off by the child. In fact, all the evidence suggests they cause far greater and more lasting damage than occasional smacks and slaps. I must make it clear I am not advocating physical punishments which are demeaning to both child and adult and lack even the merit of being effective. But in terms of injury done to children such physical punishment is likely to produce far fewer long-term difficulties.

In the world of computers there is an expression – GIGO. It stands for Garbage In – Garbage Out and means that if the machine is given a program which is rubbish one should not be surprised if rubbish is all it produces!

In some ways the child's brain is like that computer. It processes information and comes out with a particular way of behaving in the world. The major difference is that the human mind has an emotional as well as a purely logical response so that the impact of psychological garbage is all the more devastating. Research shows that a great deal of verbal garbage is pumped into the average child during the process of growing up. It is hardly surprising, therefore, that many children respond by producing a good deal of 'garbage' behaviour.

There are twelve especially harmful pieces of verbal rubbish which are frequently used to criticise children. When repeated often enough they can cause lasting harm to feelings of competence and self-worth. They either undermine a positive ideal-image and so bring about changes in the real-image, or else create a negative ideal-image to start off with. The outcome is the same in either case. A child whose behaviour and abilities are unproductive and self-destructive.

Children learn lessons from each of the GIGO comments which are usually quite different from those intended by the adults. As you read through them I would like you to consider how many times a week you use any of these comments when correcting your child's conduct.

Comment One: 'Do as I say – not as I do!'

When made in earnest such a remark indicates that the child

has issued a challenge. A parental command has either been refused, or seriously questioned. As I have already mentioned, children quickly develop an understanding of moral behaviour which, while it may lack sophistication, still provides them with a standard against which to judge their own – and other people's – conduct. Certainly their parents are not exempt from critical scrutiny and any behaviour, whether this takes the form of actions or comments, which are inconsistent or hypocritical will be noticed. Such parental responses place the child in the well known 'double-bind' situation. They are pulled in opposite directions by the conflicting demands of those who exercise power over them. On the one hand the child is being told *not* to act in a certain way, while – at the same time – the activity is being implicitly condoned because the adults are doing it themselves.

Children learn both by instructions from their parents and by *imitating* their behaviour. From the earliest weeks of life they pay close attention to what their parents do and to copy them as accurately as possible. Anybody who has watched a two-year-old toddling after his father and managing an almost perfect imitation of the paternal gait, will appreciate just how carefully the child watches and attempts to reproduce the same responses.

This means that double-bind situations, created by the 'Do as I say . . .' comment are especially confusing and unsettling to the young child. As he grows older, and beginning to seek a more independent approach to life, this type of criticism almost always produces frustration and anger, especially in the child whose intellectual ability has developed successfully. They, perhaps better than other youngsters, can appreciate the lack of logic in such abrupt and dismissive remarks.

Children who are frequently exposed to comments like this are unlikely to achieve a stable self-image since they never feel certain of their own judgements.

Dr Eric Berne, the creator of Transactional Analysis, points out that the use of this kind of remark on the part of the parents has a deeper significance. Adults who make such demands on their children, while ignoring it in their own behaviour are often saying effectively :

'It is all right to do this so long as you don't get caught.'

The child who comes to this conclusion may well perform the

forbidden act in private and be perhaps not unreasonably aggrieved if caught and punished for it.

The most likely GIGO additions to self-image are :

I am powerless.

I have no say in what I should do.

I have an inferior status.

I am unimportant.

Comment Two: 'Because I say so ...'

This conveys only a flat refusal. No explanation for the instruction is offered and any possibility of discussing the matter further ruled out. The child's right to know has been dismissed in the most abrupt manner possible.

The comment contains two hidden meanings which are understood by any intelligent child. The first is :

'My word is law and my laws must be obeyed without question. You are powerless to resist my orders and wrong to question them.'

When a decision, which appears no more than simple common-sense, has been taken, it is obviously irritating for adults to have a child naïvely question their commands. But a brusque refusal to offer any explanation and to insist on blind obedience is likely to make the child overly submissive to authority.

Since most parents want their children to show increasing independence this type of remark places the child in the same double-bind situation I described above. On the one hand they are being ordered to obey and not to reason why, but at the same time they are being urged to think for themselves in other situations. This can be damaging to self-image as the child comes to question his own competence. They have no firm guidelines as how best to behave in order to win their parents much needed approval.

The second hidden meaning is that children are of no real importance. Effectively they are being told :

'Your status is so insignificant you have neither the right to a fuller explanation nor the ability to understand it.'

The most likely GIGO additions to self-image are :

I am the kind of person who lets others think for them.

I am the kind of person who obeys authority.

I am not sensible enough to make my own decisions.

I am incompetent.

Comment Three: 'Why didn't you try harder?'

Parents often say this without trying to discover if lack of effort was the real reason for failure. Such comments are frequently made by adults who, like Jimmy's parents, are perfectionists. It can lead to over-motivation on the part of the child anxious to win affection and approval. This state of 'trying too hard' is as damaging to performance as a lack of motivation, as I will explain in a later chapter.

If used on numerous occasions, the comment leads the child to believe that nothing he can do will ever be good enough to satisfy his parents. It undermines self-image by constantly bringing into question both competence and self-worth. The anxiety which is aroused by the need for perfection diminishes performance and so makes failure more likely. In time the conflict between real-image and ideal-image is liable to lead to a rejection of all those goals which the parents valued.

The most likely GIGO additions to self-image are :

I am lacking in ability.
I am a disappointment.
I am a person who lets down those who love him.
I am not worthy of love.

Comment Four: 'Why didn't you ask me before you did that?'

This comment is usually followed by a lengthy explanation of how much better the child might have done if only the adult had been consulted earlier. The lesson learned here is that he should seek parental approval before reaching any decision or attempting some new course of action. As a result he becomes uncertain of himself and fearful in unfamiliar situations. This restricts the desire to find out, to explore, and to discover. Inevitably healthy intellectual growth is damaged.

The most likely GIGO additions to self-image are :

I am the kind of person who avoids trying anything unfamiliar.
I am helpless.
I am unable to understand things without being told what to do.
I am cautious.

Comment Five: 'Why can't you do as well as . . .'

In this comparison the tone of voice usually makes it clear that the child is *less* effective than a brother, sister or friend. Parents often use such a comment in the hope it will motivate the child to try harder by arousing envy or jealousy. Half the objective is usually realised. The child *does* become envious but performance rarely improves. Instead a bitter rivalry may develop between the children. This leads to the admonished child seeking to outpace the paragon in everything except the activities the parents had in mind! The child may fight, argue with, tell lies about, insult, tease, belittle and seek to humiliate the paragon – especially if younger or smaller. This not only harms the child who is aggressive but also the victim of the attacks. Children held up as 'good examples' to others often reduce their performance abruptly in order *not* to stand out from the crowd. Most young children are extremely conformist and match their performance to those around them.

The most likely GIGO additions to self-image are :

I am an inferior person.

I am not so competent as others.

I am less worthwhile than others.

I am not as deserving of love as others.

Comment Six: 'You'll never amount to anything'

The repeated use of such a comment leads to the creation of a self-fulfilling prophecy of failure. The child comes to believe what adults tell him and so ends up failing in virtually everything he attempts.

A basic technique of brain washing is simply to repeat an accusation or command over and over again. In the end the victim ends up actually believing himself guilty of the crime or in agreement with the order.

If repetition can have such a profound effect on the mature adult brain, how more effective must it be with the still developing mind of the child! Children aged between six to ten are especially receptive to the feelings and attitudes of their parents which, through a process known as internalisation, they then make their own. Effectively they are brain washed into believing the ideas handed down to them were theirs in the first place. Tell the child repeatedly he will fail and the child will come to see this not as *your* judgement or opinion but his *own*. The powerful effect of repetition applies to all the GIGO remarks but it is especially damaging where this direct attack on competence and self-worth is concerned.

The most likely GIGO addition to self-image is just one this time. But it is a big one:

I am a failure.

Comment Seven: 'Don't be stupid'

Here the parent is actually saying:

'You *are* stupid.'

It is a harsh and hurtful judgement that conveys no constructive advice or useful information. The parent seldom even defines the actions which led to that conclusion on their part. It is seemingly an objective statement of fact.

Even if children do not know why they should be considered 'stupid' they know how stupid children behave. If used frequently enough, so that the child internalises the judgement in the manner described above, it is likely to result in markedly changed behaviour by the child.

Again there is usually just one GIGO addition to self-image and, again, it is a big one:

'I am a stupid person.'

Comment Eight: 'Can't you do anything right?'

It may be used like a question but it always *sounds* like a statement:

'You *can't* do anything right!'

The key word here is *anything*. The child learns that not only has he made a mistake in that particular task but that adults see him as generally incompetent.

The comment might seem like nothing more than a momentary and harmless exaggeration on the part of an impatient or disappointed parent. When used very occasionally it may do little harm. But young children, like some immature adults, tend to see life in terms of black and white. There are no shades of grey. Everything is an absolute statement, which is probably why TV dramas with clearly defined 'goodies' and 'baddies' are so popular with the young and the immature. But this attitude towards life results in statements such as 'You can't do anything right!' being taken at their face value. When used frequently this absolute rejection of the child's competence becomes a part of his own self-image. As a result he no longer makes any attempt to be competent so that self-worth and performance decline abruptly.

The most likely GIGO additions to self-image are :

I am an unsuccessful person.

I am not the sort of person who can be trusted.

I am the kind of person who makes mistakes.

I am an unreliable person.

Comment Nine: 'Stop acting like a sissy/tomboy'

Such a comment is usually an attempt to change the child's behaviour by making him/her feel humiliated. Without attempting to understand *why* the child is behaving in a particular way, the adult passes a hurtful and sarcastic judgement on them. It is most frequently made to boys when parents interpret their conduct as excessively emotional and hence – by the standards of Western society – 'effeminate'. We have for example developed a folklore which says that girls cry and boys do not. The fact that boys cry far more easily than girls up to the age of five is generally ignored.

Fathers with strong views about what constitutes 'manly' activities and attitudes use such comments against sons who appear insufficiently interested in 'masculine' pursuits. Mothers who value 'feminine graces' make disparaging remarks to girls who dress boyishly or show an interest in anything considered a male preserve.

The intention behind both kind of comments is to make the child feel so ashamed and embarrassed by the label that he or she will behave more appropriately in the future.

The result is often a child unable to show emotions and finding them hard to handle in others. Since young children lack sufficient maturity to conceal their feelings, and may not understand why they should try to behave in a way which seems unnatural to them, considerable psychological harm can be done.

It is ineffective to try and teach 'appropriate sex roles' by direct instruction. Children acquire such knowledge through *modelling*, that is imitating the behaviour of a same-sex adult. It is also important to note that the child will imitate the parent who offers the most rewards, in terms of affection, warmth, interest, stimulation and so on. This means that the boy who is punished by his father for being 'effeminate' is *more* likely to turn to the mother and so imitate more of her behaviour. The daughter who is constantly reprimanded and criticised by her mother for being a tomboy, will similarly turn to her father. Fewer lessons will be learned from the avoided same-sex parent and there may be a tendency to increase the activities they found upsetting.

The most likely GIGO addition to self-image here is the confused plea:

Who am I?

Comment Ten: 'You are a bad boy/girl'

There can be few parents who do not make fairly frequent use of this comment. The point to remember is that 'bad' is a powerfully emotive term for the child. As I explained when discussing Comment Eight ('Can't you do anything right?'), young children see life in terms of absolutes. To them 'good' and 'bad' are the opposite ends of a yardstick by which actions are measured. There can be nothing worse than 'bad' and there can be no shades of meaning within 'bad'.

If told that they are 'bad' often enough the idea will become part of their self-image. The child will conclude that there is no way in which to win approval and love through 'good' behaviour since this is beyond them. They may, therefore, set out to win the approval of those who value 'bad' behaviour. This usually means the most unruly and least academically successful group in class. Because of this they will also be classed as difficult children and poor students. They will be denied access to intellectual stimulation and suffer as a result of both this and their general lack of interest and attention in class.

The most likely GIGO additions to self-image are:

I am a bad person.

I am the kind of person adults think badly of.

I am not liked very much.

I cannot win people's love.

Comment Eleven: 'How can you be so lazy!'

The word 'lazy' lacks any precise meaning in the English language. It is avoided for this reason by psychologists but much used by parents and teachers. A child who is judged lazy by an adult may feel that he is actually working hard. It is essential, therefore, to investigate the reasons behind an apparent lack of enthusiasm or interest on the part of the child before simply branding him as idle. Frequent use of the word damages self-image and may lead the child to the conclusion that no amount of effort will satisfy adults. The child who sees himself as working sufficiently hard may feel that, if he is to be criticised for laziness, he might as well enjoy the benefits of being really idle!

The most likely GIGO additions to self-image are:

I am not the kind of person who works hard.

I am not interested in trying.

I am never going to be appreciated.

I am not the kind of person who takes much trouble over life.

Comment Twelve: 'I'll do that – you're too young to manage it'

The child may indeed be too young to perform a particular task and will need help. But such a direct emphasis on his inadequacy does little to encourage the creation of a positive self-image. Demanding that the youngster only does something after consulting an adult, emphasising his helplessness while at the same time insisting on an increasing self-reliance is a common source of conflict in many families. The situation produces confusion and doubt in the child's mind and prevents the formation of a constructive, positive self-image. In some instances the use of this kind of caution reflects a fear on the part of the parents that their child will become independent and grow away from them. It is a method of applying the brake to their mental growth and it usually works, inhibiting intellectual development by curbing the freedom to explore and the natural desire to discover.

The most likely GIGO additions to self-image are:

I am helpless.

I am unable to make decisions for myself.

I cannot do things on my own.

I am dependent on others.

These are the kind of 'inputs' to the child's biological computer which result from remarks widely used in child rearing. As you can see considerable intellectual and emotional damage can be caused. When this happens it is the children who are blamed, but we must remember that what they put out by way of behaviour is no more than a reflection of the kind of things that we, the adults, have programmed in.

In stressing the harm which can be caused to self-image by frequently used critical comments, it may seem like I am advocating a completely laissez-faire approach to child rearing with the youngster being allowed to do anything he pleases as and when he pleases. This is certainly not the case. There is a considerable amount of research to support the view, held by many parents, that children like and need a structured environment in which to develop. They prefer clearly established rules – although the fewer there have to be the better – so as to guide their conduct. Studies have shown that in families where discipline is haphazard and inconsistent, with occasional bouts of severity being interposed with a parental indifference to the behaviour, bewilderment and self-doubt are created. The child simply does not know how to behave because there seems to be no direct relationship between what he does and what happens. An activity which is ignored on one occasion may produce a punishment the next time it occurs. Self-image cannot form satisfactorily under these circumstances. Children need firm and definite guidelines by which to construct their own rules of behaviour. In attempting to establish these rules, however, parents must be careful not to damage the child's feelings of self-worth and competence. The GIGO rule applies to child rearing just as it does to computer programming. Everything you input to the child's mind, by word or deed, will be somehow reflected in the output.

If you have become accustomed to expressing yourself to the child in any of the ways I have described then it is essential, in order to safeguard their self-image, for you to adopt a more constructive approach. Since your repeated use of certain comments has produced a deeply engrained habit of self-expression, it may not be enough simply to make a decision to respond differently in the future.

Necessary change *can* be achieved without too much difficulty, however, provided the right psychological approach is adopted. This means exploring the emotional forces at work within your family since, as with the formation of attitudes, self-image is created by a dynamic interaction between what you and your partner say and do, and the perceptions of your child.

To discover your own contribution to this interplay, consider how often you use any of the GIGO comments when criticising or scolding the child. The exact words are unimportant, it is the sentiments behind them that matter. So when calculating your score include remarks which are similar in content or effect. Be honest if you want the result to prove helpful. As with the assessment of attitudes, I strongly suggest that both you and your partner work out a score. This is done simply by counting up how many times a week, on average, you use any of the comments. Give yourself one point for *each* use of *each* remark. The GIGO table below tells you how your overall total rates, shows you the percentage of parents in our survey of 1,200 European and American families using a similar frequency of comment and suggests the likely effect on the child's self-image.

Score	Rating	Likely Effect on Your Child
1–4	*Low.* Of parents interviewed 33 per cent used a similar frequency.	Little harm is likely to be done by such an infrequent use of critical remarks. But make a note of those which you do use and then consider what I have to tell you about them in the next chapter.
5–10	*Medium.* Of parents interviewed 55 per cent used a similar frequency.	The use of GIGO comments with this regularity can cause damage to the child's self-image. You would be wise to take steps to reduce the frequency. I will describe how this can be achieved in the next chapter.
11+	*High.* Of parents interviewed 8* per cent used a similar frequency.	This high use of GIGO comments can only damage the child's sense of self-competence and self-worth. It is essential to take prompt action to develop more constructive ways of bringing up your child.

* The remaining 4 per cent of parents claimed not to use any of the above comments or make remarks which expressed similar sentiments. This may be a true reflection of their child-rearing approach. It might also be due to a lack of awareness on their part that this kind of statement is being used. If you are at all uncertain I suggest that you observe yourself in action for the next couple of weeks. Should you do let such a comment slip

out make a note of it, in writing preferably. At the end of the period you can count up exactly how often the GIGO comments are used on the child.

The next step is to discover the strength of your child's self-image. To find out how positive his sense of competence and self-worth actually is. Even if you and your partner scored low on the GIGO comments possible damage may still have been caused by the views of other influential people in the child's life, especially teachers and older brothers or sisters. In the next chapter I will be showing you how this important assessment can be quickly and easily carried out.

Chapter Eleven

ASSESSING YOUR CHILD'S SELF-IMAGE

I am sure you will agree that understanding and helping children would be a great deal easier if one could get completely open and honest answers to such important personal questions as '. . . are you feeling unhappy . . . why are you so miserable. . . . what has made you so angry. . . . has something upset you . . .?' and so on. But the direct approach seldom produces worthwhile information. The child may refuse to answer at all, insist that nothing is wrong, or mumble some confused explanation that leaves you little wiser than before.

A lack of openness when it comes to self-disclosure is not confined to young children of course. Adolescents and adults are generally just as reluctant to reveal their more intimate feelings or admit to emotional problems even when their listener is discreet, sympathetic and only too willing to help. The older we get the more wary we tend to become about wearing our heart on our sleeve or allowing the world too much insight into our true selves. In part this may be from a fear that any such indiscretions will be used against us in the future, in part because we feel embarrassed about some of the things we think or feel. But a major reason is that the real facts frequently contradict the self-image we are so concerned to present to the world. The businessman who is determined to appear tough and self-confident will not easily admit that he is actually torn by self-doubt and riddled with uncertainty. A teenager eager to seem worldly-wise and independent will take great pains to hide his anxieties from others.

Young children are much less likely to protect their self-images by being deliberately devious or deceptive. They are usually fairly uninhibited and lacking in embarrassment when it comes to expressing their true feelings. The problem is that when deep emotional difficulties are involved they generally lack both the necessary insights and the language skills needed to turn those feelings into words. They avoid your questions because they do not know how to reply rather than through any basic unwillingness to do so.

In order to assess a child's self-image, therefore, we need to take a rather less direct routine. Not out of a desire to trick them or put words into their mouths, but to provide them with the means of giving the kind of answers which will be most useful in helping them most effectively.

I think I am . . .	I feel that way . . .
1. Smart	Never__Now and Then__Almost Always__Always__
2. Able to do things well	Never__Now and Then__Almost Always__Always__
3. Good at school work	Never__Now and Then__Almost Always__Always__
4. Careful in what I do	Never__Now and Then__Almost Always__Always__
5. Good at sports	Never__Now and Then__Almost Always__Always__
6. Able to do things on my own	Never__Now and Then__Almost Always__Always__
7. Happy	Never__Now and Then__Almost Always__Always__
8. Helpful	Never__Now and Then__Almost Always__Always__
9. Obedient	Never__Now and Then__Almost Always__Always__
10. Friendly	Never__Now and Then__Almost Always__Always__
11. Kind	Never__Now and Then__Almost Always__Always__
12. Liked by others	Never__Now and Then__Almost Always__Always__
13. Good looking	Never__Now and Then__Almost Always__Always__

Work with your child through the list of thirteen statements. Note, on a separate sheet of paper to avoid marking the book, how often they see themselves in the way described. If you are reading the list aloud to a younger child it is very important to keep a neutral tone so as not to suggest which answer you want him to make. If the child asks:

'What do you think . . .' just reply that he must answer for himself. Never try to prompt, by saying for instance: 'Well, you did something pretty smart the other day . . .' or 'I think you are always helpful at home.'

Do not allow the child to think about any of the statements too long. The best answer will be the one which occurs immediately.

Scoring The Assessment

The only responses which matter are the first two. Award one point for 'Now and Then' and two points for 'Never'.

Total Score	Child's Self-Image
0–10	Self-image is *high*. Child is well adjusted.
11–18	Self-image is at a *moderately high* level, but may need help in enhancing specific aspects.
19+	Self-image is *low*.

What self-image says about your child

Our studies have shown that certain kinds of behaviour can be expected from children in each of the three categories of self-image.

If your child obtained a score of between 0-10 the comments under *High Self-Image* can be expected to apply.

A score of 19 or more means that the behaviours described under the *Low Self-Image* heading can be expected in most situations.

A medium score (11-18) suggests that the child will behave in ways described under both the High and the Low headings depending on the situation. However, these behaviours will seldom be found to an extreme degree.

High Self-Image

Children whose self-image is high are active, alert and anxious for new experiences. They are friendly, confident, articulate, readily expressing their ideas, feelings and desires. They may be rather mischievous at times and tend to enjoy practical jokes, even when they themselves are the victims. They are curious about anything unfamiliar and eager to explore strange surroundings. They ask a great many questions and cannot easily be fobbed off with foolish answers. They will show higher levels of ability than average and be eager to seek out problems and solve them. Tasks will be carried through with persistence and they will give an answer or voice an opinion even when not completely certain of being right. Since such children often feel slightly superior to others they seldom need to lie, cheat or bully to get their own way. They mix well, socially and in school, show less anxiety about life and appear happy most of the time. When difficulties do arise they seem to take them in their stride.

Low Self-Image

These children are less active than average and often avoid new stimulations or unfamiliar situations. They seem shy, withdrawn, passive and are unwilling to mix socially. They are over-sensitive to teasing and taunts by others and are made very anxious by bullying. They tend to live in a world of fantasy, responding to stress by day dreaming. In class they may find it hard to concentrate and will worry excessively about any problems confronting them. They seek help frequently and doubt their ability to find the right solution unaided. They may attempt to compensate for feelings of inadequacy or isolation by bullying, or through cheating and tale-telling, by displays of stubbornness and passive resistance. They are more anxious than the average child and worry about things which a youngster with a stronger self-image might dismiss or ignore. They appear miserable and depressed much of the time – especially in school – and may have difficulties such as bed-wetting, inability to sleep, nightmares, loss of appetite, school refusal or truancy and a constant series of minor illnesses which seem to have no physical cause.

Competence and Self-Worth

You can assess these two components of self-image by adding up your child's score for the first seven statements. This indicates the current level of *competence*. The score on the remaining statements provides a guide to *self-worth*. The table below shows you what your child's standing on each indicates.

You should make a special note of your child's score on these two components of self-image in order to discover if the overall evaluation which he/she has made is related to feelings about competence, or self-worth or both. When we come to look at the best course of action for you and the child, these two dimensions of self-image will be taken into account.

As with attitudes, it is essential to consider all the forces interacting within the family before deciding how best to help the child. This means looking at your own role, and that of your partner, in creating the atmosphere from which their sense of competence and self-worth develops. You can use the assessment results and the Check Sheet below to guide you to the appropriate situation. There I will explain the most effective ways of guiding your child towards a stronger and more positive self-image.

	Score	What it Means
Competence	0–3	Child feels highly competent. Should experience little self-doubt over this component of self-image.
	4–9	The child feels moderately competent. May need some help in improving this component of self-image.
	10+	The child feels incompetent. Needs sympathetic help to bolster feelings of competence.
Self-Worth	0–3	The child has strong feelings of self-worth and is satisfied with personality behaviour and appearance.
	4–9	The child is moderately confident and has a reasonable level of self-worth but may need some sympathetic help to enhance this aspect of self-image.
	10+	The child feels generally worthless and is dissatisfied with personality, behaviour and appearance.

Child's Total Self-Image Score	Parent's GIGO Score		
	High	Medium	Low
High	Situation One	Situation Four	Situation Seven
Medium	Situation Two	Situation Five	Situation Eight
Low	Situation Three	Situation Six	Situation Nine

Situation One

Although it appears you use potentially damaging criticisms far too frequently, the child has retained a strong self-image. In such situations one usually finds that some other influential adult, your partner, a favourite teacher, another relative or an older friend, has adopted a more positive and constructive belief in the child's abilities. As a result he has simply stopped paying attention to your views, and now forms judgements about his competence and self-worth from the comments of these people. This is an unfortunate situation, and not simply because he has stopped taking your opinions seriously and so placed an emotional barrier between you. Research has shown that when one of the parents has a high GIGO score it is very likely to lead to either a complete alienation of child and parent or the eventual undermining of self-image. This is because parents are, obviously, a far more permanent feature of his life than either teachers, friends or other relatives. Where one partner supports the child while another attacks him the result is friction and tension in the home. The anxiety which this creates, especially in a sensitive youngster, is quite sufficient to destroy a belief in himself. I suggest you read my suggestions in the next chapter about how you can improve this currently unhelpful state of affairs.

Situation Two

Your frequent and damaging comments are taking their toll of the child's self-image. Although no lasting harm may yet have been caused, the need for improvement is fairly urgent to prevent harm being done to that sense of competence and self-worth so essential for successful mental development. Once self-image starts to decline its downward progress can prove rapid. Instead of approaching life, and his own abilities, with confidence the child becomes increasingly anxious. This makes it more likely he will fail and, by doing so, simply provide confirmation of his own lack of talent. I suggest that you read my suggestions in the next chapter about how you can reduce the frequency of GIGO comments and help your child improve his self-image.

Situation Three

Of all the possible interactions this is the most unhelpful and harmful. You seem to use damaging criticisms with considerable frequency against a child whose self-image is already far too low. The fact that you have been honest enough to complete the assessment frankly and interested enough to read this book in the first place, suggests a strong desire for change. In the next chapter I will suggest ways in which you can both develop a more constructive approach to your child and improve his sense of competence and self-worth.

Situation Four

Your child's self-image has remained high in the face of rather too regular GIGO comments. To ensure this sense of competence and self-worth stays at its currently helpful level you should start to use a more constructive approach to guidance and criticism. You may believe that, now the damage which such comments can cause has been pointed out, you will be able to refrain from using them in future. If you have any doubt about your ability to break what is, by now, probably a well established habit of response, then the methods suggested in the next chapter should be considered.

Situation Five

The fact that you fairly frequently criticise your child in a destructive manner appears to be taking its toll on his self-image. If your child is aged from six to eight, your attitude is likely to be especially damaging since youngsters of this age have very few outside sources of reference. They rely on you and your partner for information about how they *should* behave and how they *are* behaving. The older child, with access to a wider range of adults and greater experience of life, may be able to disregard some of your more harmful comments. This does not mean, however, that he will be entirely immune to their effects. It is essential both to reduce the frequency and type of criticisms currently being used and to start helping your child towards a more positive self-image. I will suggest ways in which this may be accomplished in the next chapter.

Situation Six

Although you only use a moderate amount of criticism, the child has an unhelpfully low self-image. This must be improved in order to enhance performance and improve mental development.

Start by reducing the level of critical comment. If judging the child rather harshly has become a habit, merely taking the decision not to use such an approach in the future may now be sufficient. The method suggested in the next chapter should prove helpful here. It could also be that your child responds powerfully to even mild criticism. Some children are especially sensitive to any sort of adverse comments and take them far more to heart than a less sensitive youngster. Such a response stems from inborn features of their nervous system which has given them a lower threshold of anxiety arousal than most children. This is an important topic which I shall be looking at in more detail when describing ways of helping the anxious child over his difficulties. To assist your child towards a more positive self-image I suggest you consider the methods outlined in the next chapter.

Situation Seven

This is the best possible combination of scores. You use few harmful criticisms and the child has a strong self-image. Make sure that this favourable situation is maintained by continuing to avoid the type of comments listed in the GIGO assessment.

You should monitor your child's self-image regularly, either using the assessment or simply by keeping a watchful eye on the kind of things they say about their competence and self-worth.

This is especially necessary if the child is subjected to any drastic changes such as moving to a different school; the family going to live in a new neighbourhood; serious illness in the home, or the arrival of another child. The physical changes associated with puberty can also cause difficulties and sometimes lead the child to reassess himself in a negative way.

Puberty can begin as early as seven years in girls (the average is eleven) and by eleven years in boys (the average is thirteen). It sometimes, but by no means inevitably, brings with it difficulties of adjustment. The child with a strong self-image should not experience any great self-doubt, but if this does occur, and either competence or self-worth decline, be prepared to help to sustain self-image using the procedures described in the next chapter.

Situation Eight

Despite your generally favourable approach, the child's self-image is rather too negative. Although it has not been seriously undermined at the moment it will be useful to find out what has been causing the difficulties.

Talk to the child, gently and tactfully, about problems at school, in the family or among friends. Try to discover if a particular teacher, some other pupils or even brothers and sisters are picking on them and being too harshly critical.

If you do discover that such a difficulty exists then it may be possible to put matters right by a quiet word to the school principal or the rest of the family. But proceed with caution. Children with a fairly negative self-image are quick to see confirmation of their own lack of competence or self-worth in adult interventions on their behalf. They easily take the view that: 'I'm not capable of fighting my own battles. They have to do it for me.' Naturally this can only lead to a further decline in self-image.

If you are at all doubtful then the best answer may be to do nothing to change the situation itself. Rather work to improve the child's self-image by making use of the procedures described in the next chapter.

Once this has improved they should be in a stronger position to tackle the problems for themselves.

It may also be that your child is more anxious than others and responds adversely to situations – such as a critical teacher or teasing companions – which others are able to take in their stride. It is quite wrong to blame the child for this. We all react to the world in a unique way which depends, to a great extent, on the way our bodies deal with stimulation. Some people have a much lower threshold of arousal than others and quickly find certain stressful conditions intolerable.

A third possible reason for difficulty is that your comments, although not very frequent, create the double-bind situation I have already mentioned. Problems like this are bound to occur when children are both encouraged to be independent and then criticised for taking decisions for themselves, especially if they lead to mistakes. Under these conditions the child cannot decide what to do for the best. This will certainly lead to anxiety and may also result in the child either never venturing any independent course of action or ignoring anything the parents have to say about his behaviour. Consider whether this situation may not be occurring in your own family. If it is, make sure the double-bind does not feature in your future comments to the child. In the next chapter I will explain ways in which the child's negative self-image can be restored.

Situation Nine

Your child's self-image appears to be rather poor, despite the fact that you do not seem to be over-critical in your comments. This suggests that somebody else in the family, or at school, is creating the problem. If your partner obtained a high GIGO score this could be the cause of the difficulties. If not then I suggest you try to find out whether a particular teacher is responsible. Do this by gently and sympathetically discussing the situation at school. Try to find some suitable pretext for this, so that your interest appears casual. Do not turn the talk into an interrogation and avoid saying anything which suggests *you* doubt the child's competence or self-worth. Children with a rather negative self-image are quick to read confirmation for their opinion into the most casual adult remarks. If there is a teacher who persists in harsh criticisms then you will have to arrange a meeting to talk about this problem with them or with the principal. Do not approach the school aggressively. Rather explain that the child seems worried about a particular subject and ask why difficulties have arisen.

In the next chapter I will explain how you can help your child develop a more positive self-image. But the methods can only be effective if influences which tend to undermine feelings of competence and self-worth are dealt with first.

Chapter Twelve

GIVING YOUR CHILD A STRONG SELF-IMAGE

I call children with a strong self-image 'Can Doers' because that is how they approach each new challenge. They see the unfamiliar as something which *can* be accomplished if they try hard enough. This does not mean they are unrealistic about any difficulties involved. But their confidence is such that they are able to consider what needs to be done coolly and carefully before adopting a particular line of attack. In this way their chances of success are greatly increased. Such achievements enhance their belief in themselves still further.

The usual response of a child with a negative self-image is to protest: 'I can't do it . . .' whenever confronted by some unexpected demand. The 'Can't Doers' usually start by doubting their competence or self-worth in one particular area but rapidly spread this lack of confidence across any related problems. For example a 'Can't Doer' may start out by saying: 'I can't do these sums . . .' when presented with a new set of calculations. Unless something is done to improve his feelings of competence this response quickly becomes 'I can't do any sums . . .'

The 'Can't Doer' sees insurmountable obstacles in even the simplest tasks and makes life far more complicated than it need be. The world of such children is filled with impossibilities while that of the 'Can Doer' is full of possibilities. The reaction of many adults to the persistent 'Can't Doer' is to dismiss them as stupid. In fact it is their self-image which lets them down so badly, not their mental abilities.

An interesting experiment, which demonstrated how 'Can't Doers' can easily be transformed into efficient 'Can Doers', focused on the supposed differences in mathematical abilities between girls and boys. In the past the explanation for the poor performance of females in maths tests was to claim they have 'non-mathematical' minds. But a study in the United States has shown that the fault lies in learning rather than any inborn differences in the workings of the brain. Like all other aspects of intelligence it stems from early lessons in life.

From their first experiences of education, most girls are conditioned to believe that maths is a subject at which only males can expect to excel, a skill of such complexity they could never understand its subtleties.

Judy Genshaft of Ohio State University, and Michael Hirt, of Kent State University, decided to see what would happen if these negative expectations were changed, and the girls were encouraged to believe they could do well. If they were turned into 'Can Doers' would their ability to manipulate numbers improve? To find out, thirty-six schoolgirls were randomly divided into three groups of twelve. All the pupils were about the same age, had been attending maths classes regularly and were of similar intelligence. Girls in the first group received two extra maths lessons each week for eight weeks. These periods were designed to improve their interest in the subject as well as their problem solving skills; girls in the second group were trained in problem-solving but also had instruction aimed at reducing anxiety and enhancing self-image; those in the final group only had extra coaching in solving mathematical problems.

At the end of the experiment no change in attitudes or abilities was found in the third group. Girls in the first two, however, had not only improved their understanding of mathematics, but showed a far greater interest in all science subjects. Their maths had improved as their self-image changed. The researchers commented that:

'These subjects were underachieving because of . . . generally negative stereotypic attitudes.'

Behind the psychological jargon there is a simple message. Change the self-image and you change the abilities.

In this chapter I want to tell you how to turn the underachieving 'Can't Doer' into a confident and successful 'Can Doer' by bringing about two essential changes within the family. The first is a reduction in the use made of GIGO comments, the second an increase in responses aimed at enhancing a child's image of himself and his abilities. The assessments should have revealed which of these changes is most likely to be necessary. If you are interested in gaining the widest possible understanding of how self-image can be improved, I suggest you read all of this short chapter. Otherwise you need only look at the methods which are appropriate to your particular family situation.

Building Family Feelings

If you have used destructive criticisms for a number of years you may have grown so accustomed to responding to your child in this way that it will take more than good intentions to break the habit. So here is a method which has proved very effective in building better feelings in the home.

You start by constructing a 'GIGO box' from any medium sized cardboard container with a slit cut in the top. Now copy down any of the comments from Chapter Ten which you use regularly and add any other frequently used remarks which are equally harmful to the child's self-image. Attach this list to the front of the box.

Explain to the child, or children, that you should be told: 'GIGO Dad . . .' or 'GIGO Mum . . .' each time you use any of the comments on the list. When this happens you must place a small sum of money in the box. Wait until the total reaches a reasonable amount and then spend it on some activity which you can enjoy *together*.

Describe the rules of the GIGO game carefully so that the child is able to distinguish between reasonable comments and those remarks whose main effect, you all agree, is to attack their competence or self-worth in a damaging way. The child is not allowed to designate as 'garbage' commands or criticisms which arise from your rights as a parent. For instance, you are perfectly entitled to tell the child to wash his hands before sitting down to lunch. But to express this order in terms of a personal attack such as:

'You're a filthy person. Don't you know what soap and water are for?' is not legitimate.

Similarly a constructive criticism like:

'Your writing is hard to read, I suggest you go more slowly,' is fair and helpful. To tell the child: 'You are a messy little idiot who will never write properly,' is not!

The GIGO box serves as a constant reminder of the comments which undermine the child's self-image and focus on a harmful habit that needs to be broken. The method has the additional advantage of improving family communications. As the child becomes more aware of the difference between fair comment and verbal assaults he learns better ways of expressing his own feelings. Temper tantrums and outbursts of fury in which a child may yell abuse at his parents usually occur because he has no other means of explaining his anger or distress over what has been said or done.

You may feel that the GIGO box concentrates on the parents' responses but takes no account of the poor conduct or bad behaviour which caused them. This method does nothing to prevent you from criticising, commenting on or complaining about the child when you feel the need to do so. I am not suggesting you stop providing instructions or issuing commands when this is necessary. So long as these are reasonable and made in a way which respects the rights of the child, no harm will be caused to self-image. The test for a GIGO remark is really very simple. Ask yourself how you would feel if an adult, especially one in a superior position, said the same thing to you. Now try to imagine the effect this would have on your sense of competence and self-worth if you accepted what was said at face value. How would you feel if you believed them to be telling the absolute truth about your personal merits or capabilities?

It will quickly become clear which of your comments are destructive. You should also begin to see more easily why damaging verbal attacks are unlikely to bring about the desired change in behaviour. If you were constantly being abused in this way by a powerful adult, wouldn't your conclusion be that nothing you could ever do would meet with his approval? That it was pointless to try and make him like you, or have regard for your abilities? That the best thing to do was close your eyes and your ears to those hurtful, hateful comments?

You can guide the child's behaviour in the direction you want it to go without resorting to any sort of punishments and at the same time create a strong, positive self-image. Here's how it can be done :

Rebuilding A Shattered Self-Image

Kind words alone are never enough to restore the self-image of a child who has come to believe himself incompetent and worthless. It is essential to take practical steps to improve his perceptions, enhance his confidence and rebuild his faith in his own capabilities. This takes time and requires not only patient under-standing but a knowledge of the correct psychological procedures. The methods I shall describe are used successfully by family therapists in Europe and America, but have not previously been generally available. Experience has shown, however, that parents who are sufficiently motivated to help their child can use them just as effectively as skilled practitioners.

I will begin by describing the procedures and then tell you how to create a teaching programme precisely tailored to the unique individual needs of your child.

The Effect Of The RP Factor

The RP Factor is the balance between rewards and punishments used when controlling the child's behaviour. Dr Kaoru Yamamoto of Arizona State University has found that a 5 : 1 RP Factor is the most effective. This means that the child is given five rewards for every one punishment. Dr Yamamoto's studies have shown that if the RP Factor is less than 5 : 1, in other words where the child is punished more frequently, self-image is almost inevitably dam-aged. Not only that, but the conduct for which the punishment is being inflicted seldom vanishes. It is merely transformed into some other kind of equally undesirable activity. For example, the child may show such signs of disguised hostility, as stubbornness, passive resistance, dumb insolence, indifference, or sullenness. If these too are punished he may retreat into an intense fantasy world. Children treated like this quickly give up hope of being able to win their parents' love and approval. They see them-selves as too inadequate ever to meet their demands and so abandon the attempt.

I am not suggesting that you give up all forms of punishment. Clear limits on the child's behaviour must be established, for their own sake as much as anybody else, and infringements of these family rules may justifiably be penalised. What has been made clear by the research is that for every punishment inflicted in response to an undesirable piece of behaviour, there must be at least five other occasions on which desired conduct is rewarded.

The first step to improving a child's negative self-image, there-fore, is to adjust the RP Factor to the correct level. In the case of most families whose children I have helped, this called for little or no reduction in the number of punishments. Rather it entailed the parents becoming aware of, and responding to, opportunities for rewarding good behaviour on the part of the child. Before any changes can be made you must have an accurate record of the relationship between rewards and punishments in your own home. Memory and guesswork are too unreliable for this purpose, so you will need to keep notes for a short period of time. Most parents find that a fortnight is long enough to get a clear idea about how often they reward and how frequently they punish – either verbally or physically. Select a couple of weeks when the family situation is as typical as possible of the whole year. For example, it is best to avoid holidays away from home or occasions when you have guests staying in the house. Both may lead to an unrepresentative decrease in punishments and an increase in rewards. During the observation period you should make no attempt to change your approach, continue to reward and punish just as before.

The simplest way to keep a record is to use a pocket diary and put a 'p' for every punishment and an 'r' for each reward. Do this on all the occasions that you strike or threaten a blow, when you scold the child or deprive him of some treat as a result of his behaviour. Even punishments as mild as a raised tone, angry expression or frowns of disapproval should be noted as a punishment since children usually, and rightly, see them as such. Keep a note of rewards in the same way, writing an 'r' each time the child receives praise, is kissed, cuddled, hugged, given your favourable attention or a material present for good behaviour.

At the end of the observation period count up the number of 'p's' and the number of 'r's'. To find the RP factor simply divide both numbers by the *smallest* to provide a ratio of rewards to punishments. For instance, suppose you noted twenty rewards and five punishments over the fortnight. This is an RP factor of 4 : 1 (*ie* 20/5 = 4 and 5/5 = 1). On the other hand, if there were only thirty rewards to ten punishments the RP factor would be 3 : 1 (*ie* 30/10 = 3 and 10/10 = 1). If there are ever as many or more punishments than rewards there is no need to carry out the calculation since the RP factor is bound to be 1 : 1 or less. This will direct you immediately to the final column in the RP Factor Chart below. The Chart tells you what effect various

RP Factor ratios have been found to exert on the child's self-image.

RP Factor	Influence on Child's Self-Image
4:1	A reasonable ratio and probably rather better than average. However you should still adjust this to the optimum 5:1 level since your child's self-image is somewhat negative.
3:1	Still not dangerously out of proportion, but in the case of your child probably a contributory factor to the rather negative self-image. Research has shown that this proportion of punishments to rewards will adversely affect self-image in the majority of children.
2:1	This ratio has been found to decrease self-image strongly and produce emotionally disturbed behaviour in the majority of children studied. You should take immediate action to adjust the ratio since the disproportionate number of punishments will have a damaging effect on your child's development.
1:1 (or below)	Your child is likely to be in despair of ever achieving behaviour which will satisfy you. He/she may well feel that nothing which is attempted will ever be right or meet with your approval. It may be that the child has already abandoned any effort to please you. Certainly he or she is unlikely to be showing the kind of adventurous or risk-taking behaviour necessary to achieve a high level of intelligence. There is a lot of repair work to be done.

If it becomes perfectly clear after only a week or so that the RP Factor is going well below 5:1 there is no need to wait until the end of the recording period before starting to take positive action to improve the situation. As you begin to do this, however, continue to take a record since it is important to monitor your efforts.

To improve the RP Factor simply start to reward the child more often than usual for all behaviour which you consider desirable. Perhaps in the past you have tended to take the 'good' behaviour for granted, as something the child should be 'expected' to do, while being quick to punish any 'naughtiness'. Unless the situation has deteriorated very badly indeed there will certainly be a considerable number of desirable things which the child does that can win your approval. Do not be surprised, however, if your initial efforts are met with a degree of suspicion or even disbelief. After all, if the child has come to expect a punishing home environment, the sudden introduction of praise will be surprising. The child may become anxious, fearing some kind of a trick or an attempt to lull him into a false sense of security. I must emphasise that such a response is only likely in families where the breakdown in understanding and communications between parent(s) and child has become critical. However the point must be made since some parents seem to expect an instant improvement in the youngster's self-image and become dis-illusioned with the procedure when no such spectacular trans-formation occurs.

Rewards do not have to be elaborate and costly. Indeed simple, but sincere, ones are far more effective than expensive gifts which may give the child the impression that you are trying to buy your way back into their favour. They can range from a warm smile, or nod of approval and a few words of praise, to privileges such as staying up later than usual, being taken out for a trip, watching a favourite TV programme, or having their favourite food.

Where the RP Factor has been very low do not attempt to make any dramatic changes in the first week or so. Raise the proportion of rewards slowly to bring them up to the desired 5 : 1 level within a month or so.

When increasing the RP Factor make a note of your child's scores on the competence and self-worth scales. If the child shows a normal score on self-worth but a poor competence score, then you should centre your additional rewards on displays of competence. If the competence component of self-image is strong but there is a negative feeling towards self-worth then direct your extra rewards to this area of behaviour. Praise the child's appearance when he makes an effort to look especially attractive or neat. Praise the child's honesty and obedience. Congratulate him on making new friends or on performing some act of kindness.

The type of behaviour on which you focus when adjusting the RP Factor depends on the balance between these two components of self-image. It is a good idea, therefore, to make a written note of your child's score on both these scales so that you have a constant reminder of the area where increased rewards are needed.

The second procedure is simple and easy to use, but has proved remarkably effective in helping to restore a poor self-image. Use it right away, even if you are still recording RP information.

Earshotting

Have you ever been pleasantly surprised to overhear some highly complimentary remark about yourself? The fact that the comment was not intended for your ears makes it all the more agreeable and flattering. When people say something nice to our faces we can never be sure that it is not an attempt to talk their way into our good books. But no such suspicion clouds the pleasure of an eavesdropped remark.

Therapists make deliberate use of the 'overheard' comment in the procedure known as 'Earshotting'. It has achieved remarkable results with low-image children and studies have shown that this approach is likely to prove more successful than direct praise alone. The child with a very poor opinion of himself finds it hard to believe that grown-ups could ever think well of him. When offered a compliment he tends to be suspicious and look for the trap. Often he will reject it as an adult trick and become suspicious about the person who offered such an unlikely comment on their abilities.

Earshotting clearly needs prior agreement between the adults concerned and it has to be done carefully. There must be no suspicion on the part of the child that pre-planning is involved. A typical 'earshotting' exercise might work as follows. The mother is working in the kitchen and talking to her husband in the next room. Both are aware that the child is playing just beyond the half-open door and can hear what they are saying. She takes advantage of this situation to speak in glowing terms of something good the child did :

'John did his homework as soon as he got home,' she might say. 'He certainly is getting on well these days.'

The father then responds by echoing his wife's praise and pleasure.

It is, of course, essential not to speak unnaturally loudly or to emphasise the words in such a way that the child becomes aware you are really holding the conversation for his benefit. This would defeat the whole purpose of earshotting. Nor should you make excessive use of the techniques. Use it sparingly and only at times when it can be achieved effortlessly and naturally.

Do not underestimate the power of this procedure. Child psychologists have found it to be an extremely effective method whereby parents can provide a much needed boost to a negative self-image. Remember that all young children crave the approval of their parents above everything else, even if they do not always seem to demonstrate such a need.

Contrived Losing

This technique simply consists of letting the child beat you at some game or sport, then showing your respect for his ability. Naturally it is important to lose in such a way that the child has no suspicion you have 'thrown' the game. Such a procedure works best to enhance the competence component of self-image, but it is also helpful in improving feelings of self-worth. No matter what the game is you should begin to make a series of deliberate mistakes, slowly but surely placing yourself in a losing position. When the child takes advantage of these 'blunders' you should respond with some complimentary remark such as – 'that was neat . . . you are certainly on form today . . . that was a good move'. Avoid criticising yourself as this suggests you see your failures, rather than the child's ability, as being responsible for the level of success achieved.

This easily adopted procedure has been found to have a powerful, positive effect on the child's self-esteem. To win against an adult, a being most young children regard as all-knowing and all-powerful, is regarded by most youngsters as an accomplishment of major proportions.

Positive Self-Talk

What we say about ourselves plays a considerable part of determining how we see ourselves. If a child succeeds at some task and says:

'That must have been easy because I was able to do it,' he is diminishing his own abilities and his faith in himself. If he says, on the other hand :

'That was pretty tough but I am good at problems' he gains in self-regard.

A technique based on this seemingly elementary idea has been developed by Dr Lloyd Homme of the Westinghouse Research Laboratories in Albuquerque, New Mexico and is based on the fact that if you tell yourself something often enough you will come to believe it.

The ability restricting effects of negative self-talk are most often seen in the area of memory and mathematics.

'I can never remember anything . . .' people will tell you. 'I've a memory like a sieve . . .'

When it comes to simple arithmetic many are equally pessimistic about their chances of success :

'So long as it doesn't involve any numbers I can manage. But I'm hopeless at maths. No head for figures at all.'

One of the first things to do when trying to improve either your memory or your maths ability is to stop convincing yourself about how badly you are performing.

The parent can start to put this procedure into practice by getting the child to put a desirable piece of behaviour into words in order to describe them to somebody else. The mother may say, for example :

'Go quickly and tell Daddy how well you did that,' or

'Go and tell your teacher how much time you spent on your homework last night.'

These are the kind of remarks the child with a low self-image longs to think about himself but doesn't dare to believe. At first a great deal of encouragement will be needed, especially when the self-image is very poor. But persist. Get the child to tell first other people, and then himself, how well something has been done. I am not suggesting that you encourage them to adopt an unrealistic approach towards tasks, and to claim perfection when the results fall far short of this. Merely to start to say positive things about their ability rather than either ignoring achievements or seeing them in a negative light.

Family Participation

Many children with a low self-image feel excluded from the

family group, especially if there is a brother or sister whom they see as much more capable or worthwhile than they are. You may reply that all your children are encouraged to take part equally in making family plans and decisions. But experience has shown that it is hard to be completely even handed if one child is apparently so much more competent, enthusiastic and articulate than another. It is also important to bear in mind that *your* view of the family situation may be quite different to the way the child sees things. And it is *their* perception of the role they have within the family group that determines self-image.

Listen to the child's views patiently and treat all suggestions with serious consideration if they have been proposed in a sensible manner. Thank the child for the contribution and discuss it, do not dismiss the comment with an impatient shrug. Ask for help from all the children, not just those who are the most vocal and ready to give advice. The more you reward and encourage participation the more readily it will be provided.

When using this procedure – and the same applies to all those in this programme – make sure you are sincere in your comments. If praise, congratulations, compliments, encouragement or thanks are given in a half-hearted or patronising manner the child will be aware of this and disregard them.

Teaching the Procedures
How frequently you should use each of the procedures described in this module, and how best you can introduce them to the child, will depend on the current self-image. The score obtained in the assessment can be used to help you here. Remember that the two components of self-image – competence and self-worth – should be balanced. If one is much lower than the other (and the assessment should have revealed this) then pay special attention to building it up.

The Teaching Timetable
This should only be regarded as a guide. Modify the timetable, by introducing more training with one procedure than another, as the circumstances demand. Be flexible and watch out for changes which will require you to adjust the schedule. If the self-image is very low do not expect miracles. It may take weeks or even months before the child starts to respond in a more effective

manner. Do not become discouraged or disillusioned. What you are attempting is difficult, delicate and time consuming. It will demand all your skill, sympathy and patience. But the rewards will more than justify the investment, for yourself and – especially – for your child.

Procedure	How Often You Should Use It		
	Child's Self-Image Score		
	11–15	16–20	21+
RP Factor	In all cases adjust this so that it is 5:1		
Earshotting	1 in 2 weeks	1 per week	2 per week
Contrived Losing	1 in 3 weeks	1 per week	2 per week
Positive Self-Talk	1 per week	3 per week	5 per week
Family Participation	As often as a suitable occasion arises in all cases. Where the self-image is especially low try to make certain that occasions *do* arise at least once a week.		

Chapter Thirteen

IS YOUR CHILD AFRAID OF INTELLIGENCE?

Children very often behave in an apparently stupid manner not because they lack mental abilities, fail to understand what is expected of them, or are incapable of doing what is required, but simply because they do not *want* to act intelligently.

To understand why this curious situation should have arisen, and appreciate how a child learns to be afraid of intelligence, we have to consider the sort of rewards people expect for behaving in a particular manner. For there is only one way in which any child can appear intelligent: if he has the *desire* to do so.

Psychologists have long recognised that behaviour occurs in response to various *needs*. These range from needs essential for the survival of the species, eating, drinking, mating and so on, to needs which may be regarded as equally vital for psychological survival; affection, recognition, self-fulfilment, success and that powerful need described in Chapter One, to feel in control of events.

Different needs produce various behaviour, the main function and purpose of which is to satisfy those needs as quickly and completely as possible. Where intelligence is concerned this driving force is termed the *need for achievement*. It is to energetic and efficient mental activity what the powerful physical drives of hunger and thirst are to bodily responses.

Need for achievement produces a motivation for seeing and solving problems whose potent influence on performance is seldom fully appreciated by parents or teachers. Psychologists, however, have no doubt about its importance. After twenty-five years research into its impact on intelligent behaviour, one of America's foremost authorities on the subject, Professor John Atkinson of the University of Michigan, has concluded that:

'Any measured differences in what had been called general intelligence, scholastic aptitude, verbal or mathematical ability . . . can be given a motivational interpretation.'

This is an extremely significant statement. What Professor Atkinson is saying, in simple terms, is that classroom success or failure depends, more than anything else, on the need for achievement felt by a particular child. This need exerts an effect over any sort of intellectual task, from doing an IQ test to taking an examination. His claim is backed by hard evidence gathered in experiments going back over a quarter of a century.

But it would be a disastrous mistake to suppose that if a certain level of motivation is essential for effective performance, a far greater amount would prove even more beneficial. The research clearly shows that quite the opposite is true. Too much need for achievement is every bit as harmful as having too little.

The Drive Towards Achievement

If your child badly wants to attain some goal a high need for achievement will be created. This results in a strong motivation, or drive, to overcome any obstacles standing between him and success. If the problems are solved the goal will be gained and the need for achievement satisfied. This leads to a decline in the motivating force. To give a simple example, we can imagine a child showing intense interest in finishing a large, complicated jig-saw. As soon as the final piece has been pushed into place, however, the puzzle is abandoned. The need for achievement was satisfied the moment the picture was completed.

This process can be thought of as progressing through the three steps shown in the diagram below.

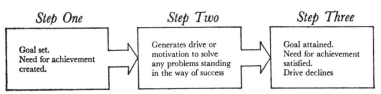

Step One	*Step Two*	*Step Three*
Goal set. Need for achievement created.	Generates drive or motivation to solve any problems standing in the way of success	Goal attained. Need for achievement satisfied. Drive declines

Here's how it might work in real life. A girl wants to come top of her class in mathematics. This creates a *need for achievement* (Step One) and produces a *drive* to reduce the need (Step Two). She can only do this by behaving in a certain way, for instance by concentrating hard during lessons, working patiently through exercises, performing all her calculations carefully, and checking the answers she gives. These activities should help her attain her goal of top marks and so reduce the drive generated through her desire to excel in the subject (Step Three).

This is what will happen in an ideal situation. But many things may go wrong. The goal may not be considered sufficiently important to the child so the need for achievement remains low and the drive generated is inadequate to overcome the obstacles encountered along the way. Suppose the girl in my example had not been especially interested in getting high marks in maths, but was merely trying to please her parents. Instead of responding to setbacks and mistakes in a positive way, as a correctly motivated child would have done, she used them as an excuse to abandon the goal as hopeless. Equal harm can be caused if the need for achievement is too high. The girl might then have done well during the routine exercises but gone to pieces under the pressure of a final term test. In this case she might have been tempted to blame 'nerves' for her failure, and her teachers might well have agreed. In fact the true culprit would have been her unhelpfully high need for achievement.

You see we all have an optimum level of drive, whether this is being generated by the need for achievement or the desire to satisfy some other physical or psychological need.

For most people this optimum lies about halfway between the state of no drive at all and extremely powerful motivation. If we drop below this level there is a reluctance to make any real attempt at all, it simply does not seem worth the effort. If the need rises too high we may revert to old ways of behaving which are better established than the newer, more efficient, but less well learned responses.

This happens because we can only acquire new skills gradually and, in the early stages of learning, spend more time doing things wrong than getting them right. As each fresh level of ability is reached there stretches behind us far greater experience of error than of accomplishment. The way in which complex tasks are mastered is shown in the diagram below which represents what psychologists term a *Learning Curve*.

Let's look at the way the girl works her way up this learning curve as her knowledge of maths slowly improves. During the first few lessons she has little ability and makes a great many mistakes. By learning from these, and acquiring fresh strategies, she becomes increasingly capable. At day twenty she feels con-

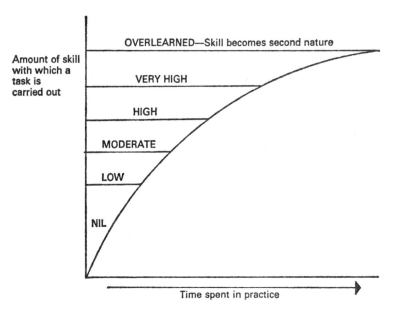

fident of her ability to tackle any problems to that level of complexity. But behind her skill on day twenty are nineteen days of
lesser achievement. Under pressure she is likely to slip back to
an earlier level of performance whose tactics are more familiar
to her. We can compare the situation to that of a learner driver
who has progressed beyond grinding the gears and stalling the
engine, except in moments of emergency. Then his new found
motoring confidence deserts him and he starts to make the same
errors as when he was a raw novice. The only time we can be
confident of performing consistently well, under almost any conditions, is when the necessary techniques have been *overlearned*.
This is the way one describes an ability which is so well practised
that it comes as second nature. We all possess many skills which
come into this category, including reading, writing and – for
experienced motorists – driving a car.

A high need for achievement puts a person, especially a child,
under great pressure. As the goal comes closer and closer, this
stress increases and so makes it more likely that performance
will slip back down the learning curve. The girl coped well under
the pressures of everyday class work but was let down on the
crucial test by her excessively high need for achievement.

Most people have had the experience of wanting something so badly, and trying so hard to achieve it, they failed because of stupid mistakes and foolish errors of judgement. On other occasions, when the goal is seen as less vital, a relaxed and almost carefree approach is adopted which brings success with hardly any effort. In such situations the need for achievement is at its optimum to produce strong motivation without the accompanying anxiety.

But this is not the only way in which need for achievement affects performance. It can also influence the way we approach a problem and the information we consider when deciding how it should be tackled.

Attention and Achievement

Every waking moment we are bombarded with messages from our five senses. If equal attention were paid to all these signals life would quickly become impossible. So the brain only takes notice of some of them while filtering out any not considered important. The mind is focused only on those aspects of the world seen as significant to the needs of the moment.

As you sit reading these words for example, the majority of information should be coming from the printed page. However, it is quite easy for you to change the selection of messages. If you switch to 'touch signals' you will become aware of the texture of the book under your fingers, the pressure of the chair against your legs and so on. Switch to 'hearing signals' and a whole range of previously suppressed or dimmed messages will be attended to as noises from the rooms around you or from the street beyond come flooding in. The more familiar we are with our surroundings the less attention is paid to routine sounds and sights. Which is why people can tolerate living close to railway lines or under the flight paths of airports.

The ability to filter out everything except material relating to the task in hand is what we mean by concentration. When a child sets about solving a problem, learning new material or trying to understand an unfamiliar idea, he must selectively attend to certain pieces of information and ignore others. For example, suppose he is asked to find a solution to the following question : *What is 'x' when* $2x + 3 = 5x - 3$.

To find the answer the child must first bring all the 'x' terms onto the same side of the $=$ sign. This demands the ability to filter out, or ignore for the time being, any number in the equation which is not followed by the letter 'x'. If he is unable to attend to the question in this way he will become confused by irrelevant numbers and unable to find the right answer.

Whenever we are asked to solve a problem or to understand a new idea it is essential to have the ability to concentrate on one idea at a time while temporarily forgetting anything else. Without the correct amount of filtering, confusion and failure must result.

The work of the American Psychologist Professor John Easterbrook has established a clear link between the need for achievement and the effective use of selective attention. It works like this.

In any problem solving task or learning exercise there are certain essential *cues* which tell us how to proceed. If we can recognise them and interpret their meaning correctly, these cues act as signposts directing us along the right road to an answer. Children are taught which cues matter in a particular task and how to make use of them once they are identified. But it is up to the child to discover which are relevant and which have no bearing on the required answer. In the maths question above, for example, relevant cues are the numbers with an 'x' after them. For a child able to recognise their significance they showed quite clearly the steps necessary to solve the problem. To see what I mean, try your hand at this question. Working out the answer depends on a knowledge of differential calculus. Yet even a non-mathematician can solve the problem if bright enough. *As a guide, an intelligent person takes six seconds to come up with the correct solution.*

Two cyclists are on a track 20 miles apart. At the same instant they begin to pedal towards one another at a steady speed of 10mph. There is a fly on the handlebar of one bike. As soon as the cyclist begins to move, the fly takes off, travels to the oncoming bike and then returns again. He continues to do this, flying at 30mph, as the cycles draw closer and closer to one another. The distance which the fly covers clearly decreases from one flight to the next. But, assuming no time is lost in turning around at the end of each trip, how far will he have flown when the bikes meet?

Did you get the answer? It is, in fact, *30 miles*. You see the only relevant cues in that problem are the distance and speeds. It is clear the cyclists will meet in one hour. You are told the fly's speed is 30mph. Therefore he *must* have covered that distance when the bikes meet. I told you that an intelligent person could solve the problem in six seconds simply to put you under pressure. To give you a high need for achievement – we all like to prove ourselves bright – and so, I hoped to focus your mind too narrowly on the question. To make you pay attention to irrelevant cues while ignoring the only facts needed to provide an answer.

Professor Easterbrook suggests that motivation acts rather like a telescope. It narrows the field of view, magnifying what is important and excluding the insignificant. Up to a point this helps us concentrate on essentials. But, if the need for achievement rises too high, you can quickly reach the state where it is impossible to see the wood for the trees.

Imagine a fairly typical classroom scene. A bright boy is reading a dull book with little interest. His need for achievement is low. His attention wanders. He looks out of the window, daydreams, listens to a whispered conversation between his neighbours, and only takes in an occasional word from the text. Then the teacher announces a test at the end of the lesson. As he is a child who usually gets good marks and wants to come top in class his need for achievement immediately increases and his attention becomes far more selective. He focuses his mind on the book and ignores distractions.

But suppose instead of just announcing a test, the teacher added that boys who did badly would be severely punished. The child now becomes so overmotivated that his attention is far too selective. Instead of understanding the concepts described in the book he concentrates on just a few of the facts, grasps only a small proportion of the ideas. His knowledge is incomplete so he does poorly in the test.

The illustration below shows how different levels of motivation affect our ability to attend to various features of the environment and so influence the cues we notice.

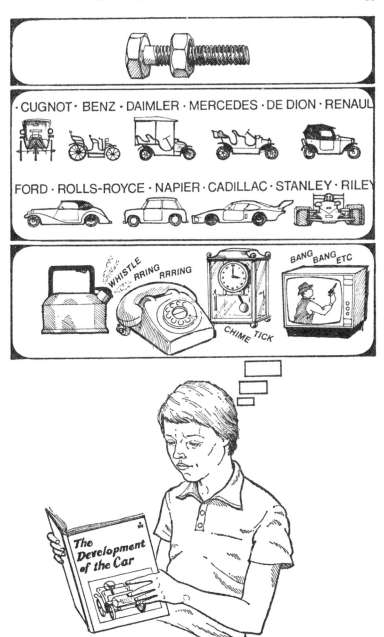

Too high a need for achievement makes us pay attention to too few relevant cues. The optimum level of need for achievement helps us select the most relevant cues. Too low a need for achievement makes us pay attention to too many irrelevant cues. As you can see, need for achievement affects the child's ability to behave intelligently in two crucial ways. First it sets the level of drive and then influences the efficiency with which selective attention operates. Where the need for achievement is too high the result is performance reducing stress and tunnel vision. When it is too low there is not enough motivation to persist in the face of setbacks and attention is so general that irrelevant cues confuse the issue.

But need for achievement is not the only factor involved in motivation. Studies conducted by Professor R. C. Birney, Dean of the School of Social Sciences at Hampshire College in the United States, have shown it to be opposed by an equally powerful counter force. This is called the *fear of failure*.

How Fear of Failure Works

The child with a strong need for achievement works in such a way as to achieve success. A youngster whose thinking is dominated by the fear of failure has the same goal in mind. But the motivation is very different and so is his approach to the challenge. He tries to ensure success by making failure almost impossible. This means setting himself very modest goals which he is certain to attain, by having humble aspirations which can easily be satisfied, by keeping his expectations so slight that they are almost incapable of remaining unrealised. The self-image of a child motivated by fear of failure is low, both in terms of competence and self-worth. His attitude is unhelpfully negative, his problem-handling skills massively inhibited by a refusal ever to take a risk or move boldly forward into unfamiliar intellectual territory. Children with a fear like this are often found among the kind of youngsters I described in Chapter One as Middle Classers. Gerard, aged nine, is a typical example of that type of child. At school his average termly position is fifteenth out of a class of twenty. He might come far higher if he stretched himself a little, but this would be taking too much of a risk. He knows that he can remain at fifteenth place without any fear of failing. He does not appear a complete dunce and is easily able to compete with boys who offer little challenge to his position.

The attitudes of these students can be compared with those of the achievement motivated children like this. They tell themselves:

'I am going to avoid failure by making certain I always succeed.'

The attainment orientated child says to himself:

'I am going to achieve success even if I have to run the risk of failure.'

Why should some children set their sights so low? What makes the child with a powerful fear of failure do almost anything to succeed except try harder to become a success? It depends, you will hardly be surprised to hear, on the lessons that youngster is taught.

Need for Achievement v. Fear of Failure

I once heard a consistently underachieving child described as somebody who had 'let failure go to his head!' That remark contained a good deal more psychological truth than the speaker probably realised. For the perception of failure, and the fear which this generates, is very much a learned response to life.

At birth the infant has no notion of what it means to achieve something. He knows neither success nor failure. He simply behaves. It is not until much later that the idea of *not* being able to do something comes to assume such importance in his life.

This is hardly surprising since one response to a particular performance is highly subjective. A poor student who scrapes through a tough exam may be over the moon with joy. One who expected straight A's may consider a single B to indicate humiliating failure.

Whenever we start to do something unfamiliar we bring to that task an expectation of the outcome based on past experience. The poor student expected to fail because this was what had happened in earlier exams. The good student anticipated an 'A' on the basis of previous marks. It is the unexpected result that gives us pause for thought and makes us reconsider our abilities. The failure that was predicted or the success that everybody knew would be achieved does nothing to influence the need for achievement or the fear of failure.

Consistent failure to achieve an expected result creates a condition known as *learned inadequacy*. It is the seed from which a fear of failure grows.

The child who starts to fail becomes increasingly sensitive to those failures which may soon come to dominate his thinking. Such successes as he does enjoy are regarded, by him, as much less important indications of his true abilities. Selective attention functions to focus his mind on every mistake and misjudgement, to blow them up out of all proportion, while causing him to overlook the good points of his performance. Expectation of failure leads to a lowering of goals which may also prove unattainable because the child has become so obsessed with his inability to do things well. If failures are punished by parents or teachers, as they often are, he also learns to fear the outcome of everything attempted.

The child with a high need for achievement will usually hazard a guess even when not quite certain of the right answer. If he is right it will be a success the others did not achieve. If he is wrong it won't do much to damage himself either in his own eyes or those of others. A child with a high fear of failure, on the other hand, hesitates to respond, even when confident of the answer, because a mistake would cause him further humiliating loss of face. The rewards just do not seem worth the risk.

In order to transform a fear of failure into a need for achievement the child must be allowed to start experiencing success in situations *where failure was anticipated*. It is not enough merely to point out to the child his achievements in areas where such success was the most likely outcome. Remember what really gets through is the unexpected result. The victory that was snatched from the jaws of defeat against, as the child sees it, overwhelming odds.

The first step towards helping your child develop a constructive need for achievement is to discover whether he is in any way hampered by a fear of failure or handicapped by too great a desire for success. You must also find out what influence your own view is exerting on this level of need. Both these important factors can be assessed using the simple procedures I shall outline in the next chapter.

Chapter Fourteen

ASSESSING ACHIEVEMENT NEED

Young children have such powerful imaginations that they often live in a world where fantasy seems more real than reality itself. We can make use of this ability in order to gain valuable insights into their level of motivation and need for achievement. This assessment, based on the pioneering studies of Professor McClelland and Professor Birney, allows the child to project his own feelings onto imaginary characters in order to achieve far greater self-disclosure than would be possible by direct questioning however gentle and well intentioned. You can use it to discover whether your youngster's mental development is being restricted either by a fear of failure or by an excessively high desire to succeed.

Ask the child to look at the three drawings and then select just *one* from each of the six pairs of statements which appear beneath them. This will produce a total of six responses for every drawing.

Make a note of their replies on a separate sheet of paper to avoid marking the book and then turn to the scoring chart to assess the level of motivation. When reading the questions out to a younger child remember to keep both your tone and expression neutral. He must be allowed a completely free choice if the assessment is to prove valid.

Picture One

'Mary is studying for an important test at school . . .'

1. (a) She is determined to get a high mark and win a prize.
   (b) She is afraid that if she does badly her parents will be cross with her.
2. (a) She enjoys studying.
   (b) She is bored and would like to do something else.
3. (a) She wants to show the others how clever she is.
   (b) She is afraid of doing badly and being laughed at by her friends.
4. (a) Her grade on this exam could make up for poor class-work in the past.
   (b) If she does badly on the exam, she will be put into a lower class.
5. (a) She has been given much help by her teacher and parents.
   (b) She has often been scolded by her teacher and parents.
6. (a) She is proud of having learned a lot for the exam.
   (b) She is afraid her friends will call her a 'swot' and stop playing with her.

Picture Two

'Philip is getting changed for an important match . . .'
1. (a) He is determined to help his side to victory.
   (b) He knows that if he plays badly he will be dropped from the team.
2. (a) He has trained hard for the match.
   (b) He only trained hard because he would be unpopular if he let the team down.
3. (a) He is confident he will play a good game.
   (b) He is afraid he will be hurt during the match.
4. (a) His game has improved tremendously this season.
   (b) He had to practise because the coach kept on criticising him.
5. (a) He has been given special training for the match by the coach.
   (b) He found the training session dull and wished he could avoid them.
6. (a) He is worried that he may make mistakes and let the team down.
   (b) He is angry because he has just been dropped to the reserves.

Picture Three

'Mark was talking to his father one night . . .'

1. (a) He explained that he wanted to become a doctor.
   (b) His father scolded him for doing badly in class.
2. (a) He asked his father what exams he would need to pass to become a doctor.
   (b) He told his father how much he hated school.
3. (a) He said he was sure he could become a doctor if he worked hard.
   (b) He said he felt the work needed to become a doctor would be too hard.
4. (a) He told his father that he would like some extra coaching to do better in school.
   (b) He told his father that he didn't have any friends in school because he was bad at sports.
5. (a) The father promised to help him get on well in school.
   (b) He was relieved when his father said he need not do any more chores around the house.
6. (a) He told his father he was excited by the idea of becoming a doctor.
   (b) He told his father that he was angry because a teacher had made him stay behind after school to do some work again.

How to Score the Assessment

Add up all the 'A' and 'B' statements. Take the lower score from the higher to get a single figure. For example 12 'A's' and 6 'B's' would give you a final total of 6 'A's'. The table below shows you the level of motivation revealed by the assessment.

Child's Score	Child's Need For Achievement Level
High 14-18 A's	Your child has too high a need for achievement. This can easily produce the problems of stress and tunnel vision which I described in the last chapter. Ways of resolving the difficulty are described in the next chapter.
Normal 4-12 A's	The need for achievement level is optimum and should be maintained at this level. This can be done using the procedures given in the next chapter.
Low 2 A's-18 B's	Motivation is too low and there is a fear of failure which is likely to restrict intelligence. You should start to improve the situation as rapidly as possible. How this may be achieved is explained in the next chapter.

With this general idea of the motivation levels suggested by each score, let us now look in greater detail at the implications of these three levels of achievement need.

Need for Achievement Too High (Score 14-18 'A's')

A child with too high a level of motivation is not only likely to suffer from excessive, performance inhibiting, stress and selective attention problems but will also be unable to learn from his mistakes.

Any failure, when used constructively, is an important learning experience. The child who refuses to acknowledge that mistakes have been made is, therefore, denying himself essential lessons. At present setbacks are likely to be blamed on bad luck, an inexplicable but transitory drop in confidence ('I just wasn't in the mood' . . .) or seen as the fault of somebody else. The child may grumble that a teacher wasn't up to the task of preparing them for a particular test; that the parents failed to provide the right kind of support and encouragement; that the classroom was too hot and stuffy or the other students too noisy. There may, of course, be more than a little truth in any of these statements. But the child with an excessively high need for achievement is more concerned with shifting responsibility for the failure than voicing a legitimate complaint. Once they have cleared themselves of any blame in the matter, at least to their own satisfaction, the failure is pushed aside and forgotten as swiftly as possible.

The risks involved in this approach were shown by a research project in which poor maths students were given extra coaching in the subject. In one class the children were never allowed to experience failure. Their miscalculations were brushed aside by the teachers. The second group received identical instruction, but all their errors were clearly pointed out and they received special help in learning from their mistakes. At the end of the experiment the children sat a test. Those in group two showed a considerable increase in ability, while the 'faultless' first group did extremely poorly.

Children with a very high need for achievement often set themselves goals which are unrealistically high. This makes them walk a tightrope, with the risk of plunging into a state of fear of failure always a possibility. Such a switch can take place so swiftly that it may be missed even by attentive parents and teachers. From a high class position and good marks the child suddenly becomes an underachiever whose previous uninterrupted successes are transformed into unending failure. This shift in performance often occurs when the child moves to a higher form, or following a change of schools. The tendency is then to blame the decline in competence on these changes rather than seeing them as a reversal of motivation. As a result inappropriate measures are often taken to try and bring about improvements in performance.

As well as this ever present risk, these children are often emotionally difficult because they are subjecting themselves to consistently high levels of anxiety. They may be irritable, hard to get along with, easily upset, tearful or moody. Your job is to reduce the level of need for achievement without diminishing, too greatly, the motivation essential to successful intellectual growth. In the next chapter I will explain how this delicate task can be safely accomplished.

Need for Achievement Level Normal (Score 4-12 'A's')

Your child has a healthy desire to succeed, which will provide sufficient motivation to do well and attend effectively to intellectually demanding tasks. This is the optimum range for the growth of intelligent behaviour. He sets goals which are high, but within his capabilities, and do not cause undue anxiety. He can learn from failures without allowing himself to be discouraged from making future attempts at similar tasks. Although some fear of failure statements were picked out, the high need for achievement score indicates that the child does not actually fear failing but rather respects the learning aspects of setbacks. If school performance or intellectual ability in other situations seems poor you must look to some of the other factors discussed in this book to provide the explanation.

Need for Achievement Too Low – Fear of Failure Present (Score 2 'A's'-18 'B's')

The assessment score suggests that your child is more anxious to avoid failure than to achieve success. He dislikes situations where his abilities will be compared with others and, were it not for pressure from parents and teachers, would avoid all activities which carried any risk of failure. To reconcile their fears with the unavoidable necessity of facing classroom challenges such children are likely to adopt one of two very different strategies. The first I have already described. It consists of setting themselves such trivial goals that success is virtually guaranteed. The second is more subtle and leads to a paradox which often baffles adults. The child with a high fear of failure frequently takes on tasks where there is *hardly any hope at all of success*! Where the very failure they fear so strongly is almost certain to occur.

Why should such children cheerfully, almost casually, accept a challenge which would give even the child with an excessively high need for achievement pause for thought? The answer to this mysterious attitude is perfectly simple. If success is impossible because the task is too tough, then failure can always be blamed on the activity itself rather than on the ability of the child.

In practice this leads to the child with a high fear of failure behaving in one of two ways. He may either give up trying almost as soon as an unexpected setback is encountered. This happens when goals which the child thought could easily be won turn out far harder to attain. On other occasions he may press stubbornly on in the face of constant setbacks and certain failure. At a point where a child with a constructive need for achievement would accept that the task was beyond his capabilities and seek further help, the youngster dominated by a fear of failure just carries on regardless.

Such determination usually seems praiseworthy to adults who can admire the child's 'fighting spirit' even while doubting his good sense. Persistence is considered an admirable attribute and we all warm towards a trier. But the approach is really neither sensible nor helpful because it wastes time, increases anxiety and prevents the child from being given the assistance and instruction so badly needed. The child motivated by a fear of failure adopts the 'never give up or admit defeat' tactic because this is the only way he can bring himself to respond.

Such youngsters are unable to admit that they have failed even to themselves, far less confess it to an adult by asking for help. As Professor Birney has rightly commented :

'The dogged persistence is really rigid, apathetic compliance, as is his tolerance for continual routine success at tasks offering virtually no possibility of failure.'

The conduct of children driven by a fear of failure may appear perplexing in many ways because it often seems so paradoxical. If they *fail* in a task where such *failure* was anticipated one might assume that they would be reluctant to make similar attempts in the future. In fact they tend to become *more* ambitious following a predictable setback. On the other hand if they *succeed* in something where failure was predictable they do not necessarily become more confident and adventurous, as logic might lead us to assume, but are often less willing to make another attempt. How can these puzzling contradictions be explained and what do they tell us about the thinking of the child?

The key to both responses lies in the arousal of anxiety. This is such a distressing experience that we all work very hard either to avoid it or, when it arises, to eliminate its mental and physical effects as quickly as possible. What happens when the child with a fear of failure is forced to attempt a task in which there is very little likelihood of success, is that a great deal of anxiety is generated. The very thing which such a youngster fears now seems unavoidable. It is as if somebody suffering from claustrophobia was being obliged to step inside a small, windowless room.

The child carries out the task and, as anticipated, fails dismally. This is the terrible outcome they were so concerned about. But, once it has happened, the worst is over. They experience an abrupt reduction of anxiety and this encourages them to try a similar task immediately afterwards. We can liken their response to the phobic feeling just as bad as they feared inside the room but, having endured the intense anxiety produced by the experience, finding a certain sense of relief that it is over and done with and they managed to survive the ordeal.

If the child expects to fail and succeeds, however, the anxiety is not reduced. They think :

'That was a fluke . . . I can't really do it. I could never do it again . . .'

So they continue to feel stressed and miserable. This response is further heightened by the fact that, because they have attained a goal nobody considered possible, adults are likely to demand a better performance from them in future. To give them unfamiliar tasks to accomplish instead of letting them travel comfortably along in the same, reassuring, rut. Exactly the same response could be expected from the phobic who stayed in that small room without feeling the anticipated terror. They might tell themselves that it would only be worse the next time and that now people would expect them to enter even more confined spaces, such as a lift, because they had coped so well.

Bear in mind that the child motivated by fear of failure is an anxious child. He is a child who feels mentally and/or physically distressed when confronted by an unfamiliar intellectual challenge. His natural reaction, like that of the phobic, will be to reduce the anxiety and attempt to avoid it in the future. When seen in this light even his more bizarre and apparently illogical responses are usually found to serve a purpose and possess a meaning.

Having considered the role of the child we must now turn to your own part in establishing the driving force behind his intellectual behaviour.

Your Role In Motivation

The score achieved by parents on the assessment below has been found to be closely associated with achievement/failure motivation in their children. It is based on research carried out by Dr Sheila Field of the Mental Health Study Centre, National Institute of Mental Health in Maryland and Dr Richard Teevan of the State University of New York at Albany in their intensive investigation of the link between what parents teach their children and the level of motivation which those children come to possess. Read the questions carefully and answer as honestly as you can. To discover the truth it is essential to *tell* the truth.

The Assessment

This test is divided into two parts. The first consists of a list of fifteen statements about things you may teach your child. Note those to which you answer 'Yes' on a separate sheet.

Part I: Expectation Test

I encourage my child to . . .	
1. Do well in competitions	Yes
2. Learn to speak well before a group	Yes
3. Learn dancing and go in for contests	Yes
4. Be successful in hobbies	Yes
5. Be willing to give up some interests in order to do well in others	Yes
6. Try to be good at a sport	Yes
7. Do well in school without help	Yes
8. Try hard to excel in all he does	Yes
9. Try hard to be independent in all he does and not rely too much on others	Yes
10. Show pride in his ability to do things well	Yes
11. Be able to be alone at home during the day	Yes
12. Stand up for what he believes is right	Yes
13. Do household chores well	Yes
14. Earn his own spending money	Yes
15. Make his own decisions about what to wear, how to spend his money etc.	Yes

For the second part of the test I want you to read through

the six different kind of responses listed below. Select just THREE which you regard as typical of the way in which you react when your child's behaviour comes up to your expectations in any of the above fifteen situations to which you answered 'Yes'.

Part II: Responses Test

> When my child does any of the things listed above (to which I answered "Yes") my usual response is to . . .
>
> 1. Give him a hug or kiss.
> 2. Tell him how good he is.
> 3. Give him a special treat or privilege.
> 4. Do nothing to indicate I think he has done something special.
> 5. Show that he has done no more than I expected from him.
> 6. Point out ways in which it could have been done better.

Now look through the six statements below and, once again, select just THREE which are most typical of your response when the child's behaviour *fails* to meet your expectations on those items above to which you answered 'Yes'.

> When my child fails to do any of the things listed above (to which I answered "Yes") my usual response is to . . .
>
> 7. Spank or scold him.
> 8. Show him how disappointed I am by his failure.
> 9. Deprive him of something which he likes to expect, such as a treat or privilege.
> 10. Hide my feelings about it.
> 11. Point out how he should have behaved.
> 12. Ignore his behaviour until he does something I can admire.

Scoring the Test

Start by awarding yourself 1 point for every 'Yes' which you gave in response to the first set of statements. This will give you a maximum score of 15 points.

Now score the second part of the test, which looked at your responses to occasions when your child either met or failed to meet your expectations, as follows :

Statement Number	Award Yourself
1, 2 or 3	Two A's for each of these statements ticked.
10, 11 or 12	One A for each of these statements ticked.
7, 8 or 9	Two B's for each of these statements ticked.
4, 5 or 6	One B for each of these statements ticked.

Proceed as follows:

1. Total up ALL the A's and all the B's.
2. Subtract the smaller score from the larger one so that you are left with either all A's or all B's or a zero (if you had an equal number of both).
3. You now have two separate scores. A number representing the total 'Yes' responses noted at the end of the first part of the test, and a certain number of A's and B's (or a zero score) obtained from the second part of the test.
4. The final step is simply to *multiply* the first score by the second. If, for example, you responded with a 'yes' to eight of the first fifteen statements and were left with 4 'A's' after carrying out the second scoring instruction, the final calculation will be to multiply 8 x 4 to give you the total number of 'A's' i.e., 32 A's. This number will direct you to the correct part of the scoring chart below. There you will find a brief analysis of what the final assessment reveals about your approach to motivating the child. A more detailed explanation, which examines the role of each parent separately, follows the chart.

What the Scores Tell You

Your Score	Motivation Influence	Comments
36 + A's	High	You are applying a high level of achievement motivation. You value success and usually reward your child for a good performance.
3-35 'A's	Normal	You are applying an average level of achievement motivation. You value success in your child but are not insistent on it.
1-2 'A's *Any* number of 'B's A Zero score on the Response Scale	Low	You are influencing the child more to fear failure than to value and strive for success. You deplore failure and see achievement as something which should be taken for granted. If you score 5 + 'B's you are in a danger zone and may become the chief cause of the very thing you so dislike – your child's failure.

As in previous chapters it is now possible to discover the interplay of forces between parents and child by comparing the assessment results. This will suggest which of a variety of possible situations exists in your own family. In the next chapter I shall describe the likely effects of each type of interaction and explain how any difficulties being created can be overcome.

Motivation Check Sheet

Child's Need for Achievement Level	Parents' Motivation Influence		
	High	Medium	Low
High	Situation One	Situation Four	Situation Seven
Normal	Situation Two	Situation Five	Situation Eight
Low	Situation Three	Situation Six	Situation Nine

Chapter Fifteen

GIVING YOUR CHILD GREATER MOTIVATION

Although the differences between children with an excessive need for achievement and those held back by a fear of failure have long been obvious, it is only recently that the reasons for these different approaches to life have become clear.

In the past few years experimental studies have established that children learn a need for achievement by being given a clear understanding that independent, successful behaviour is expected of them and will be rewarded by their parents. American researchers have found that the greater the emphasis which parents place on their children acting independently in every-day situations, the stronger their motive to achieve. When child-ren are encouraged to work out problems on their own, with perhaps the occasional helpful nudge from adults, they develop a healthy self-confidence in most activities demanding intelli-gence.

In a study carried out by Dr Winterbottom, a well-known educational reseacher, mothers of boys with a high need for achievement reported that both they and their husbands had expected the child to act independently from an early age. This approach had been encouraged by frequent rewards and few restrictions had been placed on the child's behaviour. They were allowed to explore freely and satisfy their curiosity by direct experiments. This approach to child rearing was not found in families where the child had a low need for achievement.

When the level of motivation is at its optimum to encourage healthy intellectual development, both parents may claim an equal share of the credit. In cases where there is a harmfully high need for achievement or a restricting fear of failure, how-ever, the contribution of each parent is rather different. In general it is the mother who creates the fear of failure while it tends to be the father who generates the excessive drive towards success.

How The Mother's Influence Works

Dr Richard Teevan of the State University at Albany, New York, has shown that where mothers respond to their child's accomplishments in a neutral manner (as in items 4, 5 and 6 of the Response Scale), but react to their failures with punishments (as in items 7, 8 and 9 of the Response Scale) the result is to create a fear of failure rather than a need for achievement. As I have already explained, children suffering from this fear set themselves very low goals – so as to ensure achieving them – and refuse to take many chances when it comes to intellectual challenges. As a result they tend to be frequently punished by their mothers, thus further decreasing their motivation towards achievement.

Although the mother's attitude towards her child produces long-term effects, the fear of failure motivation can be reversed and a need for achievement substituted.

How The Father's Influence Works

Studies by Professor John McClelland have revealed a close association between the father's attitude and the child's level of motivation. Children whose need for achievement was excessive, frequently had fathers who were both remote and overly demanding. While showing little real understanding of their children's true needs or abilities, they insisted on a generally unrealistic standard of excellence in all that was attempted. Nothing short of complete perfection was good enough and children who failed to meet their expectations, by no matter how small a margin, would be treated to scathing criticism. I remember watching one child excitedly telling such a father:

'I came second in French but first in geography and history.'

His only reward was a frown of anger and the scornful reply:

'Well you've obviously got to try a lot harder in French, Paul. Frankly I find that a very disappointing result!'

Investigating the backgrounds of overly demanding fathers, Dr J. H. Turner of City University, New York, found that the critical factor appeared to be the parents' occupation. Such men more often worked with objects rather than having to deal with people. They usually had little real responsibility and few chances to take independent decisions. Their role as father seemed to provide them with a sort of compensation for their restricted opportunities to exercise authority at work. They supervised their children very closely, showed them quite a lot of physical or verbal aggression and placed strict limits on their self-expression.

By comparison, fathers whose children had a healthy need for achievement were more likely to deal with people than things in their daily work and usually had jobs which gave them responsibility and control over others.

In a moment I will look at the different situations identified by the assessments in order to give you advice tailored to meet the specific needs of each. But, for general guidance, here are six golden rules for creating constructive levels of motivation in your child:

* Encourage independence in thought and action from the earliest moment.

* Let the child do things for himself, even if you become irritated when they fumble and make mistakes.

* Reward children for their successes – a word of praise is usually quite sufficient. But your response to failure should be neutral. Try not to show any disappointment. Look at the positive aspect of the outcome. Used correctly, mistakes can provide an invaluable learning experience.

* A good motto is – 'If the job's worth doing it's worth doing badly!' That is to say tasks should never be avoided just because they cannot be performed perfectly. Let your child try to do anything, within reason, he wants to do even if you know it will end in failure. It is much better for the child to find out his own limitations by experience than have these boundaries set by adults.

* In learning independence of thought and action the child is bound to do things which you find silly and objectionable. Protect them against life's hazards but do not try to save them from every knock and upset.

* Finally I urge you not to look on your child as an agent who will realise all the ambitions you were never able to achieve during your own childhood. Many parents try to use children in this way and the result is almost always to damage their levels of motivation. There is, for instance, the musically inclined mother who longed to win piano competitions as a girl but never had the chance. Now she sees, in her daughter, a chance to relive her youth and make up for those lost opportunities. Then there is the father who always wanted to be a good sportsman but never achieved the first team. He may regard his son as a means of gaining second-hand glory by insisting he does well at games.

It may be that your child is equally interested in the activities which you value and just as keen to excel in them. But that must be *their* decision. An effective need for achievement will only be generated by goals which are truly important to the child himself. It cannot arise from somebody else's dreams or ambitions.

Now let us consider the different family situations which may have arisen to see how each can best be handled.

Situation One

Your child appears to be over-motivated and is striving too hard after success. The result of your own assessment suggests that your emphasis on achievement is at least partly responsible. As you now realise this situation is in many ways restricting to intellectual development and steps should be taken to teach your child a more relaxed approach to life. Ways in which this can be done are described under the heading **Reducing Need for Achievement** on page 178.

Situation Two

Your child's level of motivation appears to be just right. Although you emphasise the importance of success this does not seem to have done any damage. Your ways of rewarding constructive behaviour appear entirely satisfactory and do not require any modification. However, bear in mind that by placing such a strong emphasis on achievement there is the risk that your child might become over-motivated. Watch out for this possibility and be ready to reduce the pressure for achievement if difficulties occur. The Fantasy Assessment should help you identify a sudden rise in motivation as it can be used successfully on several occasions.

You should also bear in mind that behaviour you now regard as independent and success-seeking may come to be seen as precocious when the child reaches his teens. Dr Sheila Field of the Mental Health Study Centre, Maryland, USA, found that children who had a high need for achievement and were independent at an early age came to be considered over-assertive and too independent when they reached adolescence. This led to difficulties at home and in school, leading to the breakdown of previously good relationships and a feeling, on the part of adults, that the youngster was conceited or impudent. The punishing responses which such behaviour produced were harmful to all concerned and frequently led to an abrupt reduction in achievement and ambition.

Situation Three

The results of the assessment indicate that your child has a fear of failure and is under-motivated. This is preventing successful performance and limiting intellectual growth.

However your own assessment, if it was honestly answered, suggests that the fear of failure is not being created by anything which you say or do. The motivational climate seems to be high. Indeed this might be part of the problem. Sometimes an over emphasis on success results in children adopting failure as an easier way of coping with life. It is just possible that your child has given up hope of ever meeting your high standards and deliberately opted out. If you have other children in the family who appear to be much more powerfully motivated, this could be a contributory factor in the child's decision. Where brothers or sisters of more or less the same age seem able to achieve so much more, the less successful child will often dismiss all possibility of attainment from his, or her, mind.

A possible approach would be to reduce the emphasis on success so far as this particular child is concerned. Try to lower your sights and, at first, set more easily attainable goals. Where the required behaviour is seen as being almost impossible to achieve a child may well not bother. But if it lies only a little way beyond the perception they have of their own abilities it might be accomplished. For example, rather than insisting that a child who usually comes in the last five places move to the top of the class, suggest that they try to improve their position by just a few places. If they achieve this, then offer warm praise and congratulations. Do not suggest they have done badly by not coming *top* but stress how well they have done by moving up at all. The next step is to move from a middle position into, say, the first ten and so on. Create numerous stepping stones between the current situation and the desired position. These sub-goals should be carefully worked out so that the gap between them is neither too great – which might invite a feeling of despair – nor too close together. This would lead to even the underachieving child regarding them as too easy to attain and so insufficiently interesting to bother about.

If there are other, more achieving, children in the family then be careful never to try and motivate this type of child by making an unfavourable comparison with brothers and sisters.

Finally you should check that your partner does not use responses which induce fear of failure. The assessment should reveal such an approach to the child and he or she should have been directed to a different situation. If your partner is unwilling to take the assessment then simply observing the way he or she responds to the child's activities ought to provide you with a fairly reliable guide to the partner's attitudes. Try to persuade your partner to read Situation Nine and, if he or she refuses, go through it yourself to see if your partner might not be encouraged to adopt the procedures suggested.

If you are certain that the fear of failure has not developed as a result of anything which has happened within the family, then it is likely that school is to blame. Read my suggestions in Situation Six for dealing with this situation.

You must also, as a matter of some urgency, build up a stronger need for achievement in the child. Do this by making use of the methods I suggest in the sections headed **Raising Need For Achievement** and **Banishing the Fear of Failure** on pages 180 and 184.

Situation Four

The assessment suggests that while your own influence on motivation is perfectly satisfactory the child still has far too great a need for achievement. This may have arisen because he responds very readily to the rewards you offer. Despite their moderate frequency these rewards produce a more powerful effect than you realised. As I explained earlier in the book children differ markedly in their response to stimulation. Bear this possibility in mind when rewarding. Do not suddenly withdraw your praise, but avoid excessive encouragement. You should also take steps to reduce the child's level of motivation. Methods for accomplishing this will be found on page 178 under the heading **Reducing Need For Achievement**.

Situation Five

Both you and your child obtained ideal scores on the assessments. If these were answered honestly there seems no reason for making any changes in the current situation. The need for achievement is at its most helpful and your level of rewards and encouragements are perfectly in tune with the child's requirements. If you feel that his intellectual ability is not sufficiently well developed it will be necessary to look elsewhere for the cause.

The only possible problems created by the current situation lie in the future. As I explained in Situation Two, behaviour which is well thought of when the child is aged from six to twelve may appear less praiseworthy as they reach their 'teens'.

Situation Six

The result of the assessments indicate that your child's intelligence is being limited by a pronounced fear of failure. However, your own influence on their level of motivation appears perfectly satisfactory. You offer rewards and encouragement for achievement and do not place undue emphasis on failure. If the assessments were honestly answered, then the cause of your child's current lack of motivation lies elsewhere, and the most likely culprit is the school. If you have more than one child then a check on the level of need for achievement in the others may provide some clues. If different schools are attended and the fear of failure exists in only one child it strongly suggests that some aspect of their education is actively damaging their level of motivation. Go back through previous reports, including those from earlier schools, to see if any changes in the child's attainments or behaviour have been noted by the teachers. If there is a sudden decline in performance you may be able to pinpoint more or less the precise moment it occurred. The influence of just one dominant and harshly critical teacher can be quite powerful enough to create a fear of failure in only a short space of time. Notice too if there are any particular days of the week when the child seems especially reluctant to go to school, or has spent a disturbed night beforehand. A glance at that day's timetable should reveal the class, subject or teacher responsible for the difficulties. By quietly and gently questioning the child you may then get to the root of the problem. Once you feel you have identified the cause you may be able to help the situation by talking to the head teacher or the one directly concerned. But proceed with great caution. Older children, especially, may resent your 'interference' and feel you are treating them like babies. An informal discussion during a regular PTA meeting is often a better way of sorting out the situation.

It is important to help the child fairly quickly, however, since the current low need for achievement is restricting both the growth and expression of intelligence. The advice contained in the sections headed **Raising Need For Achievement** and **Banishing the Fear of Failure** on pages 180 and 184 of this chapter will help. You can put the methods of work right away without waiting to pinpoint the precise cause of the difficulties.

Situation Seven

If the results of the assessments are accurate they have revealed a rather unusual situation. While your child seems to have a high need for achievement and is, indeed, over-motivated, you appear to be trying to bring about quite the opposite response. The way you behave towards the child is more likely to produce a fear of failure with the attendant lowering of goals and refusals to take chances. It may be preferable to set aside these results for the time being and retake both assessments in a few days. The possibility, at least, exists that either you or your child were what is termed 'faking good'.

This is a problem frequently encountered when people take tests and have some idea of the kind of responses expected of them. To show themselves up in the most favourable light, they select answers on the basis of what they *think* will give the best impression. Some tests contain special 'lie' scale which are especially designed to detect subjects who are 'faking good'. Because this is a fantasy based assessment no direct lie scale has been possible, but a result like this does suggest the possibility that the child has tried to answer in a way which he believed would please you most. The next time you give the test follow the instructions carefully, and try hard not to influence the replies either with words or, just as effectively, by body language.

If you get a similar result it suggests that, despite the unfavourable circumstances, your child does indeed have a powerful need for achievement. This usually indicates such an intense fear of failure that he is 'running scared'. The striving for success is a way of reducing his deep rooted anxiety over failing and a means of boosting a basic lack of confidence. The situation he faces is rather like that of soldiers under fire. So long as he has plenty to do and think about, the dangers seem less frightening and the hazards less daunting. In the short term this may lead to success, but the long-term prospects are far less attractive. Such over-motivation, in the face of excessively critical responses, can cause damage to health and may lead to a sudden collapse of ability, self-image and motivation which is difficult to prevent and very hard to reverse. This can create emotional problems during adolescence even though the current level of success is maintained. The fear of failure can also damage other aspects of life, including social relationships.

Instead of punishing the child for failures and ignoring successes you should start to reward achievements while paying much less attention to failures. That does not mean you should simply shrug them off, since this in itself may seem like a punishing response to the child. Instead take a long, careful look at what was attempted and what was actually achieved. Virtually every mistake and setback contains, within the overall failure, a number of successes and useful lessons. Rather than dismiss the whole attempt as useless, take it apart step-by-step. Praise those things which were done well, analyse what went wrong and use this as the basis for constructive help and creative criticism.

Suppose for example, that you had expected high marks in a school test but only an average grade was obtained. You might normally have commented on all the mistakes in a critical manner, perhaps saying things like :

'You were stupid not to pay more attention to the instructions . . .' 'if only you hadn't been so lazy when it came to studying' . . . 'why does your writing always have to be such a mess?' 'No wonder you let me down so badly. . . .'

If these problems seem to have caused failure to achieve higher marks, then by all means draw attention to them. But frame your criticisms in a helpful way and lace them with encouragement for what was done well : you might, for instance, say :

'I thought the overall presentation of ideas was excellent. You have certainly grasped the main points of the subjects and I liked what you had to say about. . . . The next time you take the exam it would be a good idea to read the instructions very carefully. You see it says you should only answer one question from each part and you tried to do two. I know it's easy to get flustered but that left you too little time to answer as well as you could have done. . . .' and so on.

This helps and supports the child. No harm is caused to self-image or to motivation.

Adopting this approach may not be easy if you have got into the habit of using destructive comments. However, the fact of your reading the Programme suggests you have your child's best interests at heart and will be willing to make the necessary changes. In Situation Nine you will find some ideas for reducing damaging criticisms from your responses toward the child's successes and failures. It will also be useful to help them reduce their currently excessive need for achievement. Ways of doing this are described on page 178 of this chapter under the heading **Reducing Need for Achievement.**

Situation Eight

Your child appears to have a healthy desire for success and a satisfactory need for achievement. This is slightly unexpected since your own score on the assessment suggests behaviour which is more likely to have produced a fear of failure and a decline in achievement. If you continue in this way it is likely that the need for achievement will be diminished or replaced by a fear of failure. Once this occurs the decline in ability, self-image and motivation may be rapid and hard to reverse. Now is the time to make changes, while the child is still well motivated. Read the advice contained in Situation Seven and Nine then put it into practice as soon as possible.

Situation Nine

Your child appears to have a fear of failure which, the assessment suggests, is brought about by your own responses to their behaviour. It seems that while you are quick to point out and punish failure you tend either to take achievements for granted or criticise them as, in some way falling short of your expectations. This approach inevitably reduces the need for achievement and makes the child afraid of failing.

If you work outside the home I suggest you start by examining your attitude to this occupation by answering the six questions below:

1. Do you have as much authority as you would like?

2. Do you get opportunities to make decisions and put them into practice?

3. If you do, then are you given credit for your ideas?

4. Does your job demand a high level of training?

5. Are you seldom reprimanded by superiors in a condescending or humiliating manner?

6. Does your work involve dealing with people rather than things?

If you replied with a 'no' to more than two of these questions this could be an important factor in the way you respond towards the child. Explore your feelings further by looking at the six questions below.

1. Do you sometimes get a feeling of relief after a row with your child or having punished him?

2. Are you able to exert more authority over your child than you can achieve at work?

3. Do you find more things to criticise about your child after a bad day at work than on those days when things have gone well?

4. Do you feel resentment if your child comes to an important decision without consulting you?

5. Do you find it irritating if your child offers a suggestion about a problem you have been discussing with your partner?

6. Do you resent it if your child and partner make family plans without fully consulting you?

If the answer to any of these is *yes* then I suggest you consider your attitude carefully. Do you think it is likely frustrations from work are being taken home and worked out on the child? Perhaps especially on one child who has become a scapegoat for your irritation? In my experience such feelings often arise from resentment – of which you may be unaware – over the child apparently enjoying a freedom of thought and action which is denied to you. It is your way of responding to the child which may well have become a habit and changes are unlikely to occur merely from a realisation that they might be causing harm.

An approach which I have found helpful in the past is to use the GIGO technique described in Chapter Twelve. There it was designed to improve self-image, but it can equally well be used to change damaging attitudes towards the child. Read the procedure described on page 131 and construct a similar box. Write down a reminder that you will make a small contribution to the box each time you express hostility towards the child, who should be encouraged to point out such verbal aggression as it occurs.

Before doing this it is, of course, essential that he appreciates the difference between comments which are reasonable and constructive and those which are unreasonable and destructive. I am certainly not suggesting you should no longer make judgements, which may well be critical on occasions, about his behaviour. Indeed self-confidence and effective motivation are more likely to be enhanced than harmed by providing clear guidance about what is expected of the child. In Situation Seven I explained some of the ways in which you can offer criticisms in an encouraging and helpful manner that turns failure into a learning rather than a punishing experience. However if you tend to use a great number of damaging comments, in addition to those intended to be of practical value, the child may not be able to see the difference between the two sorts of criticism. Try and establish, in both your minds, what sort of remarks are seen by him as unnecessarily harsh. Perhaps the easiest way of doing this is simply to watch the reactions of the child as you make the criticisms. If he appears upset and confused, or apathetic and sullen, then it is probably being viewed as a form of punishment.

It will also be necessary to improve your child's level of need for achievement by using the methods described on page 180 of this chapter.

Reducing Need For Achievement

The purpose of the methods I am going to describe is to help you reduce your child's overly powerful need for achievement which appears to be having an adverse effect on performance. When the level of motivation has been slightly reduced you should find that the child not only enjoys greater success but derives more pleasure from the things he does. At present the excessive striving after achievement leads to activities being seen as a means to an end – obtaining a reward from you – rather than being enjoyable for their own sake.

Turn back to the Expectation Test which formed Part I of

the Parent's Assessment (page 162). Look through the list of those statements you ticked as being pursuits or achievements which you expect from your child. From these select just *two* you consider to be most important.

Now I want you to continue to reward your child, exactly as before, for these activities but to cease to reward them for the remainder. Since providing such rewards has probably become a habit it may be necessary to help yourself bring about this change by proceeding in a methodical way.

The most effective approach is simply to keep a record in a pocket book or diary, of all the occasions when either of the two selected activities are carried out by the child and rewarded by you. You should also note any lapses on your part when rewards are offered for the activities which are now no longer to be rewarded. This will help you to keep in mind the new policy and so make it less likely that you slip back into the old approach.

Those pursuits which you have decided shall no longer be rewarded should not now be punished or ignored. Merely acknowledge them in a neutral way, saying for example: 'O.K. now let's do this . . .' or 'I see you've finished that, shall we try this now . . .' and so on. Never show disinterest or disapproval.

You need not fear that a withdrawal of positive rewards will cause the child to abandon any activity which is of real interest. If it actually gave the child little or no pleasure, and was merely done as a means of obtaining praise or recognition from you, then it may indeed suffer a decline. But this is all to the good. Giving it up will allow the child to devote more time, effort and enthusiasm to activities which he finds truly rewarding. Furthermore, the child will be able to behave in a more relaxed way towards those pursuits which do interest him. He will start to take chances and to experiment more imaginatively with his skill and abilities now that he is deriving satisfaction from the activity itself. You may also find that interest increases for other reasons too as rewards decline. Research has shown that where children receive strong external encouragement to carry out a particular task, the value of that activity decreases in their eyes and they do it more reluctantly.

The final step is to look at the first six items in the Responses Test, which formed Part II of the Parent's Assessment. Notice how you have been rewarding your child for the activities ticked in the Expectation Test. From now on you must offer the same kind of rewards when the child does something which is desirable but not specifically success-orientated. For example, suppose he tidied up his room neatly without being asked to do so. In the past you might have ignored this behaviour or simply taken it for granted. From now on you must be certain to give active encouragement and positive rewards for all these activities. There is no need to provide material rewards the whole time : a smile, a few words of affection or praise are quite sufficient.

You may find it helpful to use the same notebook to jot down the sort of activities which could come into this category to help fix them in your mind. This part of the procedure is important because, in the past, the child may have been mainly rewarded only for activities which led to some obvious achievement or success. By distributing your rewards more equally around a whole range of desirable behaviour you take the pressure off the constant need to achieve.

Raising Your Child's Need For Achievement

Your child's need for achievement appears to be too low to ensure sufficient motivation. This probably means he gives up rather easily and allows himself to become discouraged by initial setbacks. It also seems likely that the low level of drive is associated with a fear of failure and I will be explaining how this can best be tackled in a moment.

All the methods I am going to suggest are simple and straight-forward to use, but have been shown to be extremely effective in bringing about the necessary improvements in intellectual growth and performance.

Start By Setting Goals

Work with your child to establish some realistic goals, the steps which will have to be taken in order to attain those goals and the rewards which will be won once they are achieved. I will discuss each of these stages more fully in a moment, but we should begin by examining the nature of those goals.

To prove effective any goals you decide on must fulfil three essential conditions. These may seem little more than common-sense, yet are often overlooked. They must be :

Achievable : Any goals you agree on must be within the

child's grasp. Do not pitch them too high. For example suppose you decide, with the child, that a goal is learning to swim. This could mean anything from dog-paddling across the width of the pool to crawling the length of the baths in record time. Clearly an achievable goal for a non-swimming youngster would be to manage a width without putting a foot down. Set this as the goal level. You can always progress to a more demanding goal when this has been achieved. Similarly, where an intellectual task is involved, keep it realistically attainable. To tell a child that the goal is to get every question in a test right is excessively demanding. A more realistic goal might be 50 per cent correct. By introducing a goal which is too far out of reach you run the risk of either increasing the motivation to a level that it reduces performance or raising anxiety about failure to a damaging degree.

The easier it is for them to attain a goal, the more they will be encouraged to set and achieve future goals by themselves. Although you will have to help think up and carry out goals at the early stages of this training it is essential that the child takes responsibility for setting their own targets in life as soon as possible. Only in this way can the level of need for achievement be raised and maintained.

Believable: The child must, of course, believe that the goal *can* be attained. This qualification for any goal is important because many parents set goals for their children which *seem*, to them, to be achievable and which they – incorrectly – think the child also regards as believable. The non-swimmer who *cannot* believe that he will ever manage a pool width may well be too anxious to make an adequate attempt. So the goal would have to be reduced still further. To perhaps half a width, or even to a few strokes without arm-bands for support.

The only way of setting believable goals is by working them out in true collaboration with the child. Do not try to impose your ideas on them. There is no point in saying: 'Of course you can do this, it isn't hard . . .' when the child *believes* it to be impossible. Do not insist. Trust the child's judgement and bear in mind that a youngster with a very low need for achievement may well believe that very little is possible. Rather than over-riding this pessimistic viewpoint go along with it. Let the child establish the goal and help them to plan ways of achieving it. The important thing is that the goals are present at all.

Desirable: Find out what your child really wants, and give it to them as a reward for success in achieving the goal. The rewards need not be material. Praise, recognition that something worthwhile has been achieved, even a warm smile of congratulation are often more than sufficient reward. Furthermore, if the child has been allowed to select a goal which is desirable to them, its accomplishment alone will provide sufficient reward.

Planning the Goal Steps

Once the goal itself has been decided the best ways of achieving it should be discussed with the child. Really these steps in attainment can be regarded as a series of sub-goals through which you both have to work in order to reach the final target. Make sure there are plenty of sub-goals. Taking too big a step at once can lead to failure and a loss of confidence, especially with a child whose need for achievement is already low. It will certainly be necessary for you to make most of the suggestions when it comes to planning ways of reaching the agreed goals. The best approach should be carefully worked out and then written down. As each step is achieved it can be ticked off and rewarded in some minor way in order to sustain interest and motivation. A good way of judging whether the chosen goal is too high is to look at the sub-goals which have to be accomplished in order to achieve it. At first there should be no more than three or four steps between the current situation and the final realisation of the goal. If there are too many the risk of failing is excessive and the time needed to achieve the goal may be too great.

For example, suppose that the goal in learning to swim is to do a width without touching the bottom of the pool. Step one might be to do a few strokes without arm-bands. At this stage the adult can be in the water and providing some support for the child to ensure confidence.

The second step might be to swim a few strokes with the adult at a distance. The third step could be to swim halfway across the pool, while the final goal is reached in the fourth stage.

In collaboration with the child set a date by which each of these stages is to be completed. How long you both decide is needed should be left up to the child. It does not matter, at first, if the child elects to have plenty of time. This will reduce anxiety and provide greater confidence. Finally you will agree upon the final reward.

All these components of the goal programme should be written down on a large sheet of paper and pinned up somewhere you can both see it each day, perhaps in the child's bedroom or on the family noticeboard.

Exactly the same approach is taken when teaching an intellectual skill. Start by setting a reasonable overall goal. Then establish sub-goals and help the child work through them. Write down each of these stepping stones to success and tick them off on the chart as they are achieved. In this way you sustain motivation and allow the child to see how much progress is being made. I have used the example of swimming deliberately, even though it may not appear to have anything to do with intelligence. If you can give the child confidence in some enjoyable pursuit which is not directly associated with school subjects, such as playing a sport, it often enhances a sense of competence and self-worth in other areas as well. This improvement in self-image can lead to a greater need for achievement in the classroom as well as outside it. Always remember that each of the four factors is intimately interconnected. Change one of them for the better and it is quite likely the others will be enhanced as well. But you should, of course, tackle all the problem areas at the same time. Do not focus on motivation alone, for instance, in the hope that this will automatically increase problem-handling ability or create a better self-image. Reinforce any spin-off benefits you get from helping the child over one source of difficulties by working on the others simultaneously.

In later chapters I will be explaining how you can organise intellectual activities into a series of goals and sub-goals.

Independence Training

I have already remarked on the importance of helping your child develop an independent attitude towards establishing and accomplishing goals in life. You can set about this most easily by looking at the Expectation Test in the last chapter. Note four of the activities which you failed to tick and begin to encourage your child to behave in the ways suggested. For instance by earning their own spending money, showing pride in their ability to do things well or learning dancing. All the activities listed have been shown to help increase the need for achievement.

As with the goal setting method above, it is helpful to keep a written note of all the occasions on which your child carries out any of the desired activities and whatever rewards were used to sustain their interest. I especially recommend encouragement to undertake some household duties – boys just as much as girls – and to assume responsibility for certain, specific, domestic chores. Research has established that such tasks are associated with an optimum need for achievement.

Banishing The Fear of Failure

In an earlier chapter the child's powerful sense of fantasy was used to assess the need for achievement. This strong imagination can also be used to banish the fear of failure. You take advantage of it using a technique which psychologists term 'cognitive rehearsal', but do not let that piece of jargon put you off! All it means is mental practice. Not only is the method very easy to employ but it usually produces rapid results.

One of the foremost practitioners of mental practice is Dr Richard Suinn, a psychologist at California's Stanford University. He has used the technique to bring about almost any kind of response his clients request, including relief from excessive anxiety, enhanced personal relationships and more skilled social behaviour. His grateful subjects include members of America's Olympic ski-team who have used cognitive rehearsal to improve their performance on the slopes. You can use it to banish the fear of failure and create achieving attitudes in the classroom.

You should start by establishing goals in collaboration with the child and setting up sub-goals as I described on page 180. Now go with the child to a room where you can be undisturbed. Sit down comfortably, close to one another and help the youngster to relax as much as possible by talking quietly about familiar topics. When any initial suspicion or unease has been reduced, look at the list of sub-goals and, starting with the first, get the child to work through them in his imagination. Ask the child to picture himself carrying out that activity as vividly as possible, to not only see what is happening in his mind's eye but to hear, taste, touch and smell the fantasy scene. Help the child, if necessary, to build a very realistic image; almost a mental film show which starts with the child setting out to accomplish the task and ends in success and praise. Because children have such powerful imaginations this should be far easier for them than it is for adults. The only problem may arise from some initial embarrassment or a reluctance to commit himself fully to the fantasy. This will come with practice, so long as you are able to maintain a relaxed, supportive atmosphere throughout the session. Keep each fantasy practice short, so as to avoid the child becoming bored, but make them regular. Just before going to sleep is often a good time. Tucked up warmly in bed, perhaps following a story, the child is already in a relaxed state. What is more, the fantasy images often become a part of the dreams that follow and so are established even more firmly.

If the child is unwilling to participate you should try to persuade him by saying it is a new game. Explain that you are going to see how much imagination he has. As the child starts to build the scene in his mind ask questions about what he can see and hear. If any anxiety is created then quickly go back to an earlier stage in the activity and revise your set of sub-goals, as this indicates that you are attempting to go too far too fast. Whenever possible imagination training should be backed up by real life practice in that particular activity.

To show you how such a programme might be developed, here is the way a mother helped her eight-year-old son overcome a major classroom difficulty.

Although the boy's strong fear of failure affected performance generally, one particular task seemed to be causing him more distress than the others, so this was chosen as the first target for change. A regular part of the English lessons was having to read aloud from the course book, something he found almost impossible to do. Although his ability was above average when reading silently or to his mother, the boy became tongue-tied and confused in front of others. His mistakes over the easiest words and his mixed up sentences brought sniggers from classmates and rebukes from the teacher who, perhaps, felt he was deliberately acting the clown.

The overall goal was set as reading one page from the course book aloud to the class. This might seem a rather tough target, but the mother felt that anything less than complete achievement in this difficulty would be self-defeating. The child would *have* to carry out the task in its entirety when it came to the point.

Over the holidays she started to work through a series of sub-goals which had this as the ultimate target. The first step was to have the child reading aloud to his mother, grandmother, aunt and uncle. This was done, at first, in the imagination. When the boy was confident of being able to do it in fantasy he actually read out the page to this small, familiar, audience at one of their weekend get-togethers. In the fantasy he had been encouraged to imagine his relatives all looking pleased and congratulating him. This was, of course, exactly what they did in real life.

The second goal was to read aloud at home to a small group of children. Again this was carried through first in fantasy and then in real life. But the child was carefully prepared by going over all that would happen several times in his imagination. The next step was for the boy to imagine talking to his mother in the class-room. Again practice in fantasy was followed, thanks to the co-operation of the school, by a practice session in the empty classroom.

The last but one sub-goal was to speak in the classroom with the teacher and some other children present. As before this was carried out in fantasy on several occasions and then in real life.

Finally came a dozen fantasy sessions with the child going through the process of reading to the whole class and ignoring any sniggers.

By this time he was able to picture the scene very vividly and describe to his mother how he felt as his turn came closer, what he could see and hear, how the book felt in his hands as he picked it up, the way he stood up and what the words looked like when he began to read. When the reading was completed he imagined the teacher thanking him and congratulating him for doing well. He then saw himself becoming one of the best readers in the class and getting good marks. At the end of six weeks of training he was able to face the prospect of reading in class with con-fidence rather than anxiety.

It is not always possible to carry out actual training to back up the fantasy teaching, but try to do this whenever you can. However, simply by rehearsing the activity vividly in the imagin-ation and enjoying a fantasy success the child can be given tremendous encouragement and a far greater belief in his own potential for achievement.

When carrying out this procedure, bear in mind these six guidelines:

1. Keep the sessions fairly short. Ten minutes is quite long enough.

2. Remain as relaxed as you can. Prompt the child but do not put ideas directly into his, or her, mind. Let the child's imagination work as hard as possible.

3. Encourage vivid imagery by asking questions such as 'What does it look like . . . what can you hear . . . what does it feel like?'

4. Do not be discouraged if, at first, the child seems unable to build much of a fantasy. He may be made slightly anxious by this rather strange activity and uncertain what is expected of him. Let him get used to day dreaming out loud so that any inhibitions about putting his mental images into words are removed.

5. Plan the stepping stones towards the overall goal carefully. Do not make the sub-goals too numerous or too far apart. This may mean setting a target which is, in effect, a big sub-goal itself. That is it represents a major stepping stone on the road to complete achievement.

6. Be certain to include the rewards which might be achieved, both in the short and long term, as a result of success in this activity. Have the child vividly picture himself being praised, congratulated or admired, feeling good, getting a prize and so on.

As a guide to how often these sessions should take place, look at the results of the Fantasy Assessment in Chapter Fourteen. If your child scored from 6 B's to 2 A's have three of these sessions each week until the fear of failure starts to decrease. If the child scored from 7-18 B's have four sessions per week.

Keep a regular check on the child's level of motivation by administering the Fantasy Assessment several times a year.

We have now explored three of the four factors which unlock intelligence. I have described how you can change negative attitudes, improve self-image and adjust need for achievement so that motivation is at its optimum level of intellectual attainment. In the chapters that follow we must consider the nature of the problem handling skills themselves so that you can discover the best way to help your child achieve maximum success when performing the two essential tasks involved in intelligent behaviour. The seeing and solving of problems.

Chapter Sixteen

TEACH YOUR CHILD SKILLED PROBLEM SOLVING

Perhaps this seems a rather unnecessary subject to talk about in a book on teaching greater intelligence. Here, you may feel, is the one skill your child is bound to learn well at school. Surely problem solving is a major classroom activity, the essence of maths and science lessons, and an area of learning emphasised everyday throughout the child's academic career. So why bother to give any additional help at home? What can a parent do that teachers are not already doing a great deal better?

It is certainly true that much of the timetable is taken up with children being given specific problems and shown how to find answers for them. What they never learn, at least not in any school that I have encountered, are techniques for *solving problems in general*. That is with mental strategies which, if put into practice, would make success a more likely outcome than failure no matter what type of question was being asked.

So far as healthy intellectual development is concerned this is a devastating omission. As I have already explained, intelligence is largely a matter of seeing and solving problems. The child who produces rapid, accurate answers will do well in tests and assessments of all kinds, tackle the challenges of school subjects with confidence and be regarded as extremely clever. The youngster who has learned just as much but cannot apply that knowledge to the practical demands of efficient problem solving will usually obtain poor marks, low grades and be thought of as rather dull.

Successful problem solving involves not a single mental ability but a number of related skills all of which have to be learned. They include the capacity to analyse problems effectively; the speed and accuracy with which thinking takes place; learning which is sufficiently well organised to ensure essential information is acquired in the first instance and a memory which allows swift and reliable access to that knowledge even under pressure. In this and the next four chapters I will tell you how each of these vital skills can be taught most easily and successfully. Then, in Chapter Twenty-one, I will discuss the equally important task of creative problem seeing and explain ways in which this too can be greatly enhanced.

The idea that problem solving is a basic component of intelligence goes back at least half a century. It was in the late 'twenties that Professor Otto Selz, one of Europe's most distinguished educational psychologists, conducted a massive and detailed investigation into the thinking skills of German school children. He concluded that problem solving strategies were normally acquired haphazardly and ineffectively. By teaching them in a deliberate and organised manner the child was not only provided with a greater range of strategies but was able to use them far more efficiently. He developed such a teaching programme and had it tested in German schools. To the astonishment of parents and teachers, pupils previously regarded as classroom failures suddenly surged ahead, while those at the top of the class became capable of even greater attainments. Intelligence tests showed a dramatic increase in scores for all those who had received the special instruction and this remained high even after the teaching programme came to an end.

With the start of World War II, Professor Selz's work ceased. His remarkable discoveries were largely forgotten and interest in his findings declined. After the war the belief that IQ was inborn and largely unalterable came to dominate the thinking of teachers and psychologists to such an extent that any suggestion that intelligence could be taught was regarded as ridiculous. It was not until quite recently that further studies of the role of problem solving in intellectual accomplishment were carried out by Dr D. H. Scott of Guelph University in Ontario, Canada. Like Professor Selz, this Canadian psychologist considers that children acquire their problem solving strategies by a process of trial and error. But his major interest has centred on the way in which unfamiliar challenges are dealt with, since how the child behaves when given a problem *for which he has no specific strategy* is also a reflection of the efficiency with which these strategies have been taught. The bad solution finder becomes confused and anxious. He is very likely to give up or blurt out the first answer to come into his head as a means of ending the agony. The effective solution seeker selects the strategy which seems to come closest to what is needed and then cunningly adapts it to meet the novel demands. The better the child is at carrying out such adaptions, Dr Scott points out, the more intelligent he is likely to appear. This opinion is echoed by the American teacher and author John Holt, who probably came closer than anyone to expressing the true nature of intelligence when he wrote, in his book *How Children Fail* :*

'By intelligence we mean a style of life, a way of behaving in various situations, and particularly in new, strange and perplexing situations. The true test of intelligence is not how much we know how to do, but how we behave when we don't know what to do.'

The Problem With Problems

The first problem most people have when solving a problem is discovering what that problem is really about! Fail to come up with the right answer to this basic question and you can hardly expect to find an accurate solution to the problem itself. This may seem to be stating the obvious to an absurd extent. But, as any teacher who has marked examination papers will tell you, more children seem to miss the point of a question than get it 100 per cent right the first time.

A wit once parodied Kipling's famous line in his poem 'If' . . . by remarking that :

'If you can keep your head while all around you are losing theirs – you obviously don't have the first idea of what's going on !'

In problem solving what usually happens is that people *lose* their heads because they fail to understand what is going on. Facts and figures swim before their eyes. They become confused and begin to panic. They are transformed by the unfamiliar into the 'Can't Doers' I described in Chapter Twelve. Let me give you an example of what I mean. Supposing you were told that you had *five seconds* to perform this calculation : *Multiply together all the numbers in the series: 5x7x45x8765x98x0x3x5x 76543 without using pen and paper or a calculator.* Could you do it ? Well even if you felt it was an impossible task in the time allowed, the truth is that you almost certainly could have done

* Penguin Books, 1977

it. Look again and take your time. Don't try to multiply any of the numbers, simply let your gaze wander across them. See that zero fourth from the end? Now I am certain you understand that any multiplication by zero is zero. So the answer to that tough looking sum is a large nothing! If you saw it then congratulations. If you did not, don't worry. The point I wanted to make was that a failure to understand what a problem is all about invariably results in a wrong answer or no answer at all.

Many children approach unfamiliar problems in this way, even if they only have to make very minor changes in a well learned strategy in order to find the right solution. They never give themselves time to understand what is actually being asked. They see facts or figures which look daunting, are confronted by a familiar question packaged in some unusual way and instantly conclude it must be beyond their powers.

So the first step is to teach the child a basic problem solving skill which can be applied to each and every question which is asked them, whether these crop up in class or in an examination. This skill can be compared to a street map which directs them to wherever the problem setter expects them to go. In the next chapter I will explain how the same 'street map' approach can be used to help your child become a super learner as well as a super problem solver.

To start with I would like you to read through and think about the following pair of problems :

Problem One
The third number in this series is missing. What is it?
4; 8; ?; 96; 480.

Problem Two
On my bookshelf are four volumes of a dictionary standing side-by-side in sequence. The covers of each book are one sixth of an inch thick, the pages are two inches thick. If a bookworm begins to bore its way through the dictionary, starting with the first page of volume one and continuing to eat steadily until it reaches the final page of volume four how many inches will the worm have travelled?

If these problems seem baffling, don't worry. I will be showing you how to work out the answers in a moment. My reason for asking you to think about them was to illustrate an important aspect of problems in general. However different they may appear on the surface they are always similar in structure. By analysing this structure carefully and breaking each one down into its basic components we can achieve not only a far greater understanding of the problems themselves but also see, much more easily, how a solution may be found. By teaching this skill to your child you will greatly increase the speed, accuracy and confidence with which all kinds of problems are tackled.

Three Steps To Solving Problems

Research by Professor Wayne Wicklegren of the University of Oregon, has shown that beneath their outward differences all problems consist of three component parts. These he describes as *Givens, Operations* and *Goals*. By understanding what these three steps to problem solving are and how to use them correctly the child acquires a general strategy that enables him to tackle almost any problem he will ever have to deal with.

Givens are all the elements of the problem of which we are aware. Not just the facts contained in the particular task, but every scrap of relevant knowledge which has been learned in the past. *Operations* are the procedures needed to solve the problem. They refer to all the techniques used for moving the *Givens* around, changing, transforming, adjusting and adapting them to meet the needs of the situation. The *Goal* is the ultimate achievement, the end product of manipulating the *Givens* by means of the *Operations*.

To illustrate these three components, consider the following problem : *Jack is as old as Jill was three years ago. John, who is twelve years old, is two years older than Jill. What age is Jack?*

It may look complicated. Many adults – and probably most children – would immediately be put off by its apparent complexity. But let us apply the three components of problem solving in a methodical fashion.

The Goal is clear because it is stated in the problem. We want to find out Jack's age. Many problems provide a clearly defined goal and this is especially true of the kind that children are given in school. However, one should be absolutely certain, in every case, that the Goal is clearly understood. A mistake here and all the rest of the procedure – however efficient in itself – becomes valueless.

The next stage, having clearly established the goal, is to identify the *Givens*. This is quite easy since they must be the statements which refer to the ages of Jack and Jill. You will also, clearly, require some very basic knowledge of mathematics.

Now consider the *Operations*. These are the logical steps that must be taken in order to work out Jack's age from the Givens. A careful study of the problem shows that the operations must include first finding Jill's age and then taking away three years from it.

In a step-by-step strategy the problem is solved like this:

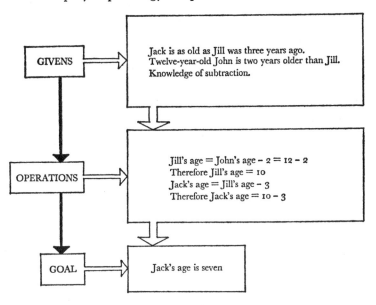

GIVENS

Jack is as old as Jill was three years ago.
Twelve-year-old John is two years older than Jill.
Knowledge of subtraction.

OPERATIONS

Jill's age = John's age – 2 = 12 – 2
Therefore Jill's age = 10
Jack's age = Jill's age – 3
Therefore Jack's age = 10 – 3

GOAL

Jack's age is seven

As with all problems, the ones I described above, can be similarly analysed into these three steps. In each case the Goal is provided, but either the Givens or the Operations are incomplete. In fact the real problem involved in each of them is to discover either the correct Operations to perform or fully to understand the nature of the Givens. Let's start by considering the missing number problem, the one which comes closest to those facing children in IQ tests.

Problem One

The third number in this series is missing. What is it?
4; 8; ?; 96; 480. Breaking it down into the three essential problem
solving steps we have: *Goal*: Find the missing number. This is
the *obvious* requirement. But problems like this also have a concealed goal. That is *to find the sequence of operations which
have been carried out on the numbers* in order to produce the
series shown. So we must bear the additional goal in mind when
tackling the task. *Operations*: These are not provided. In fact,
as I explained above, working out the right ways of manipulating
the numbers forms the heart of this problem. *Givens*: These
consist of the sequence of numbers plus a knowledge of simple
maths.

This clears the ground by placing all the information we have
in a sensible perspective that aids logical thinking. Now let us
look at the Givens and consider what operations might be performed on them. The only things that can be done are addition,
subtraction, multiplication or division. Because the numbers
increase so steeply it suggests that multiplication is most likely to
be involved. The first thing to strike us is, probably, that
$8 = 2 \times 4$. We could try multiplying all the numbers by 2. This
would give us 16 for the missing figure, but 32 and not 96 for
the fourth number along. So that operation is clearly incorrect.
Let us look, therefore, at the relationship between the last pair.
With a little thought it is clear that 480 is 5×96. We might also
notice that 480 is the fifth number along. This information is
also Given by the problem although it is not written down
directly but has to be worked out by the simple process of
counting how many sets of figures are provided. So $480 = 5 \times 96$
and 480 is also the fifth number in the sequence. $8 = 2 \times 4$ and
8 is the second number in the sequence. This is the clue we
need. The operation carried out by the person who thought out
the problem, in this case myself, was to multiply the number
by its position in the sequence. So 4 was multiplied by 1, then
by 2 to give 8. So 8 must be multiplied by 3 to give 24. This
will give us 96 when multiplied by 4 which gives 480 when
multiplied by 5.

So the Goal is achieved with the answer 24.

I have gone through this solution finding process in somewhat
laborious detail because this is exactly the way I want you to work

through the problems with children when teaching them how to use the three step problem solving strategy. They must understand not only what they are doing but *why* each operation is being performed. All too often youngsters apply strategies blindly and, if they get to the correct answer at all, it is by chance. It was once said of Christopher Columbus that he set off without knowing where he was going, when he arrived he didn't know where he was and when he got back he had no idea where he had been! This may not be true of Columbus, but it certainly describes the way many children approach problems. Logical thought is essential to regular solving success and it can only be taught in a logical manner.

Problem Two – Bookworm's Journey
The answer is 5″ although you may well have worked it out as being 9″. That is the solution most people come up with and it stems from a misinterpretation of the Givens. This mistake is quite understandable since the purpose of the problem is to lead you into the trap! You will avoid it by making absolutely certain you understand what information is being provided. Let's take it step-by-step as before. The *Goal* is clear: we want to find out the distance travelled by the bookworm. The *Givens* are information about four books and their thickness in terms of cover and page size, plus the statement that the worm travels from page one of the first volume to the final page of the last volume. But there is something else beside the information you saw written down. In the last problem it was the operation which remained unstated. Here it is one of the Givens. What additional information do you need? Only a knowledge of how books, any books, appear *when seen on a shelf*. It will probably help to sketch out the situation. Draw four adjoining oblongs to represent each of the dictionaries. Now where is the first page of the first volume located? Not on the left hand side, as your imagination probably suggested but on the *right*. So the worm must only bore through two covers to reach the pages of the second volume. Where is the last page of the final volume? Not on the right as your mind may have told you but to the left! Clearly the worm need only eat through two sets of pages ($2 \times 2″ = 4″$) and six covers ($6 \times 1/6th = 1″$) and the total distance travelled is 5″.

Your mind tricked you because we are used to seeing books

from page side and not the spine side. This problem is an instance of the need to use creative problem *seeing* skills when faced with an unfamiliar situation. But the point of including it here was to illustrate how essential it is to understand *exactly* what information is included in the problem. Never make an assumption. Question every conclusion you reach.

This simple technique of breaking down all problems into three basic steps helps your child in several ways.

First it provides a starting point, something they can get on with as soon as the problem has been presented. All too often the uncertain, underconfident youngster – or even the more capable child faced with a very novel problem to solve – wastes time by staring hopelessly at the mass of information presented in the question. The longer they wait before attempting to impose some logical order on the task the more likely it is they will become anxious and increasingly convinced of their inability to ever find the right answer :

'This is hopeless,' their brain tells them despairingly. 'I'll never cope . . .'

They flounder around, picking haphazardly at the question like a visitor to a strange city trying to locate a particular address by wandering randomly up and down the sidestreets. The three step strategy gives them a way of moving on from this initial bewilderment. Once they have mastered the method any problem has a point of entry. The door to the puzzle can be unlocked and they can start working at the finer details of the task in an organised manner.

The second benefit is that this approach makes it more likely they will actually read and understand all the implications of the question. As I mentioned before there is a tremendous amount of carelessness in the reading of problems, especially under examination pressure. As a result the child may provide a good answer but to the wrong question, a misinterpretation that can easily lead to a failing grade.

Finally it is helpful because experimental research has shown that children often lack an important problem solving skill which adults take for granted. That is the ability to break down problems into their simplest elements. When youngsters are presented with a visual scene, an involved question or some work to learn, they tend to look at the whole thing as a single unit. Their attention is spread thinly over the entire task and this naturally adds to their confusion. Only the simplest activities can be carried out in this way, every challenge of any complexity must be broken down into a series of sub-goals which, when efficiently performed, lead to a successful outcome. Let me give you an example from adult life. Driving a car is sometimes thought of as a single skill when it is, in reality, a whole series of sub-skills which have to be perfected if the vehicle is to be driven competently. In learning to drive, you acquire these different abilities at different rates; judging the distance from other vehicles; steering; changing gear; holding the car on the clutch; reversing; parking; driving at night, and so on. Only when all have been fully mastered can you claim to be a safe motorist. If you had attempted to learn everything at the same time the outcome would have been chaotic failure.

It is exactly the same when the child approaches all but the most trivial problem. The first priority is for him to stop thinking about it as a vast and complex challenge and to start seeing the task in terms of its component parts; that is as a collection of Givens, Operations and Goals.

When a child fails to find the right answer you should not immediately regard his inability as a sign of stupidity. Instead consider which of the three steps has been missed out or misunderstood. Find out if the Goal was correctly appreciated, then discover if the Operations were understood and properly used, then look at the child's interpretation of the Givens. If all three steps are right then the correct solution must be reached.

In order to train your child to use this strategy it is essential that you learn it yourself – you will find it just as helpful when it comes to solving problems at home or in the office. To help you do this I have provided a series of problems with a three step analysis of each. I suggest that you work through them without looking at my breakdown, and then compare results. Remember that, in every case, you are seeking to identify the Givens, Operations and Goals. Write down the information to avoid confusion. Once you have grasped the idea yourself go over the problems again with your child. Each must be tackled by the child answering three questions :

What are the Givens? – Write them down.
What are the Operations? – You will have to work them out.

What is the Goal? – Normally this will be provided by a problem, although always be on the look-out for a hidden Given.

Remember as you tackle these problems that finding the right answer is less important than learning how to use the three step strategy to take you to that correct solution.

Problem Three
George is not as tall as Sam.
Bill is not as short as Sam.
Who is the tallest?

Problem Four
Mike is taller than Jane.
George is not as short as Harry.
Jane is not as short as George.
Who is the shortest?

Problem Five
Ed has fewer marbles than Mary.
Mary has more marbles than George.
George has fewer marbles than Ed.
Who has the smallest number of marbles and who the most?

These are the sorts of problems children are often set in IQ tests and assessments designed to test their powers of logical deduction. They may look confusing when first seen. In fact the only difficulty they actually present is the psychological one of promoting an instant notion of failure :

'I'll never understand that !'

Rather than turning the information over-and-over in your mind apply the three step strategy. When you have tried each of them look at my analysis of these problems :

Approach to Problem Three

Givens	Goal
George is not as tall as Sam.	Find the tallest.
Bill is not as short as Sam.	

Operations
The best way for a child to work out this type of problem on the first few occasions is to draw the information. Tell your child

to make a stick man picture of each of the people in turn. As he does so, talk him through the Operations something like this:

'First draw George. Good, now draw Sam. That's right you've made George smaller than Sam. Now draw Bill. Good, you drew Bill taller than Sam. Now look at the drawings. You can easily see which of the three is the tallest. It's Bill. So that's the Goal we wanted.'

If the child makes a mistake do not correct him. Simply say: 'Try to draw (*name of incorrectly drawn person*) again and look at the information we are given about him.'

For additional practice it is very easy to create any number of problems similar to the one above, in the following way:

1. Change the order of the Givens and change the names of the people.

2. Ask who is the shortest rather than the tallest.

3. Change the word *tall* to *large* and *short* to *small*.

4. Use the word *short* or *small* for both the Givens.

By using any or all of these variations it becomes possible to construct a large number of problems which have about the same degree of difficulty. After talking the child through several of them, to make sure the three step strategy is being used correctly, you should explain that the next puzzle has to be done without the use of paper and pencil. Tell the child he is to make a picture of the people in his mind and compare them mentally. Once the initial unfamiliarity of the problems has been overcome and any anxiety they arouse reduced through successful practice, the strong visual sense of the child should enable them to achieve this new requirement without great difficulty. By moving from external sources of reference to internal ones you are not only helping the child to develop his powers of logical reasoning but enabling him to make full use of one of his most effective intellectual tools, the ability to create mental imagery.

Approach to Problems Four and Five
The second problem, which is harder than the first, should be worked out in his head. If this proves too difficult, then go back to the drawing method. At first help by talking through the Givens, the Operations and making sure he understands the Goal. Say something like this: I want you to picture Mike in your mind's eye. Now draw a mental image of Jane standing

next to Mike. You see she is shorter than he is. Next we'll picture George standing in line with them. What do the Givens tell us about him? Right, he is shorter than Jane. So finally we add Harry to the line-up. You see we are told he is shorter than George. So he comes at the end. Now who is the shortest? That's right, it must be Harry.'

Make up variations of this type of problem by introducing the same sort of changes that I suggested for problem three. As the child grows more proficient at constructing visual images fade out your instructions. But make certain he is following a logical progression and not just hazarding a guess. If he appears to be using a shot in the dark approach then go back to the talk-through technique. But do not do so in a critical or punishing manner.

The fifth problem should, at first, be drawn out. Get the child to sketch a pile of marbles and label them Ed. Now he should draw another, larger, pile and label them Mary. Continue to do this until all the piles are drawn and the answers (Smallest number, George; largest number, Mary) are obvious.

You can create similar problems, of the same level of difficulty, by using the changes I described for the third question. To increase its complexity add additional Givens.

When the child is able to find an answer easily through illustrating the Givens get him to do the problem mentally, talking through the Operations at first but then slowly fading your guidance away.

Finally here is a problem which you might like to tackle yourself, it is too hard for most children, just to make certain you have fully understood the three step strategy. Think about the problem, using this technique, before looking at my solution. If you were unable to find the answer then try to work out where and why your approach went wrong.

Problem Six
All flying cats wear spectacles.
All dog lovers ride unicycles.
Some cats can fly.
Flower eaters who wear spectacles love dogs.
Flying things eat flowers.
Is it possible to see a cat riding a unicycle?

Operations
In order to solve this type of problem you have to arrange the Givens (premises in this case) consecutively. That is in such a way as to ensure the key point made in one Given is the first thing mentioned in the next. This gives us :
Some cats can fly.
All flying cats wear spectacles.
Flying things eat flowers.
Flower eaters who wear spectacles love dogs.
All dog lovers ride unicycles.
Now work methodically through the Givens, from first to last, in sequence. Try to imagine each of them as vividly as possible. Picture in your mind a cat flying through the air, wearing spectacles and nibbling on a flower. It comes down to earth to shake affectionate paws with a dog! The final Given tells us that all dog lovers ride unicycles, so it now becomes clear that the Goal answer is – yes. One can expect to see cats riding unicycles!

I have deliberately chosen a bizarre problem in order to demonstrate that, even when dealing with situations outside everyday experience and seemingly very confusing, the three step strategy combined with strong mental imagery produces the right answer quickly and easily.

Show your child the simple procedure of analysing all problems into the three key steps of Givens, Operations and Goals. Then encourage them to make use of their powerful visual imaginations. Combine these two skills and you will have successfully taught your child how to be a super problem solver.

Chapter Seventeen

TEACH YOUR CHILD STRAIGHT THINKING

Children who are good at solving problems tackle them differently to youngsters whose answers are wrong more often than they are right. Research into the strategies used by these two groups has shown that lack of success can be put down to a muddled approach to the task. Instead of using straight thinking to get them to the solution by the most direct and efficient route, the poor problem solver makes a haphazard mental journey which lacks any system or method. In the previous chapter I explained how some of the confusions caused by the child adopting a global approach to problems can be removed through the simple strategy of getting him to analyse every question in terms of the Given, the Operations and the Goals. This enables key facts to be identified and isolated so that essential information can be distinguished from red-herrings. But to employ even this basic strategy effectively the child needs to use methodical thinking procedures. Only by doing so can we be sure to scan the Givens attentively, perform the Operations accurately and check the final Goal answer carefully.

Straight thinking can easily be taught, first by making use of some special mind unbending exercise which I will describe in a moment and then through the use of exactly the same techniques in the classroom.

Before you embark on these lessons, however, it will be helpful to find out how clearly your child thinks at the moment. The short test below enables you to do just that by analysing the logic employed in a simple matching task. When administering the test be careful not to arouse anxiety which is bound to make performance less efficient. The best way to avoid this difficulty is to turn the test into a game – although not one in which children are encouraged to compete with one another. As I have already explained, in an earlier chapter, competition like this only increases the stress involved and can further undermine the confidence of the less successful child. With younger boys I find that a good method for holding their attention is to explain that this test is the way spy masters check up on the code cracking skills of would-be agents.

The Straight Thinkers Test

Explain to the child that his task is to pick out the group of letters or numbers identical to the one at which you are pointing. He has five possible groups to choose from and must find the match as quickly as possible. You should only allow about ten seconds for each attempt. As soon as he identifies the group he believes is a perfect match he should point it out to you. Make a careful note of the number of the group chosen. On the next page there is a score table which gives the correct answers.

At the start of the test, for example, you will point to the letters *sdfgh* on the left of the page and tell the child to search the groups on the right for the match. Here the correct answer is group 3. When you are certain the child understands what is required begin the straight thinking test.

The table below gives you the right answers. Use it to obtain a total score for your child. This will show you how he, or she, stands in relation to others of the same age.

Straight Thinkers Test – Answers

No.	Correct Answer	No.	Correct Answer
1	3	13	5
2	4	14	3
3	5	15	2
4	4	16	5
5	2	17	4
6	5	18	2
7	3	19	2
8	2	20	4
9	1	21	1
10	5	22	4
11	2	23	3
12	1	24	1

Child Must Locate Match From Choice of Five Here

You Point To This Group	I	2	3	4	5
(1) sdfgh	sdrtg	sfghu	sdfgh	sdghf	sfgdv
(2) zxcvb	zcxbv	zxcbv	zbxcv	zxcvb	zdcxn
(3) cuoea	couae	cuoae	cuoae	cueoa	cuoea
(4) 54761	54671	45718	54716	54761	54617
(5) OOoOo	OOooO	OOoOo	OooOO	OOoOo	OoOoO
(6) !@&?%	!&@?%	!@&?%	!&@%?	!@%&?	!@&%?
(7) 31879	31987	31978	31879	38179	37189
(8) 88i8i8	8i88i8	88i8i8	88i88i	88i8ii	8i88i8
(9) HMNMN	HNMNM	HNMNM	HMNMN	HNMNM	HMNMN
(10) CGOUQ	CGOQU	CGQUO	COGUQ	GCOUQ	CGOUQ
(11) LiJll	LiJll	LiJll	LiJll	LiJll	LiJll
(12) A4Wji	A4Wji	A4Wij	4AWji	A4jiW	A4jWi
(13) DQOCUG	DQOCGU	DQOCUG	DQOCCG	DQUOCG	DQOCUG
(14) 294583	293584	295483	294583	249835	295834
(15) KKkKkKk	KKkKkKk	KKkKkKk	KKkKkKk	KKkKkKk	KKkkKkk
(16) 31311411 / 4342342	31311411 / 4342342	31311411 / 4342342	31311411 / 4342324	31311411 / 4342423	31311411 / 4342342
(17) C(CcCc(	C(CcC(c	C(Cc(Cc	C(Cc(CC	C(CcCc(	C(C(Cc(
(18) !?:*,.,.	!?:*,.,.	!?:,;.,.	!?:,;.,.	!?:*,.,.	!?:*.;,.
(19) @£+%&==?	@£+&%==?	@£+%&==?	@£+%&?==	@£+%==&?	@&+%==&?
(20) —=—_—=	—=—_—=	—=—_—=	—=—_—=	—=—_—=	—=—_—=
(21) lkbtdhrf	lkbtdhrf	lkdtbhrf	lkbtdhfr	lkbtdhrf	lkbtdbrf
(22) etdbpteg	etdbpteg	etdbptge	etdbpetg	etdbpteg	etdbptge
(23) slfnmxzm	slfnmxzm	slfnmxzm	slfnmxzm	slfnmxzm	sflnmxzm
(24) KKkKkKk	KKkKkKk	KKkKkKk	KKkKkKk	KKkKkKk	KKkKkKk

Average Scores on Test

Child's Age	Average Score
12–13	22
10–11	19
8– 9	17
6– 7	14
5– 6	13

Do not worry if your child scored below average for his, or her age. Similarly you should not assume your child is a genius if the score was higher than normal! The main purpose of the assessment is to provide you with a standard against which to judge the improvement in thinking as you give the training provided in this chapter. Keep a note of the score and repeat the test after you have completed the teaching. You should also do the test in about six months to make sure that thinking strategies have been permanently improved.

What does the test measure? If you look carefully at the problems you will see that, in order to pick the right match, the child has to use a strategy of systematic comparison with each of five alternatives. To avoid mistakes, attention must be focused, one letter or figure at a time, on each variation.

The example has to be matched to the five possible answers in turn by proceeding in a logical step-by-step manner. The test therefore demands the two essential skills involved in all types of problem solving, an ability to focus attention on the one part to the exclusion of everything else and to examine each detail systematically. Children with difficulties in thinking are usually unable to do either of these well. Instead they adopt a random search pattern which is inefficient and very prone to error. The illustration on p. 206 shows the different approach adopted by clear and muddled thinkers.

As the arrows indicate, clear thinkers look at the standard, then at the first alternative; they go back to the standard and then at the second sequence and so on until they reach the correct match.

Studies by Dr Lester Lefton at the University of South Carolina have shown that confused thinkers use a haphazard search pattern. Because their eye-flicks are more rapid than with

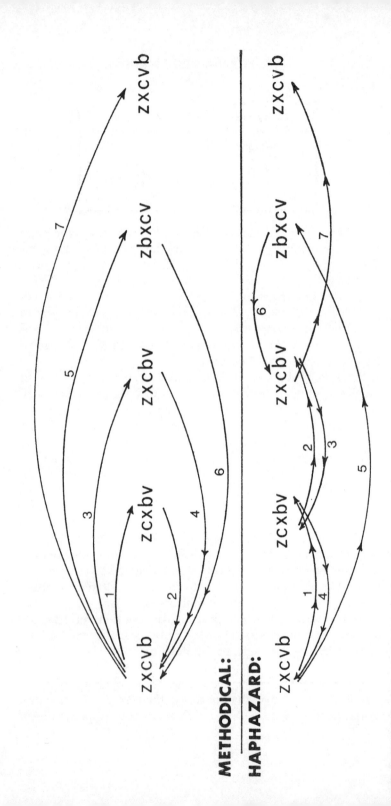

METHODICAL:

HAPHAZARD:

good thinkers, they may not appear to take any more time when carrying out this random search. But, because it is a disorganised hunt for the right answer, mistakes are almost inevitable. Only by working to a logical pattern can one be certain of avoiding errors and arriving at the right answer by the most reliable route.

There is extensive research evidence to show that children who do badly at school are those who have learned this hit or miss approach. The 'stupid' errors their haphazard strategy produce, leads adults to consider them rather unintelligent, an assessment the harmful effects of which I have already described.

In fact, straight thinking is not a matter of greater intelligence; it is merely a way to use the brain more efficiently. The more steps you have to take in order to solve a problem the longer you require and the greater the probability of error. By reducing the operations to a minimum you not only arrive at an answer faster but decrease the chances of mistakes.

If your child scored below average on the test and school achievements are not all they should be, then at least part of the answer may be found in his thinking strategies. Remember that confusions here will influence attitudes, motivation and self-image to a marked extent. Help the child to straighter thinking by carrying out the training described below. Bear in mind that efficient use of the brain is a learned skill not an inbuilt ability. Improvement is always possible so long as you are willing to invest some time and effort in order to bring about the necessary changes.

Getting Things Straight

The exercises suggested here will help your child become more efficient at the two essential components of clear thinking – focusing attention on the individual parts of a problem and examining those details one step at a time.

The essence of this procedure, which has been developed from original studies carried out by Dr Donald Meichenbaum of the University of Waterloo in Canada, is as follows:

You are going to provide a model of the way in which problems should be solved by speaking your thoughts aloud. When working through almost any kind of task we tend to use self-talk to guide us. This is usually done silently 'in our heads'. For example a motorist looking for a particular address may be saying to himself :

'Let's see, I turn left by the post office and then first right . . . there's the house with the blue shutters, so I make a right turn here . . . now on about a hundred yards and down the first left . . .'

Even when solving more formal problems we use a similar approach. It *helps* to talk to ourselves and if we are in real difficulties we may start to speak aloud. This is because it is easier to pay attention to sounds than to fleeting thoughts.

Children with confused thinking use equally confused self-talk. They also tell themselves a great many negative things while attempting to solve a problem. For example they might say :

'I'm not going to be able to cope . . . this is far too hard . . . I'd better give up . . . I'll never find the right answer.'

Such defeatist remarks only increase anxiety and confusion still further.

To banish these damaging comments and teach the child how to think straight, you must provide an example by solving problems while talking through the thought processes used. Following each demonstration the child is asked to do the same thing; solve a problem while putting into words the thoughts going on in his head.

After working through the problems set here you can use exactly the same approach on school problems.

Start the training as follows :

1. Read through the example below to see the kind of commentary you should make when solving each of the problems in this book and, later, in real life situations. Use a large number of statements which emphasise self-control and persistence, for instance :

'I am going slowly but surely . . . I am taking my time . . . I am looking at every detail . . . I haven't found the answer yet but I shall keep going.'

2. When you understand what is wanted use exactly the same approach on the first problem in Set One.

3. Now ask the child to solve the first problem in Set Two using similar audible self-talk. Do not interrupt him. Listen carefully so that you can find out where confusions arise.

4. Go through the second problem as before. But this time try to include comments which overcome some of the mistakes you heard when the child was trying to solve his problem. Watch out for negative self-talk and, if present, include more positive statements in your own approach. If the child lacked persistence you should deliberately make mistakes and demonstrate the need to keep on trying in the case of early setbacks.

5. As with all the procedures it is important to teach in a relaxed and friendly atmosphere. Never criticise, correct by demonstration. Encourage and reward effort. Do not turn the session into unpleasant ordeals or they will be worse than useless.

Here's What You Might Say . . .

This is only intended as a guide to the kind of remarks you could make while working through a problem. Naturally you will want to use your own words and deliver them at a pace best suited to the child's needs. Read through this example a couple of times so that you understand the right sort of approach to take. The sentences stressing self-control and persistence have been italicised. You should make sure to include several each time you talk yourself through a problem.

Once you have completed a problem from the twelve in the adult set, get your child to do the same with one from the child's set. Work through in sequence because they have been designed to get harder as you go along. Never do more than two or three problems at a session and spread the training over a fortnight or longer.

Here Is The Type Of Problem You Will Tackle

Find which of the five possible groups of letters matches the example underlined:

	I	2	3	4	5
UYTRE	UTREY	UYTER	UYRTE	UYTRE	UYERT

Talk yourself through the task as follows:

'OK, I'm looking very carefully at the underlined example which has to be matched. Let's see, it says UYTRE. I'll try and remember that . . . UYTRE . . . UYTRE . . . I'm going to look at each of the possibilities in turn. So I start with the first one.

Let's see, it says UTREY. Now I am going to look back at the original. I can see that the first alternative is not the right answer because it has a Y on the end and the example has a Y in the second position. So we can ignore this one.

Now I am going to look at the second possibility. *I am taking my time and looking at every letter.* The second one says UYTER. *I'll just look carefully at the original example again.* Let's see this ends in TRE and the second possibility ends in TER so that can't be right either. That means I have to look at the third one. It says UYRTE. Looking back at the example again I see that it ends in TRE and so it can't be that one either. I haven't found the answer yet, but there are two more possibilities left and *I am going to keep on trying.*

The fourth one is UYTRE and looking back *carefully* at the sample it says the same. So this is the answer. But I had better just check it again. Let's see UYTRE and UYTRE. Yes that's correct. So the fourth possibility is right.'

As you go through this procedure use a pen or pencil to point out which of the alternatives your attention is focused on, and the details of the letters within that sequence. When you switch your attention back to the example move the pen accordingly. The child should be encouraged to do the same when working through his own examples.

If you feel the need for additional training then it is quite easy to work out further sets of number and letter sequences. But do not make the child do so many he becomes fed-up with the whole affair. The great thing is that he should gain practice in *talking his thoughts out loud.* Later on, of course, these same thoughts will be expressed silently as the child talks himself clearly through the problem.

When you are satisfied that you have cleared up haphazard thinking, eliminated the frequent use of negative or defeatist statements and improved persistence, I suggest that you move to the kind of problems he faces at school. For this purpose you can work through exercises set in class or problems taken from the textbooks. Use exactly the same approach of getting the child to think out loud, expressing his problem solving strategy in the clearest and most positive way possible. To avoid embarrassment and confusion on your part, I suggest that you prepare for these teaching sessions by going through the problems selected

Problems Set One (For Parents)

	1	2	3	4	5
ABCDE	ABECD	ABCED	ABDEC	ABCDE	ADBCE

(When you have talked through this get the child to do the same on their first problem from the list below)

NHTYR	NHYTR	RTYHN	YRTHN	RYNHT	NHTYR
ITLHV	ILHVT	TILVH	ITLHV	HLTVI	LTIVH
QOUCD	DCOUQ	QOUDC	QOCDU	QUOCD	QOUCD
BPDCB	BPDBC	BPBCD	BCDPB	BPDCB	CBDPB
VEGPT	GEPVT	VEGTP	VEPTG	EVGPT	VEGPT
12679	12697	12967	12769	12679	76129
98632	98623	98236	98326	96832	98632
17411	17114	17141	14711	17411	11147
25367	27635	25376	23567	25367	25637

Problems Set Two (For the Child)
The first problem should be tackled immediately after you have demonstrated one from your own set.

	1	2	3	4	5
NHTY	NHYT	TYHN	NHTY	TYNH	YTNH
ACDB	ADCB	ACDB	DABC	CBDA	ADBC
LMNF	LMFN	LNMF	LFMN	LMNF	FLMN
PDBCE	PDBEC	PBDCE	PDBCE	CPBDE	BCPDE
IHTEF	IHTEF	ITHFE	TIFEH	FITEH	FETIH
OQDCU	OQDUC	OQUCD	OQUDC	OQDCU	QODCU
38962	39862	36928	39628	38962	69238
11147	11471	47111	14711	74111	11147
89038	89308	83908	89038	88903	88930
92145	92154	91245	94125	95412	92145

in advance. Work out a logical approach that leads to the correct solution and rehearse it a few times. It may be helpful to split the problems into two groups, as in the number and letter sequences above. You go through the first problem so as to provide a model of the thinking strategy you feel is appropriate, then get the child to complete a problem, and so on.

When looking at school questions bear in mind the three key steps of establishing the Goal, understanding the Givens and selecting the appropriate Operations. Let the child become practised at talking his way through this kind of task in an orderly progression.

Keep the practice sessions short and give your child a great deal of encouragement. Reward his efforts with your time, attention and interest. Try not to become impatient or too discouraged by any initial setbacks. Such difficulties are unavoidable when mastering any new skill and progress is often slow to begin with. The idea of talking his thoughts aloud is going to be unfamiliar and often seems rather strange to children at first. Once learned, however, this approach equips them with a powerful straight thinking technique that can be used to tackle any type of problem successfully.

Chapter Eighteen

TEACH YOUR CHILD LOGICAL LEARNING

Children may have all the facts needed to find an answer and yet fail to do so because they cannot organise that knowledge effectively. They lack any logical mental scheme which would enable them to make the proper use of the information locked away in their brains.

To the parent or teacher their failure to come up with the right solution often appears an act of almost deliberate stupidity. For adults the answer seems so obvious, that the child's lack of understanding is as baffling as it is irritating: 'Just think! It's easy . . .' complains the adult with a sigh of frustration before going through all the facts yet again. Should the patient (or increasingly impatient) reiteration of the necessary information still not lead to the correct solution being found, the child may be regarded as a dunce. But since it is not lack of knowledge that has led to a confused silence or a wildly inaccurate response, the repeated presentation of facts is no help at all. If anything it adds to the child's anguish, anxiety and apparent incompetence.

The situation can be likened to a building site on which dozens of lorries have dumped tons of materials but forgotten to deliver the architect's plans for the new house. When the builders arrive they discover mountains of bricks, stacks of timber, mounds of cement, window frames, doors and roofing tiles but no plan to explain how it should all be put together to construct a home. If they ask for help the most likely thing to happen is that the lorries will come back again and pile even more material before them. Far from sorting out their difficulties this only produces further confusion, greater chaos and the risk of a complete collapse.

The child with more than enough information to find an answer but no effective means of applying this knowledge is in much the same position as those builders. Every day in class, teachers dump more and more material before him; facts and figures; dates and place names; mathematical equations and chemical formulae; all of which he is expected to build into an edifice of knowledge and understanding. With no guidance as to how the task should be performed, it is small wonder that many children achieve only a rickety shack likely to fall down without warning. In order to make use of the information needed for an appreciation of any subject, a plan of organisation is essential. The child must be provided with a blueprint for using all that knowledge correctly.

A good teacher will, clearly, plan his course with care, working through the material logically so that each new item builds on what has gone before. The problem is that, even when teachers *do* structure their subjects with real thought – which is by no means always the case – what appears well organised to an adult may still remain extremely confusing to a child. Every student must develop their own structure of knowledge so that learning occurs methodically, each new item being clearly and logically associated with related topics taught earlier on. Only in this way can efficient use be made of that information.

To explain the best method of teaching children to acquire fresh knowledge effectively, I am going to draw on an experience familiar to most of us, that of starting to find our way around in a strange city. To do this it is necessary to construct a mental map so that confusion between streets and intersections is gradually removed.

Soon after our arrival we will probably get to know a few major junctions close to where we are staying. Let us suppose that the main through roads in this city are called North and West Street. Within a very short time we have learned that North Street crosses West Street in the city centre. This provides us with an initial concept of the lay-out which can be described like this:

Concept One

In the mental map it looks like this:

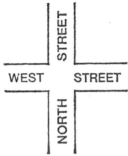

Now we have a basis for further exploration. A starting point from which to progress further. In rather the same way a child should approach any new topic by being taught the most general concept about it. We will imagine he is learning about penguins. The basic fact about penguins is that they are living creatures. This information leads to an intersection between two related concepts which can be compared to the street intersection.

Concept One

Or, in mental map form:

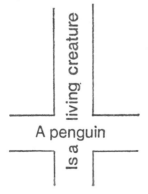

After a few more days in the city we begin to learn the location of various side streets off the main avenues. Let us say we discover where Elm St, Fir St, and Beech St, are located in relation to North and West Streets.

Concept Two

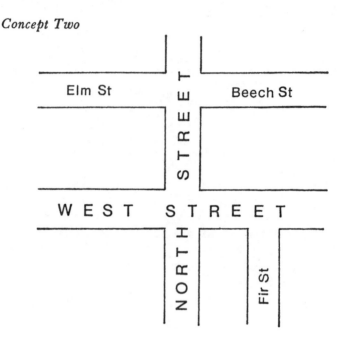

The same methods of acquiring knowledge have been found to be highly effective when children are learning new material. After being taught a general concept they should next master some qualifying facts about it. For example a penguin (which is a living creature) is a bird which breeds in Antarctica and cannot fly.

Research has shown that the most efficient way for a child to come to an understanding of any new subject is by learning it *from the top down*. This means starting with general concepts, which serve to define the area of study and to give it some form. In the example above, Concept One did just this. The child learned that he was going to be given information about a kind of living creature called a penguin. Next the child should be taught *specific* concepts about the topic area which both

Concept Two

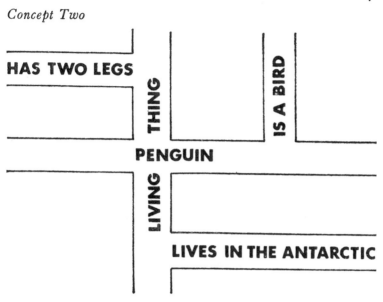

expand their knowledge and teach them to think in a creative way about the subject. That is to use particular pieces of information to draw original conclusions through logical reasoning. For instance the specific concepts that: 'Penguins can't fly' and 'Penguins live in the Antarctic' might result in thinking that prompts the child to conclude that: 'Penguins can swim.'

If the child has worked out that swimming must be the answer to how the birds manage to get around, since they cannot fly and live in a part of the world where there is a great deal of water, and this fact has been confirmed, no further strategy of memory is required. When we work something out for ourselves the process of reasoning embeds the conclusion, in this case 'penguins can swim' very deeply in the memory.

At this point the child may well experience what is often tritely termed 'the joy of learning'. It is a pleasure in accomplishment so rewarding to make the child want to repeat the experience as often as possible.

In order to encourage such reasoning, children should always be taught according to the basic structure shown on p. 218:

For Example . . .

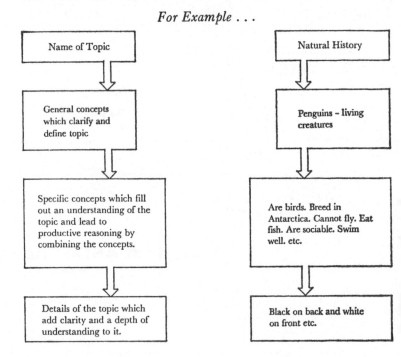

After years of research the value of this system of teaching has been conclusively demonstrated by two of the world's leading authorities on learning and memory, Professor John Anderson of Yale University and Professor Gordon Bower of Stanford. Their work established that when children are able to gain knowledge in this manner, rather than in the haphazard way with which it is usually acquired, their abilities to learn, to remember and to reason efficiently all dramatically improved.

Unfortunately, I know of no schools which approach the task of teaching in this manner. You are likely to find that your child is given a particular topic, then supplied with information relating to an entirely different concept. Next he may be told to learn facts associated with yet another idea before returning to the original concept. It is as if your street guide had the maps bound in a random order so that you got lost each time you turned to a new page. An analysis of the textbooks currently used by many British and American schools, carried out as part of the research for this teaching programme, has revealed that your child is not going to get much better organised knowledge from them either. Despite numerous studies and considerable evidence about the best methods of presenting information, the same confusing, illogical approach is still widely used.

My own conclusion is that if the child is to discover how to organise subjects in such a way that logical learning becomes possible, it will have to be taught in the home, by you. This is neither a difficult nor a time consuming task. Indeed you will probably find it as enjoyable as your child if you adopt the method I suggest. This is a device known as a Learning Ladder. It has the advantages not only of providing a straightforward means of structuring information, but also of turning learning into a game and enhancing memory through an appeal to the child's strong visual sense. As a result studying is transformed from a tedious test of memory into an exciting voyage of intellectual discovery.

How To Build The Learning Ladder

The illustration on p. 220 shows a completed Ladder. It is constructed on a sheet of board some 3' by 2' in size. The material should be soft enough to allow pins to be pressed in, even by a young child. You will also need lengths of coloured tape or string and some pins – those with coloured heads make the finished result look much more attractive. Information is going to be written on different sized cards which are best cut for the purpose from large sheets of thin board or stiff paper. Once again the use of different colours not only adds to the appearance but makes it easier to sort information into different topics. Finally you should have some cardboard boxes large enough to take all the references from one Learning Ladder.

Start by pinning out the string or tape as shown in the drawing. Leave sufficient space between the rungs for a large number of cards.

Now discuss with your child which subject you would like to begin with. I suggest that you start with a topic of special interest in order to arouse his interest and create suitable motivation. Later you can move to areas of knowledge which he may find less attractive and in which difficulties, perhaps due to poorly organised information, are occurring. Let us suppose that the subject decided on is the Civil War in England – it could, of course, equally well have been the geography of France; human biology or a personality from history. The child now writes this down on a suitably sized card and fastens it to the top of the ladder. This defines the area under study.

Now, probably with your assistance at first and certainly

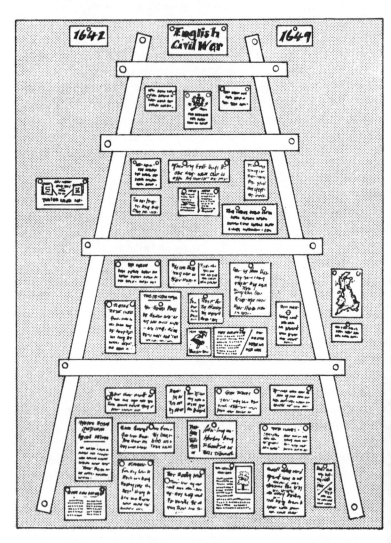

with your encouragement at all times, the child begins to gather *general* information about the subject, not only from course text-books and classroom notes but any reliable reference sources; for example magazine articles or TV programmes, radio documentaries and events such as special exhibitions in museums. All the information should be written in brief, note form, on cards. You will find it helpful if facts about a particular aspect of the subject are all on one coloured card. For example, details about the Roundheads might be on grey cards while the Royalists could be on purple. As your child moves from the general to the more specific other cards can be used; red for battles, blue for major personalities of the conflict, black for casualty figures and so on. This enables a particular item of knowledge to be seen at a glance. After the Learning Ladder has been, temporarily perhaps, dismantled so that another subject can be dealt with, the cards are stored away in the cardboard boxes. Here again the colour code proves helpful in segregating the various items.

When a set of *general* cards has been created these are pinned up in the first space on the Ladder. In this example we might expect to find on them the basic causes of the conflict, the dates it started and finished, where it began and ended. Avoid any very detailed or specific information as this comes lower down on the Ladder.

With the general outline of events in place, the child is now encouraged to fill in cards for the second and third spaces with facts of a more precise and limited type, names and dates of important battles; towns principally involved; names and nick-names of generals; casualties involved in a fight and who won. There is no need to try and collect all this information at once, and it does not matter if the wider spaces in the Ladder have only a few cards in them at first. As well as written notes encourage the child to collect appropriate illustrations, these may be pictures copied from books or cut from old magazines, they might be postcards depicting relevant parts of the country and so on. With some subjects it is possible to gather quite a wide range of additional reference material. If the study area was geography, for example, the extra items might include street maps, bus or train tickets, menus, or photographs taken by the child during a school visit or holiday.

In the final space on the Ladder goes the most specific of all information, such fine details as the name of a general's favourite horse, what the troops had for breakfast on the morning of a battle, inns where they were billeted, sidelights on the fighting and so on.

Not all the cards have to be pinned within the ladder. Material relevant to a particular topic, and this applies especially to such things as photographs, drawings etc, can be fastened outside the main Ladder frames and linked to information inside by means of coloured tape or string. Keep the reference material constantly up to date. As the child learns more, old cards can be discarded and replaced by new ones.

There is no need to have a different Ladder for each subject, this would take up more space than most homes can offer and be confusing. After building up a Ladder leave it in place for a few days and then file the cards away in the storage boxes so that you can start to construct another. Once or twice a month, or before some test or examination, the Ladder can be put together again and left up for a while. There is no need for the child to study it patiently, as if it were a large textbook. He will recall the information without any long, tedious hours swotting the facts, simply by the act of having gathered and assembled the cards. Keep the board somewhere readily accessible, for instance in his bedroom or den.

Why is the Ladder such an effective means of learning material? There are three main reasons:

1. We understand a subject most easily when it is presented in the organised form imposed by the Ladder. Ideas link together in the mind. The child has only to remember one key fact, under the pressure of a test or examination, and others will fall naturally and effortlessly into place. This process can be enhanced if you teach your child an additional skill called the *ideograph* which I shall describe in a moment.

2. It is very hard to memorise information in the way most children attempt to do, that is by sitting poring over page after page of text. What usually happens is the motivation declines to the point where, as I explained in an earlier chapter the attention is too generally focused. This causes all the information to become jumbled and confused. A far better way to remember, and hence to learn, is through active participation in the act of organising material. If you want to master a subject well,

then try teaching it! It's a strange fact but true. There is no better way of acquiring knowledge than by passing it on to others. Here the child is teaching himself rather than learning by himself.

3. Finally, memory research has shown that short but frequent exposure to material – which is what the child achieves through the presence of the Learning Ladder in his room – is far more effective in impressing facts onto the mind than long sessions of specific study. We learn best what we learn most effortlessly and easily.

The Learning Ladder can be used for *all* school subjects, including those which are strong on very precise facts and figures, such as mathematics and science.

With all topics the secret of success is to take a single area of study and then break it down in the way I have suggested; from the very general, to the less general, from the specific to the very specific. Do not attempt to cover too broad an area. For example it would be foolish to try and create a single Ladder for geography or history as such, nor could you construct one for physics or chemistry. You could, however, very easily and effectively, build one for the Ruhr valley; the Battle of Trafalgar; the physics of light; and the smelting of iron ore.

Structure and organisation are the keys to successful learning and fast recall. The mind works in a logical fashion, so by tackling studies in this way you are using the brain in its biologically most efficient manner. When information needs to be recalled without access to the references, for example during examinations, all the child has to do in order to extract the knowledge from storage is to reconstruct the original progression of ideas through the device which I have mentioned above, the *ideograph*.

Your child should not only be told how to use this device but, encouraged to practise it during examination revision. The way it works is that, during the few minutes allowed by candidates to read through the question paper and make notes – which is a feature of all important exams – he jots down on a sheet of scrap paper the key topics relating to a question he wants to answer. These ideas will trigger off thoughts about other, related ideas which can also be noted down, very briefly on the scrap sheet. Instead of having a blank mind from which anxiety has driven any notion of how to answer, your child now has a starting point for the reply. Related ideas can be linked by arrows or lines. He will find that this approach opens the flood gate of memory and everything he has learned suddenly becomes accessible. General ideas produce specific knowledge which leads to finer and finer details.

From the completed ideograph he can easily construct a thoughtful, logically presented essay or short answer that will impress the examiners not only with the depth of his knowledge but also with the organised way in which it has been developed. This kind of structured response is so rare in examination answer papers that it cannot but win additional marks and so improve the chances of a top grade. Incidentally it is a good idea for the child to hand in the ideograph with the answer papers – having first *clearly crossed it out*. This is important or the examiner may mark it as part of the answer. If it is merely provided, but at the same time shown not to be a direct response to the question, the examiner will probably still glance at the list of ideas. If the child has, through an oversight or lack of time, forgotten some important fact, its presence on the ideograph may persuade the examiner to award an additional mark, even though it was not transferred from the rough notes to the final essay. Contrary to what most students believe, examiners are on their side to a very great extent. They would always sooner give them the benefit of the doubt if offered the chance to do so.

Ideas which are presented haphazardly are the symptoms of a mind into which knowledge had been randomly tumbled, like the confused jumble of goods on a bazaar's white elephant stall. Under such adverse mental conditions failures of learning are not just likely – they are inevitable.

Chapter Nineteen

TEACH YOUR CHILD RAPID READING

Being able to read rapidly and well is not just an added bonus of brightness, but the basis on which superior intellectual skills and school success are constructed. Despite the increasing use of such visual aids as films and videotape, the child's primary source of information is still books, articles and class notes. Reading is still the main way in which children acquire knowledge and the only method by which they are able to do so at their own pace. The more effective their reading ability the more successful studying will prove. As the child progresses through education there will be ever growing quantities of material to be assimilated. To gain access to sufficient information in the time available he must, therefore, not only read accurately but as quickly as possible. This is such an important learning skill that it cannot be ignored in any attempt to teach greater intelligence.

In this chapter I want to describe two basic reading skills. The first is designed to assist children who may, currently, be having some problems in the subject. Whether or not this is a cause of difficulty with your own child can be determined by asking him to take a short test. Second, I shall explain how even children who are competent readers can be taught to read more efficiently still.

As literate adults we may find it hard to understand the difficulties which many young children encounter when attempting to comprehend a written text. Forgetting any problems we must have had in mastering the skill during childhood, we often come to the conclusion that they must be rather stupid in not making sense of something literally as easy as ABC. We also, wrongly, believe that children decipher words in the same way as we do. This mistaken belief leads to a misunderstanding over their true difficulties that can make our sometimes rather impatient attempts to help them quite ineffective. In order to find out what really goes wrong and how best to put things right we need to consider how adults read and the important role played by guesswork in interpreting written material.

Guessing Our Way To Word Sense

As you look at these lines of type, you may get the impression that your eyes are sweeping smoothly across the page. In fact they are taking in the words in a series of short, rapid flicks. Between each abrupt movement, your eyes pause for a fraction of a second on two or three words. Your brain interprets these and the eyes then jump to the next word group. At the same time your mind is making a series of predictions, really inspired guesses, about the meaning of words just beyond the range of sharp focus to the right of the word group being interpreted. This speeds up the reading process because if the word can be identified the eyes will miss it in their next flick. Instead of taking five or six separate movements to cross the line of type from left to right you are then able to do it in three or four with no loss of comprehension.

The guesswork, which takes place below the level of conscious awareness, is based on the shape of those words just out of clear sight. For example if you were given the sentence: 'Johnny threw the ball to his **l – ı**,' you would probably realise that the word 'dog' fitted the gap nicely. The oblongs indicate that the missing word has three letters, starts with one which rises above the writing line and finishes with one that falls below it. Given these clues, and the context of the sentence, 'dog' seems a pretty likely bet.

Exactly the same mental process would have taken place had the word *dog* been printed there. Your eyes, flicking swiftly along the line might have rested on the word 'ball'. At the periphery of vision, where the image is very fuzzy (there is only one small area of the eye, termed the fovea, which is equipped to provide sharp focus) your eyes would have sent back similar clues to the brain. Even though you could not clearly see the word, it would have been possible to detect that it was about three letters long, had a first letter which rose up and a last one which went down. Your brain would have filled in the gaps and slotted 'dog' into the missing space in your vision. Your eye would then have ignored it and flicked over to the next word along. Of course a mistake might have been made. It could have been a trick, such as 'Johnny threw a ball to his dig.' But the chances are you would still have seen the word as 'dog' because that was what your brain predicted.

Working at the University of Rochester's Centre for Development, Learning and Instruction, Dr Keith Rayner has demonstrated that the more skilled a reader is the greater use he is able to make of this kind of guesswork. Most young children, however, are unable to predict words from this type of clue and cannot identify them rapidly enough to take advantage of the invaluable short-cut to word gathering. Instead they have to work laboriously through every word in a sentence, seeing only those few which come under the zone of sharp focus. If this zone is restricted to two words then the average page requires at least six separate movements of the eyes, with pauses between each, to absorb it. An efficient adult reader could at least halve the time needed by cutting the flicks and pauses to perhaps only two. This failure is not due to lack of ability, it is simply that children are never taught to read this way. In fact, at school, they seldom learn more than the most basic reading skills. They may acquire the technique with practice, but even the most alert youngster takes many years to do so and many fail entirely, always being slow and inefficient readers. As a result time is wasted which might have been used to gain greater knowledge, while reading which should be an effortless joy is never more than a painful chore. By teaching your child this easily acquired skim and scan technique you will enhance both reading and learning.

The differences between the slow and rapid reader is illustrated by the figure on page 228. Fast readers understand words just beyond their zone of sharp focus. They take three eye flicks to read each line. Poor readers can only make out words inside their limited zone of focus. They take five flicks to cover the same length of text.

First Check Your Child's Reading Skills

Before you start such training, however, it is important to ensure that your child has moved from the first to the second stage of reading proficiency. When they begin reading all children have to pick out words one letter at a time in the familiar C – A – T manner. With practice, they come to identify whole groups of

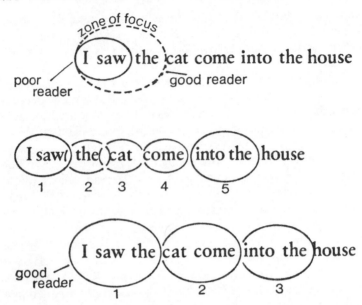

letters at the same time. But their choice of letter groups is important. If it is random, rather than rational, they remain at the first level of ability and must be helped to move to a higher degree of competence. Dr Sheerer-Neuman of the Cognitive Psychology Work Unit at Germany's Ruhr University was the first person to identify variations in letter group choice when he investigated the precise skills of children with high and low levels of ability to see how they differed. A major finding was that good readers identify words by breaking them up into syllables, while poor readers approach them in a haphazard manner. For instance, a child who reads well would see the sentence: 'Johnny and Mary rode bicycles yesterday' as: 'John-ny and Ma-ry rode bi-cy-cles yes-ter-day.' Children who have not progressed beyond the random combination level might read the words as: 'J-ohnn-y a-nd M-a-ry rode bi-cycle-s ye-sterd-ay.'

To analyse this difficulty, Dr Sheerer-Neuman presented sentences which had been split up in various ways to groups of children. Some of the words were already divided into syllables, others were not. He found that capable readers were faster and more accurate with the divided words than with the normally presented one. But the changes made no difference to poor readers. When good readers were shown words broken up randomly, however, their speed and accuracy fell sharply, while the poor readers showed no such decline in ability.

Not only do children split words effortlessly into their natural syllables read quickly and accurately, but they are more likely to remember what they read. As I shall explain in the next chapter, words are stored in the memory as sounds rather than by appearance; and the easiest way to find out what a word sounds like is to chop it into syllables. Try saying bicycles, first as *bi-cy-cles* then as *b-icyc-les* and you will immediately understand what I mean!

If you think that an inability to split words correctly could be a problem that is slowing down your own child get him to take this short test which is based on Dr Sheerer-Neuman's study. All he has to do is read the first version of the story below while you time him. Do this without it being obvious to avoid putting the child under any sense of pressure. Wait three or four days, so that he forgets what has been read, and then ask him to try reading the second passage. Once again make a discreet note of the time taken.

Version One
The gleam ing sil ver space ship rest ed on the gigan tic launch ing pad at the Mar tian ter min al, sur round ed by the death ly still ness of the de sert sands. In side her crew pre pared care ful ly for their top sec ret mis sion to an o ther world. A voy age of dan ger ous and dar ing ex plor a tion des tined to trans port them in to the deep est reach es of out er space, far be yond the fam i li ar so lar sys tem to wards the un fath omed mys ter ies of the un i verse.

Version Two (To be read three or four days after Version One)
T he gl eaming si lve r sp acesh ip rested s ilentl y on the giga ntic la unch i ng pad at the Marti an t ermi n al, surrou n d ed by the de athl y st illne ss of the dese rt sands. Insid e, her cre w p repar ed ca re fully for their t op secr et m issio n to anot her wor ld. A voya ge of d ange rous an d dari ng expl o ratio n d esti ned to tr anspo rt th em into th e dee pe st re aches of o ute r

spa ce, far beyo nd the fa milia r sola r s yste m towa rds the
unfa thome d myste ri es of th e univ ers e.

If your child reads the *first* version more quickly than the
second he naturally breaks his words into syllables – the sign of
a good reader. There is no need to take any additional steps to
help improve the skill. However, if the child reads the *second*
passage faster than, or at the same speed as, the first he is more
at home when dealing with cross-syllable groups of letters. In
this case I suggest you carry out the following exercise :

1. Make a copy, either in longhand or via a photocopier, of
some current book or school reading assignment.

2. Now give the child a pencil or pen and ask him to try and
split the words into letter groups which *sound* like syllables. You
are not looking for strict etymological accuracy here. What
matters is the way the words will *read* once he has drawn in the
lines. For instance this kind of division : 'The gleam/ing sil/ver
space/ship . . .' sounds perfectly correct while : 'The glea/min/g
si/lver spa/cesh/ip' does not. You are trying to find out how the
child says those words in his head.

3. The next step is to make a shutter mechanism that will
enable you to uncover words one at a time as shown opposite.

The easiest way of doing this is to take a sheet of opaque
material, thin card is best, and use a razor to cut a narrow slot
in it. This should be about four inches long and the width of
one line of writing. A second piece of card, placed under the
first, is used as a shutter to reveal words slowly through the slot
in the covering card.

With the child seated comfortably and a portion of writing
hidden by the card, begin to expose the words *one syllable* at a
time. As you do so he must read out those syllables. Here again
it is the sound which matters. Reveal the words in such a way
that the natural points of division within each one becomes
apparent.

This procedure will help the child read and learn better in two
main ways. First he discovers how to split words into the correct
sound sequences visually, then he finds out how to do so by sight
and sound. In this way his memory for words will be enhanced
as the reading skill improves. I suggest you carry out ten minutes'
training, two or three times a week, until the fluency of his reading has clearly increased. Reward his efforts with encouragement

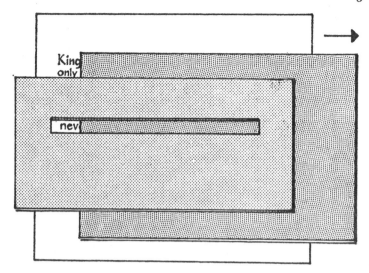

Shutter Mechanism for Speeding Reading

and praise. Try not to become discouraged or impatient if he continues to make mistakes at first. Reading is really a very difficult skill which takes a lot of time to master.

Now let me describe how the competent reader can be helped to increase his speed by showing him what *not* to read.

Teaching Skim and Scan

How much skimming and scanning can be used depends, to a great extent, on the complexity of the material. It is obviously easier, and safer, to make inspired guesses about words just outside sharp vision when reading an adventure story than a physics textbook. But even with the most difficult piece of reading, economy of effort is still possible by using this technique. It is especially helpful if, as so often happens, the child needs to look through a number of books in order to extract material for an essay. Instead of having to plough through them word by word he can move swiftly down each page to the required information and then slow to a more reasonable speed in order to absorb the necessary facts.

To teach your child how to identify words outside their zones of sharp focus quickly and accurately you can turn this book into a teaching machine.

On the next page you will find a box outline filled with squiggles and a black dot. This is a Masking Oblong which will cover the phrases you are going to prepare and place in position on the page below. The purpose of the squiggles is to break up the whiteness of the paper and prevent the child getting undesirable help from what are termed *after images*. You experience these pictures in the mind yourself whenever you stare at some bright source of light and then glance at a plain surface. There, floating before your eyes, will have been the shape of that light source. Children can often obtain such powerful after images that if they glanced from a line of type to a white sheet of paper the words might be 'projected' onto it like images onto a cinema screen. This would defeat the object of the training. We prevent it by the use of visual 'noise'. In other words the squiggles! The dot is there to provide a point at which the child must look just before the page is flicked back and the written material, briefly, presented to him. It ensures that the final word in the phrases you will have prepared lies just beyond the zone of sharp focus. The purpose of the training is to teach his brain how to make correct guesses from the vague clues available.

On the page beneath the Masking Oblong is an identical shape, this time minus the squiggles and dots, which serves as a guide to the size and position of the words the child will be shown. To find phrases, use any of your child's current reading material.

The next step is to get hold of a pad of cheap paper about the size of this book. The paper should be plain white and thin enough for you to see the guide lines of the oblong through it when a single sheet is placed over the page.

Prepare for the training session by writing, in neat block capitals, twenty or so, three word phrases extracted from the child's books. They must fit exactly inside the dimensions of the oblong. Start by making the last word in each phrase fairly short, certainly no more than two syllables and preferably just one. As the child's skill at word identification increases, make the final word longer and harder, but never go beyond the difficulty of words in the child's current reading material. When the phrases are prepared you are almost ready to start. Take the first and position the sheet of paper so that the words fit along the dotted line inside the Guide Oblong. Now fold down the

MASKING OBLONG – *Use This To Cover Your Phrases*

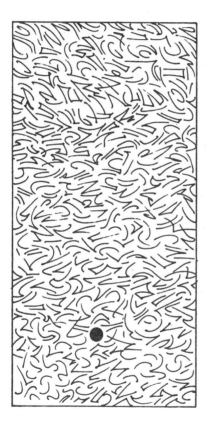

Hold page here and flick it forward and back to uncover the phrase beneath. The exposure time should be about one second.

Masking Oblong page so that the words are concealed. Place the book in front of the child who should be sitting comfortably and in such a way that he can easily see the pages.

Make certain the sheets of phrases you have prepared are hidden from view.

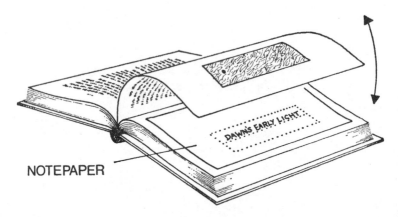

NOTEPAPER

Explain that you want him to look at the black dot on the Masking Oblong. You are going to flick the page up and down again so that he will be able to see briefly some words you have written. He should try to read these aloud as quickly as he can. When you are sure he understands what is wanted and is staring at the dot, move the top page up and back again to uncover the words for a moment.

Only give the child one chance with each phrase, you can return to any he failed to read correctly in a later practice session. Never continue for more than five or six minutes, to prevent boredom, and restrict the teaching to no more than three periods a week. The atmosphere should be relaxed and friendly. The child should never come to see this teaching as a form of punishment for not reading well enough. Stress the fact that you think he is already a very good reader and this will help him be even better. You may like to add that fast, accurate reading allows him to get through tasks like homework or holiday studies all the more rapidly !

Normally you will uncover each phrase for about one second – that is for a silent count of 'one – and'. If the child finds this too easy it is better to increase the difficulty of the final word in the

Guide Oblong – The phrases you write should fit along the dotted line shown with the oblong. Place the sheet of plain, white paper on which you have written the words (in neat capitals) over this page. The phrase should then be positioned along the dotted line.

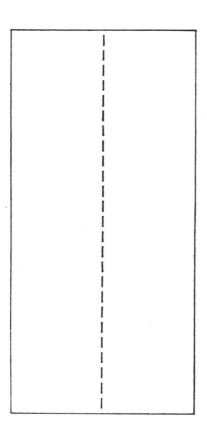

phrase rather than to attempt to speed up. It is very difficult to be consistent with your timing at speeds of much more than one second. On the other hand if your child experiences any difficulty in reading even short words at the end of the phrase at this exposure time, give him a little longer. You will have established the correct exposure speed when the child can easily read every word *but the last*.

Have two or three short sessions each week and you will be surprised at how much easier the child finds it to read rapidly and accurately when going through almost any type of text.

When using this, or any other teaching method described in the book, never be tempted to make them appear more interesting by turning the game into a competition between children. Such a contest will undermine the effectiveness of the programme for the very child most in need of help, the rather anxious, under-confident, underachiever.

Reading is the key to learning, and memory is the mental skill on which both depend. It is never enough to merely acquire information in the most logical and efficient manner. Knowledge has to be stored away in the mind in such a way that it can be recalled reliably and rapidly whenever needed. By improving reading and providing your child with a logical structure from which to extract information you will greatly improve both storage and recovery skills. But there are other, more specific aids to memory which the child can easily be taught. In the next chapter I will explain how you can help your child to remember everything so clearly and confidently he may appear to possess what one youngster on our training course described with considerable awe as a 'supercharged memory.'

Chapter Twenty

GIVE YOUR CHILD A SUPERCHARGED MEMORY

Your child's success in the classroom is primarily assessed on his ability to remember what has been taught. However much one may deplore this approach to learning, it is a fact of school life which parents and teachers are obliged to live with and children to cope with. A recent study in American Junior Schools, for example, showed that 90 per cent of all questions asked required only a precise restatement of information given in the textbooks.

Nobody would deny that being able to recall basic knowledge from memory is an important aspect of intelligence. The child who excels at logical thinking but is unable to name the capital of France, remember when Columbus landed in America or give the date of the Battle of Hastings can hardly expect academic success. Without effective storage and recall of information very little intelligent activity is able to occur.

Despite its essential contribution to intellectual success memory is frequently maligned, usually taken for granted, yet hardly ever taught as a specific mental skill. Like so much else in mind development, children are expected to create their own systems for storing and retrieving the vast amounts of facts and figures with which they are presented in school and college. Some are fortunate enough to devise efficient methods which lead to relatively effortless learning and reliable recall. Others never achieve the same kind of success. However hard they try to cram information into their brains nothing much ever seems to stick. When a child is unable to remember a lesson the usual adult explanation, which the student may almost thankfully adopt, is that his memory is 'bad'. Since we are constantly telling one another how poor our own powers of remembering are, how we can never recall faces, have no heads for figures, and cannot even bring to mind what we had for lunch two days ago, this is usually accepted as a perfectly valid reason for failure. It has now been accepted, almost as a self-evident truth, that some people have good memories while others are not so lucky. The results of modern research tell a very different story. Carefully controlled experiments in psychological laboratories have shown beyond any doubt that there is *no such thing as a bad memory*! We all possess an almost identical ability to store and recall the same amounts of information.

You may feel that this finding runs directly contrary both to commonsense and everyday experience. What about TV quiz contestants who appear to have phenomenal memories for some particular subject, or those professional memory men who can give you any sports statistic without a moment's hesitation? Surely an actor who is word perfect on all the 1,422 lines spoken by Hamlet, the longest role Shakespeare ever wrote, has a far superior power of recall to the average man in the street?

The simple answer is that he does not. What makes all these people so much better at remembering things is not their ability to store information but the manner in which they perform that storage in the first place.

To understand these differences let us consider one fairly common example of supposed superior memory, the ability never to forget a face. This often appears a very special feat of remembering since the person has no chance to practise, as one might by reading a list of facts over and over again, or of using memory tricks – such as mnemonics – to help him out. Here, surely, is a skill that clearly demonstrates basic differences in memory power? That such differences exist is undeniable. In one investigation, volunteers were shown movie films of a large number of people, then asked to identify them from still photographs. Some did so with almost complete accuracy, others were only able to recognise very few. But this same study showed that the supposed 'good memory for faces' depends not on the ability to recall details of the features seen but on the effectiveness with which that information has been put into mental storage in the first place.

When we look at a stranger, their features are not all seen at once, but are scanned with a series of extremely rapid glances. The brain takes these separate mental snapshots, showing different details of the face, and blends them together to form an overall impression of appearance. Because our minds are so occupied in carrying out this assimilation task we are never aware of the scanning process behind it. To us it appears that we take in the face before us as a whole and, the next time we see the person, recall their features in exactly the same way.

It was only when researchers employed high speed film cameras to analyse the scan systems of different people that marked variations in these patterns became obvious. Those with a 'good memory' for faces carried out the scrutiny of unfamiliar features in a precise and systematic manner. They started at the eyes and then moved down to the mouth before glancing at other aspects of the face. Each major detail was given the same amount of attention but, because their eye movements were more organised and rapid, they could take in a great deal of facial information in the brief scanning period.

Subjects who found it hard to remember faces used a much less efficient method for studying the features. Their eye glances were slower which meant they were unable to register the same amount of information in the time available and the movements were haphazard, roaming unsystematically up and down the face so that certain features had much more attention paid to them than others. This meant that when the face was seen a second time they had far less information stored away to provide essential clues. Their failure to make a correct identification was not a fault of memory but an inability to gather information effectively in the first instance. The more clues we have when trying to recall something to mind the greater the probability of successful remembering.

The same applies to remembering words or people's names. You may have felt in the past that somebody who 'never forgot a name' has remarkable powers of recall. But, as with faces, success depends on the efficiency with which information has been stored away in the first place. Professor Max Coltheart of London University, one of the world's foremost authorities on memory, has shown that letters and words are most easily recalled by paying attention to their *sounds* rather than their visual appearance. People who can remember words easily store them audibly rather than by appearance. They also break each one down into its smallest unit of sound so as to make the task of storage and recall even easier. By doing so they provide themselves with a large number of mental 'hooks' on which to hang each word in the mind.

To see how the system works let's look at how two people with apparently different 'memories' for words might set about the task of recalling an unfamiliar noun such as *Engastrimyth*, meaning a ventriloquist.

The person with an inefficient system of storage and recall will attempt to learn the word as a whole and bring it to mind by picturing the noun in its entirety. If you would like to prove how ineffective the method is look at the word for a moment and see if you can write it down correctly, or even bring it to mind at all, in a few hours' time. The individual with a 'good' memory for words, probably without realising what he is doing, automatically breaks it down into its smallest sound units and stores it away as *En-ga-stri-myth*. This 'hooks' it into the brain as four separate sounds. Recall one of them and the word will leap back at you without effort. You might care to try this method as well to discover for yourself how much more success-fully you remember it.

Storing information in this way is rather like having a jig-saw puzzle instead of a single picture. If that one image gets mislaid you may not be able to remember a single thing about it. But several pieces can go temporarily missing from a puzzle without the overall image being lost.

All the many research findings of the past few decades of memory study can be boiled down to two golden rules for better remembering.

1. Focus your attention on the smallest possible details so as to give yourself as many memory clues as possible. The more mind-hooks there are holding a piece of information in place the more likely it is to remain there.

2. Examine everything that has to be learned systematically giving equal attention to every important detail.

Although simple in principle these rules are hard to put into practice. Indeed, children spend the greater portion of their time in primary education attempting to apply them to learning school subjects. Many fail to do so efficiently and some never master the skills at all. It is a major area of failure in modern teaching. Little effort has been made to include lessons on effec-tive memory skills into the timetable, despite the fact that numer-ous studies have shown that such training enhances mental per-formance and so increases intelligent behaviour.

You can teach them to your child, not in any set periods of instruction but by your whole attitude towards analysing and storing information. Show them how to separate out the whole into vital component parts and look at topics methodically. The Learning Ladder I described in Chapter Eighteen will help provide the basis for this organised approach. Never tell your child he has a bad memory. Like so much else in mental development this creates a severely restricting self-fulfilling prophecy.

As well as these general methods for enhancing recall here are two special techniques which can be used to help the child whose memory – and self-confidence over remembering – may have taken a battering from experiences at home or in school. They can, of course, equally well be used to further improve the abilities of an achieving child, especially if he has special difficulties in recalling certain types of information : history dates, geographical place names, chemistry formulae or maths equations for example. Both are straightforward to use and easy to apply.

Remembering Through Recall

Research by Professor John Yuille, at the University of British Columbia in Vancouver, has shown that the best way to remember something is to recall the information almost immediately. It seems that, by storing away facts and then rapidly retrieving them, you open up more efficient pathways in the mind. This method is far superior to the usual technique of repeating the same material over and over again, the way most children are taught to commit something new to memory. Not only does remembering through immediate recall enhance storage and retrieval it also improves the organisation of information inside the brain so that the child can make sense of what has been learned more easily.

Here is a simple procedure by which your child can make use of this extremely efficient system of learning and remembering. All he need do is to keep a diary of what is taught in school. For this purpose you should provide him with a notebook small enough to be carried around but with sufficient space to make daily notes of what happened in each lesson. The child should be encouraged to write up this diary twice a day, once at the lunchtime break and again immediately on returning home.

Although the main function of the book is to record the main things learned, you should not insist that the entries confine themselves only to classroom subjects. A child who is keen on sports, for instance, might be far more motivated to keep up the diary if he were able to note details of school matches.

What *must* be recorded are details under the headings: 'I learned in class this morning . . .' and 'I learned in class this afternoon . . .' It is essential that the information be specific. Simply stating that: 'I studied maths', or 'We had a history lesson' is no help at all. Instead the child should make such comments as: 'I learned that to multiply fractions you must find the lowest common denominator' and 'I learned that Columbus reached America in 1492'.

In order for this procedure to be effective your own role is of great importance. At the end of the day you must find ten or fifteen minutes to go quietly through the diary with the child. When doing so avoid any kind of destructive criticisms or comments which would turn the daily diary inspection into an anxiety arousing chore. If you need to point out mistakes or offer suggestions for improvements do so warmly and constructively. Raise points and ask questions designed to increase the child's recall by discussing the entries in greater detail. For instance you might say:

'I remember the story about Columbus. What port did he sail from. . . . What was his ship called . . . where did he land . . . was he really looking for America . . . what happened after that?'

All this will help the child to organise and understand newly-acquired information in an extremely effective way.

You may feel that this idea, while perhaps fine in theory, could never work in practice. No child, eager to play with friends at the lunch break, or watch TV at the end of school, is going to bother to spend even ten minutes writing notes! I can only reply that the child certainly will do so, and will enjoy it as well, if the pay-offs are great enough. By that I do not necessarily mean you should offer material rewards for a well kept diary, but that you should repay their investment of time with your interest and enthusiasm. If you feel that more than this will be needed in order to sustain motivation. I suggest you make use of a system of rewards known as the Token Economy. All you have to do is get hold of some suitable objects to serve as tokens, such as buttons, plastic counters, or even small pieces of coloured card. These are given some 'value' which makes them worthwhile for the child to collect. For instance six tokens might be exchanged for an extra half-hour's TV, or some extra pocket money; a dozen tokens could be worth an outing or some toy the child wants.

The great merit of tokens is that you can hand them out *immediately* after the child has shown you his completed diary and you have discussed the entries with him. There is ample evidence, from studies of learning, to show that any activities which produce a prompt reward are very likely to be repeated. Some parents find it helpful to create a Token Chart on which the numbers awarded can be marked down in some way, either by colouring in a space on the chart or sticking on a coloured tag. Agree with your child how many tokens each entry is worth. As soon as the discussion session is completed hand them the tokens and let them make the appropriate record on their chart.

The Token Economy system is now widely used, by parents as well as psychologists, as a means of establishing desired behaviour. You can use it equally well to reward any activities which you are especially eager to encourage. The great thing to remember is that the token must be handed over as soon as that task has been performed. Any delay will weaken its effect and undermine the chances of success.

You should never use material rewards, and this includes tokens, in place of your attention and affectionate encouragement. Your child will only remain interested in the memory diary if you constantly involve yourself in the entries.

Creating A Memory Movie

As I explained earlier in the book, children have great imaginations and live in a world rich with fantasy. Their ability to conjure up vivid mental images can be used to enhance their powers of information storage and recall through what I call Memory Movies. This has the added advantage that, by making subjects come dramatically alive it usually arouses their interest in learning even more.

Studies by the eminent child psychologist Dr Jean Piaget have revealed that while we adults live in a world dominated by the power of words, the child reasons by making visual associations. This profound and important difference in thinking can best be illustrated by the following question :

'What shape is a turtle's tail?'

If you are able to find an answer consider for a moment how you did so. Unless you are an expert on turtles you almost certainly tried to form a mental picture of the creature which you then inspected in your imagination in the hope of discovering the shape of its tail. Had the question been :

'How many flippers has a turtle?' your immediate response would have been four. This time there was no need to construct a mind image in order to count the legs. The answer is a *word* concept which derives from knowledge we have about the construction of animals in general as much as turtles in particular.

A young child, however, would have found the solution to the second problem in the way you sought an answer to the first. Dr Piaget has demonstrated that this is the way most children do their thinking, until they reach an age where words take over as the main instruments of reasoning.

The Memory Movies procedure takes advantage of this use of images to enhance the child's storage and recall of information. I am going to explain how the procedure can be used to improve general learning ability, and then consider the special case of spelling. This is an area where many children have real difficulties. Unless cleared up early on in the school career, these problems may stay with the child through adolescence and into adulthood, undermining the success of their academic efforts through persistent errors which devalue them in the eyes of teachers, examiners and – often – their parents as well.

For the teaching sessions you will need some book your child is currently reading. Since it is far easier to create fantasies from fiction than from facts, I suggest that you begin with the kind of light reading your child most enjoys. You start the training by having the child read, or reading to him, a short extract from some story. When this is done ask him to picture the scene as clearly as possible. Now ask a series of questions designed to sharpen the images still further and direct his attention to specific aspects of the scene. For example you might want him to tell you :

'What are the people in the picture doing? What is happening to them? What else can you see in the picture?'

Continue to request even greater details, for instance the colours and shapes of objects, how they relate to one another and what sort of sounds are associated with the images.

At first the child may find it somewhat strange either to produce the scene to order or, once created, to see it clearly enough to provide a description. Do not try to force the pace. If he is unused to using his powers of imagery this skill may have declined somewhat. But encouragement and interest will quickly bring it back to full strength.

To give you an idea of how such a session might develop, here is a short edited extract from a conversation between a mother and her ten-year-old son. The story involved is a space drama. A crippled rocket ship drifts helplessly above the Earth and the captain is going outside for an inspection of the damage:

Mother: 'How does he get out of the hatch?'

Child: 'Just floats out . . . on a long line. He's got some tools in his hand . . . a big spanner. He's come out upside down.'

Mother: 'What sort of suit is he wearing.'

Child: 'All silver . . . the sun shines right off it. He looks like a big white bird. All around it's black. You can't see his face 'cause the sun is too bright. Really bright.'

Mother: 'What's he doing now . . . ?'

Child: 'Floating on the end of the rope. He's got to the bit where the missile went through the rocket . . . the metal's all torn up and black. He can see pieces floating away through the big hole. He can see the earth behind him . . . it's very little . . . now he's going to take a closer look . . .'

Mother: 'What does the earth look like from up there?'

Child: 'Like a plate . . . a blue plate . . .'

After a few sessions like this the child should be able to form, hold and study fairly long and detailed scenes without much trouble. Now you should start to direct his images towards school subjects. Start with those which are easiest to imagine; history, English literature, geography and so on. All the child has to do is read a fairly short descriptive paragraph and then think about it as vividly as possible. Once again you should help to elaborate details and focus his mind on different parts of the image. For instance, suppose he were learning about exports through a busy European port. Not an especially exciting topic, perhaps, and usually deathly dull when presented in a textbook as a long list of facts and figures. You can help to make it come to life – and be remembered – by using Memory Movies. Your discussion might go something like this:

Parent: 'I want you to imagine you are down at the docks. Lots of big ships, giant cranes, the smell of the sea, gulls above you in the sky . . . can you see this?'

Child: 'Yes . . .'

Parent: 'Good, now let's walk down the dock. What can you see?'

Child: 'Crates, lots of boxes. Men unloading them from lorries.'

Parent: 'Where are they going?'

Child: 'Onto a ship. It's right by the crane. I can see the captain on the bridge. Smoke coming out of the funnels. He's watching the crates go down into the ship.'

Parent: 'What's in the crates?'

Child: 'Machinery from the factories outside the town.'

Parent: 'That's right. Now I want you to look at the side of the crates. Can you see printed on them £10 million? That's how much the machinery they export is worth. See it printed there in big, black letters. Ten million pounds.'

You will see that, in the discussion, the parent actually introduces key facts and figures, or prompts the child to do so, in order that the essential details of the subject can be mastered. By transforming lists on a page to images in the mind you make learning and remembering a hundred times easier. I suggest that you use this procedure as often as possible and in conjunction with the Learning Ladder described in Chapter Eighteen. This will enable you both to work out the clearest and most informative images.

To make this movie in the mind procedure work effectively make sure you follow these basic rules:

1. Keep the atmosphere relaxed and friendly. Do not force

the child to do it against his will. Avoid times when there are powerful counter-attractions, such as a favourite TV show.

2. Keep the sessions short. Five minutes is long enough at the start and they should never go on for more than ten.

3. Keep the images as vivid as possible. Help the child to imagine not only the sights but also the sounds and the smells of the scene.

4. Keep the child's mind directed on key facts to be learned. Do not let him wander too far from the main purpose of the imagery. When there are numbers or names to be remembered ask the child to picture them printed on the appropriate objects or attached to the right person.

Memory Movies can be used to improve spelling through exactly the same use of visual imagery. Start by giving the child practice with fictional images before moving on to the slightly harder task of picturing letters and words. Prepare a list of any important words which he finds it hard to spell correctly, and deal with them one at a time during short but frequent training sessions.

The child is asked to picture the letters from a particular word in his mind. Rather than trying to imagine them as lifeless symbols they should be brought to life as creatures with arms, legs and faces, like the ones illustrated below :

He is to line them up, in his mind standing at attention as if they were soldiers on parade. Suddenly they start running around, chasing one another in mad confusion. This is allowed to continue for a second or so before the child calls them back to attention. They form up immediately, spelling out the required word. He should imagine this as vividly as he can and spell the word by 'looking' at each letter in turn. If they are out of order he must try to rearrange them so that the word is correct.

Start with fairly short words and give the child plenty of practice at getting these right, then go on to longer ones. When words of more than six letters are concerned it may be better to break them up into groups. Children vary in the amount of information which can be held in their visual memories. It may be as low as two items or as many as seven, sometimes they can manage even more than this. Find your child's capacity by trial and error, then present all words – however long – in such a way as to be within this upper limit. Keep familiar word endings,

such as '-ed'; '-ing'; and '-ment' together so as to avoid confusion, and split words into sound syllables whenever possible. As I explained in an earlier chapter this enhances reading ability considerably.

Do not become discouraged if early attempts fail to produce scenes which are sufficiently detailed. Be patient and encourage the child to keep on trying. Never criticise or punish the child for failing to create the kind of images you wanted. Most children like the idea of having a movie house in the mind and will co-operate willingly if given the support to do so.

A child with a good memory is not merely able to store and recall information effectively. This would be nothing more than parrot fashion learning, of little real use to him – especially if he decides to continue his education to graduate level and beyond. An understanding of what has been memorised is essential if the knowledge is to be put to work in seeing and solving problems. Indeed provided the child possesses such an understanding, remembering will become a virtually automatic procedure. It is only when we try to cram into our protesting brains facts which are, to all intents and purposes meaningless to us, that memory is likely to break down. The clear, systematic organisation and presentation of material which I have advocated in earlier chapters is an essential starting point for effective remembering. Do not use the methods suggested here in isolation and expect success. Consider them as just one more mental skill to be employed in conjunction with all the others I have described. Just like the four key factors of intelligence, the mental skills involved in problem handling interact with one another to produce the final outcome.

So far I have described ways in which problems can be solved by learning and applying the most successful strategies. But, as I made clear in Chapter One, true intelligence is more than the ability to find the right answers to problems presented as such. It is just as much the ability to realise that a problem exists in the first place. It is this vital creative aspect of intelligence which I want to talk about in the next chapter.

Chapter Twenty-One

TEACH YOUR CHILD CREATIVE PROBLEM SEEING

The laboratory where I work has a large and costly computer. It will not only manipulate thousands of numbers in the flicker of an eye but also plays a very good game of chess. These, and many other tasks which it performs, are all activities demanding a high level of 'intelligence'. But the computer is not the least bit bright. It is, in fact, a simple minded electronic creature whose ability rests entirely on the programme which has been fed into its magnetic memory. It plays chess because somebody first worked out how the game should develop in terms of computer logic. It solves vastly complex statistical problems only because all the necessary information has been provided.

The difference between a computer and the men who built and use it, lies in an ability to identify problems that might usefully be solved. This skill is not just the icing on the cake of intelligence, it is fundamental to intellectual progress. Without creativity a person would become a mere problem solving machine, probably less capable than the computer and certainly less efficient. Unfortunately, while schools stress the need to solve problems – although, as I have explained they seldom teach effective strategies for doing so – little emphasis is placed on creativity. A vivid imagination may be necessary in the art room and helpful when writing English essays, but it is not encouraged elsewhere in the timetable. Exams are passed by the regurgitation of facts and through providing the correct answers to specific questions. This is the skill by which the child, the teachers and the reputation of the school as a place of learning will ultimately be judged and so remains the focus of attention.

Several years ago the American psychologist, Professor J. P. Guilford, at the University of Southern California, suggested there were basically two types of thought processes. One was *convergent* thinking which involved the search for the right, or the best, solution to a problem. The other he termed *divergent* thinking. Here there is no right or best answer and novelty and originality are the keys to success.

Professor Liam Hudson, of London's Brunel University, applied these ideas to a study of children in their last year at school. He found that convergent thinkers favoured the sciences while divergent thinkers were more interested in arts subjects. While the groupings may not be quite as clear cut as Professor Hudson's early findings suggested, it is reasonable to suppose that some children, as a result of their learning experiences, prefer to use a logical, step-by-step approach to problems, while others tackle them in a less systematic but perhaps more imaginative manner. In some situations the first method is certainly required in order to arrive at the right answer as efficiently as possible. When a problem is presented in such a way that the Goal is precisely stated you must proceed methodically through the necessary Operations, manipulating the Givens in order to reach the solution which the person setting the problem had in mind.

At school the convergent thinker is likely to be more successful in exams and tests where questions probably only have one right answer and marks will be lost for giving anything else.

In other subjects, and very often in real life, an imaginative approach, which takes what American technologists call a 'quantum' leap and produces valuable new insights, are likely to achieve much better results.

The danger in applying convergent thinking to all problems is that the brain can easily get into a rut – psychologists term it a 'set' – so that the wider implications of the task are overlooked. In the 'bookworm' problem, which I outlined in an earlier chapter, a 'set' was probably responsible for your failure – if fail you did – to arrive at the correct answer. You were so used to picturing books from one viewpoint that your mind never even considered the possibility of taking a fresh approach to the Givens.

Let me give you two further problems which illustrate the way a 'set' can blinker thinking.

Look at the illustration on p. 252 and decide where the rest of the alphabet should be written if AEF go inside the circle and BDC go outside it. Bear in mind the danger of falling into a 'set' trap which may cause you to define the problem too narrowly:

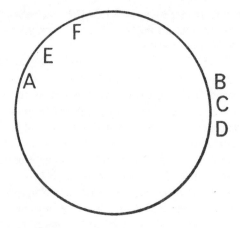

The second problem concerns a prince who was imprisoned in a dank dungeon by his wicked uncle. The walls of his cell were three foot thick and went down fifty feet into the earth. The floor was hard packed mud. The only way out, apart from the heavily locked door, was a skylight fifteen feet above the ground. The prince, though he was able to stretch up some nine feet, could never hope to reach it. There was no furniture in the bare prison on which he might stand.

One evening, after weeks of despair, he suddenly began to dig in the earth floor using a metal plate as a spade. The guard saw him but only grinned in amusement since there was no way he could tunnel his way out. What was the prince's plan?

The second problem is a great deal easier than the first, at least so most people seem to think, but both provide good examples of how the route to a solution can be blocked by an inability to use creative imagination on a situation.

If you were stuck over the letter and circle problem it is probably because you hunted for some complicated relationship between the groups of letters. This is not the right way to find the answer. The key lies in the *shape* of the letters rather than whether they are vowels or consonants. Those with straight lines go inside the circle, those with curved lines on the outside.

As for the prince, all he had to do was to pile enough earth into a mound, stand on it and reach the skylight. Here the trick was to focus your attention not on the hole but on the earth removed in order to create that tunnel.

If you tend to be a convergent thinker, and perhaps work in an occupation where it is necessary to rely on logic and to distrust intuition, you may regard divergent thinking as being less worthwhile than problem solving skills. Such an attitude is bound to diminish your child's imagination by leading them to place an unequally high premium on convergent thinking.

If you are a divergent thinker, on the other hand, a strictly logical approach to problems may strike you as pedantic and mechanical. As I have already explained, intuition and imagination have a crucial role to play in all kinds of problem solving tasks, especially those which confront us in everyday life. But the imagination is only really helpful when disciplined by an appreciation of convergent thought processes. The greatest artist in the world would never express himself adequately unless he had the self-control to transform images of the mind into images on canvas. Convergent reasoning, when properly used, does not restrict divergent thoughts but channels creativity in the most successful direction.

A good method for helping the child to develop divergent as well as convergent thinking processes is to hold occasional family brain storming sessions. These are games in which you all have to use your imagination as wildly and improbably as possible. For example, by dreaming up fantastic inventions, such as surrealistic methods of transport or incredible ways of carrying out mundane domestic tasks. These sessions must be relaxed and as good humoured as possible since it has been shown that humour actually stimulates the imagination. During the brain storming sessions all ideas should be considered however bizarre and unworkable they would prove in practice. Allow the children to develop the skill known as 'free association' in which thoughts pour out with one idea leading to another and then a third. By creating a chain of imaginings in this way you unleash the brain's full creative potential. Never criticise or attack any of the suggestions as this tends to associate fantasy with anxiety and so harms the power to imagine freely.

The same approach can also be used to solve real family problems like where to go on holiday, how to lay out a garden or what to do with a spare room. In this case allow completely free play of the imagination during the brain storming sessions but make a note of any ideas which seem just about possible, even if they are also wildly improbable. Then turn to those ideas and go through them again, allowing the child to make any contributions he desires. You may be surprised at just how interesting, exciting and original it is possible to be by this approach. Ways of doing things which would never otherwise have occurred to you may well come to light. But remember to keep the atmosphere at these sessions relaxed and good humoured if you want the best results. While tactics like this are extremely helpful in producing a sense of mental freedom, the real secret of developing the child's intellectual creativity successfully lies not in *giving* them extra skills but taking care not to *deprive* them of this inborn ability. All very young children are natural scientists, constantly exploring his environment by means of experiments; knocking things over, pulling them apart, crawling eagerly from one experience to the next. Not unreasonably, parents usually try to keep these experiments within reasonable bounds, if only to safeguard the child. But too many restrictions can harm the child's sense of curiosity and so prevent his inborn desire to seek out and solve problems from developing fully. As the child grows up, comments and adverse reactions to creative attempts are no less damaging than the physical barriers raised to contain the wandering toddler.

Experience suggests that divergent thinking can best be encouraged by sticking, as closely as possible, to six rules of child rearing:

1. Give the child ample opportunities to find things out for himself. Do not always give him the answer. It is far more mind expanding to provide the means by which that answer may be found.

2. Provide toys which allow scope for imaginative play. So many modern toys seem to have been designed with the amusement of the parents, rather than the entertainment and instruction of the child, in mind. Divergent toys are those in which there is no predetermined end result. A construction kit, for example, expands the child's mind. A painting by numbers game merely leads to foregone conclusion. If you do give expensive, mind restricting toys, do not be too surprised or outraged if the imaginative child rapidly adapts them to suit his own fantasy needs. Frequently such 'adaption' will involve what adults usually consider destructive behaviour. For the child, pulling

apart a boring toy and turning its remains to more interesting use is a highly constructive pursuit.

3. Avoid remarks which associate imagination with anxiety. Children often come up with preposterous and clearly impossible tales of the things that happened to them and their friends. Instead of scolding him for lying, or dismissing his stories with comments such as: 'What nonsense . . .!' 'Why do you talk such rubbish . . .?' see them as exercises in imagination. Rather than repressing their fantasies do your best to encourage their desire to use their minds freely and vividly.

4. Adopt the same approach when the child offers explanations as to why things happen. If you are a very convergent thinker, who believes in strict, factual accuracy, some of the fantastic ideas a child dreams up may be extremely irritating.

'How on earth could it work like that?' the convergent parent protests angrily, before demolishing the child's reasoning with a detailed account of what really happens. Of course children have to be taught the cause and effect explanations which lie behind natural events. However romantic it may be to see a volcanic eruption as an underground dragon in a rage, or to explain the tides by a giant taking a bath, then stepping out again, the realities of life demand that he learns about subterranean pressures and the effect of the moon on the oceans. But teaching should be provided in such a way that imagination is fettered as little as possible. Very often the child appreciates that his suggestion is factually wrong but enjoys exercising his mind by exploring the possibilities which fantasy allows.

5. Do not regard fairy stories as old fashioned and harmful. Many parents, in my experience, believe that only factually accurate accounts should be presented to the child even in the guise of fiction:

'Why fill his head with a lot of nonsense?' one mother asked me while another objected that this kind of tale might turn her son into a sissy. Imaginative, even fantastic, stories, feed the child's own imagination and fantasies. They are just as important as those which provide information and instruction of a more down to earth kind. Do not sexually stereotype children by allowing the imagination of the boys to feed on one sort of literature while that of the girl is directed towards more suitably 'feminine' stories. I have suggested ways in which rich fantasies can be used to improve the more convergent aspects of problem solving. So even if you are disinclined to see any merit in these tales on their own account at least recognise them as a useful means to an end.

6. Parents are often concerned that watching too much television exposes children to needless amounts of violence or ideas of which they disapprove. I believe that of no less concern should be the way in which TV restricts imagination. When images and sounds are provided together the entire creative task is performed for the viewer who becomes the passive receptacle into which other people's ideas are poured. A book or a radio programme still allow people an active part in the process of creation, since their imaginations must be exercised in order to conjure up the scenes suggested but never wholly presented by stories or sounds. In this way the power of the mind is able to develop more fully and fantasy can flourish. By all means allow the child access to television to entertain and instruct. But do not let this medium dominate the home so that every spare moment is spent before the box. It is not enough to have a radio in the home or provide access to books. Children will only listen and read if encouraged to do so both by the attitudes their parents hold and the activities they themselves enjoy.

These days a popular management tool is the conference or workshop at which executives are taught to think creatively; mind expanding sessions designed to promote the type of divergent thinking I have been discussing. Although often very effective they always strike me as rather sorry indictments of the lessons learned during childhood. These businessmen would never have to be shown how to break out of their mental prisons had not life imprisoned them there in the first place.

Chapter Twenty-Two

GROWING GIFTED TOGETHER

In this book I have talked a great deal about school achievement, tests, grades, examinations and termly reports. From this emphasis on intelligence as a means of academic attainment it may appear, despite my comments in the first chapter, that the view taken of intellectual ability is a narrow, materialistic one. It might seem that the greater opportunities I discussed at the start of the programme are all equated with paper qualifications and that mental skills which do not advance the cause of school success are dismissed as less significant.

Nothing could, in fact, be further from the truth. The purpose of this teaching programme is not to support the current educational *status quo* or to shape the child's mind in order to fit the expectations of society. Indeed it is my firm belief that the present emphasis of academic study on examinations and assessments represents the antithesis of what true learning should be all about.

This disquiet is, I know, shared by many parents, teachers and educationalists. It would be far better to live in a society where knowledge was looked on as an end in itself, rather than as a means to the relatively trivial goal of getting a passmark in an attainment test. If learning were regarded in this light then we would realise that creativity and imagination are just as valuable as the ability to solve problems correctly, often in a somewhat mechanical and basically unintelligent manner. We would appreciate the merit of other forms of mental ability, such as social intelligence, that all too rare talent for oiling the wheel of personal and professional relationships. We would be able to recognise individual worth which had nothing to do with whether a child had gained more pieces of paper in class than his companion. Liberated from the straitjacket demands of the timetable and examination syllabus, teachers would be free to encourage a more wide-ranging curiosity about the world and students would have enough time to develop at their own pace. Only then could education, as opposed to instruction, flourish in the class-rooms and children find joy instead of drudgery in learning. We do not, of course, achieve any of these important goals. Children lose interest, develop negative attitudes, come to see themselves as unfitted for intellectual activities and so leave school a little more knowledgeable but a great deal more basically ignorant than when they first sat down behind a desk! More ignorant because the lively curiosity of their preschool years has been removed and an apathetic indifference transplanted in its place. More ignorant because a natural interest in the world around them has been replaced by an unnatural acceptance of the soundness of certain views, the correctness of particular opinions and the validity of specific claims. Healthy intellectual doubt and valuable, questioning, uncertainty have been transformed into blinkering certainty in which the most palpable fictions can be elevated to the status of fact because they have appeared in print in a school textbook.

A story is told of Einstein's small grandchild coming to visit his eminent grandfather and being asked what he had learned in school:

'We were taught that parallel lines can never meet,' replied the youngster.

'But my dear child,' responded the mathematician, 'of course they can!'

It is said that the child thereafter was inclined to question everything he was taught. Were that true I would rate it as one of his grandfather's most worthwhile achievements.

For the truth is that most of the things a child learns in school are irrelevant to anything that is going to happen to him in later life, many are at best half-truths while a great number are plain nonsense. Yet all are afforded equal merit and can carry equivalent weight in an examination.

All that having been said, it is still necessary to recognise the reality of the situation rather than to pretend we are living in a more ideal and idealistic world. It is one thing for parents to build castles in the air, quite another matter to expect children to live in them. Some families, I know, manage to drop out of the conventional educational system. Rightly rejecting its assumptions and goals they teach their children at home, in their own way and according to their own philosophy. In many instances such an approach is overwhelmingly successful. But it would be totally unrealistic to suppose that all children, everywhere, could be taught by these means.

The vast majority of young people will continue to receive their education within the state authorised system and be required to satisfy its standards and meet its expectations. The notion that examination results are the most effective means of judging a person's worth has been sold so long and hard by educational establishments that this means of assessment and selection seems unlikely to go out of style in the foreseeable future. Employers, principals of colleges of further education and university admissions boards will continue to refer to paper qualifications when deciding whether a young person is suited to a vacancy in their firm or a place on their course. So classroom success *is* important. Tests and assessments *do* matter. In the context of present day demands they not only serve a valuable purpose but represent an important expression of intellectual ability.

That having been acknowledged, we should also consider in what other ways a high level of intelligence is valuable. In Chapter One I talked about its importance as a means of providing the child with choice. Of giving him the opportunity to decide which road to take in life.

Essentially, choice means deciding between alternative proposals. Of selecting which of a particular set of problems are going to be solved. For instance, the teenager making up his mind whether to study physics or chemistry to Advanced Level is really conducting a debate over which sort of intellectual challenges he is likely to find most interesting and which type of problems his mind is best equipped to solve.

Solving problems, in the widest sense, is what intelligence is really all about as I made clear in Chapter Three. It is in this ability to solve a wider range of problems more rapidly and efficiently than other species on earth that mankind has – at least in the short term – developed the power of world domination.

Natural selection, the process by which all living things evolve, has been called the survival of the fittest. It would be more accurate to describe it as the disappearance of the unfittest, since nature does not so much favour the more successful species but leads to the rapid extinction of those unable to match the changing demands of their environments.

The dinosaurs lived and flourished for millions of years yet, it appears, vanished within a generation when the climate changed and their food supplies dwindled. The unfortunate dodo, with its clumsy body and flightless wings, survived happily on Mauritius until the arrival of predatory humans who found it delicious to eat. Unable to fight or flee, the wretched creature was consumed off the face of the earth.

Intelligence, the ability to learn and adapt; to make choices rather than having them thrust upon us; the power to solve and see problems has proved the most effective survival strategy ever known on earth. It may not, of course, turn out to be the most successful *long term* strategy since there appears a better than even chance it will lead to the nuclear annihilation of the human race. But on past performance, and a more optimistic future prediction, it is unquestionably a highly efficient method for dealing with changes. Changes so dramatic that a species less flexible in its intellectual capacity might long ago have been overwhelmed.

Survival, in the Western world at least, is more concerned with psychological health than bare physical subsistence. We are less bothered about finding food and shelter than with the satisfaction of such emotional needs as recognition, affection, regard and self-fulfilment. I have already suggested some of the ways in which a high IQ can help us attain these necessary goals in life.

In helping your child towards successful mental development it is this capacity to cope with change that I ask you to bear in mind above the short term advantages of school achievement. We live in a world where change occurs rapidly and continuously. Where the ideas, standards and beliefs of yesterday may be seen as foolish, restrictive or unhelpful tomorrow. Where, instead of taking a job for life, most people will be expected to follow a number of careers during their working lives and, perhaps, go through several periods of retraining. We live in a world where men and the machines they create are likely to become on increasingly equal terms so far as problem-seeing and problem solving ability are concerned. However much we dislike the prospect it seems inevitable that society will be increasingly shaped and dominated by machines which have the ability to think, if not in the same way as ourselves then certainly to the same extent, and probably in some instances far more efficiently.

To survive and retain some degree of control over one's destiny in such a world will demand the highest possible levels of intelligence. If we fail to realise the hope of Professor John McVicker Hunt, which I described on page 11 of this book, and truly raise the intellectual capacity of the vast majority of the population then society will be increasingly divided into two polarised groups. An elite who understand and can use the technology of change and a vast, uncomprehending mass which has no real appreciation of the systems which dominate their lives and even less knowledge of how such systems can be controlled.

There is no magic formula which can transform the under-achieving child into an intellectual giant overnight. Mental ability can be enhanced and the developing brain of the young can be significantly enriched by following the programme outlined in this book. But it will take time and it will take trouble on your part to bring about the necessary increases in understanding, the essential improvements in attitude, self-image and motivation. The vital acquisition of more effective strategies for handling problems in school and elsewhere.

Your reward for such an investment will be a child better equipped to deal with life successfully. But this will not be your only reward. For the skills, attitudes and perceptions taught in this programme can benefit you just as greatly. Many of the parents who have trained their children in the use of these procedures have reported a rapid and lasting improvement in their own intellectual abilities. They have gained greater confidence, a more realistic self-image and a stronger degree of motivation as a result of reading and working with this material. They have found that the methods designed to help their child remember things more easily and to analyse problems more logically work just as well with their own difficulties of recall and answer finding.

'I started out by hoping I could improve my child's thinking ability,' said one father, 'and ended up finding that I was brighter as well.'

As I have stressed throughout this book, the development of intellect is not something which takes place in isolation. A bright child reflects not only his personal mental abilities but the interactions occurring within the family unit as a whole. All the key factors are intimately related to one another. Change one and you change them all, for better or for worse.

Your child does not grow gifted alone. You can grow gifted together. By helping him to a brighter future, I am sure you will find – like many parents have done in the past – that you teach yourself greater intelligence as well.

Bibliography

AMBROSE, A., *Stimulation in Early Infancy*. London : Academic Press, 1969.

AMMON, P. R., Cognitive development and early childhood education : Piagetian and neo-Piagetian theories. In H. L. Hom and P. A. Robinson (Eds), *Psychological Processes in Early Education*. New York : Academic Press, 1977.

ANASTASI, A., *Psychological Testing*. New York : Macmillan, 1976.

ATKINSIN, R. C., et. al. (1964). Short-term memory with young children. *Psychonomic Science*, 1 : 255–256.

AUSUBEL, D. P., *The Psychology of Meaningful Verbal Learning*. New York : Gruen and Stratton, 1963.

AUSUBEL, D. P., and SULLIVAN, E. V., *Theory and Problems of Child Development*. New York : Gruen and Stratton, 1970.

BARBE, W. B. and RENZULLI, J. S., *Psychology and Education of the Gifted*. New York : Irvington Publishers, 1975.

BELL, R. Q. and HARPER, L. V., *Child Effects on Adults*. Hillsdale : Lawrence Erlbaum Associates, 1977.

BIRDWHISTELL, R. L., *Kinesics and Context. Essays on Body Motion Communication*. London : Penguin Books, 1973.

BRUNER, J. S., *Toward a Theory of Instruction*. Cambridge, Mass. : Harvard University Press, 1966.

BURSTALL, J., *French from Eight. A National Experiment*. Occasional Pub. Series 18. NFER. 1968.

CAMP, B. W., BLOM, HERBERT and VAN DOORNINCK, 'Think Aloud' : A Programme for developing self-control in young, aggressive boys. *Journal of Abnormal Child Psychology*, 1977, 5, 157–169.

CHI, M. T., Short-term memory limitations in children : Capacity or processing deficits? *Memory and Cognition*, 1976, 4 : 559–572.

CORNOLDI, C., *Memoria e Immaginazione*. Padova: Patron, 1976.

CRONBACH, L. J., *Essentials of Psychological Testing*. New York: Harper and Row, 1970.

DANNER, F. W. and TAYLOR, A. M., Integrated pictures and relational imagery training in children's learning. *Journal of Experimental Child Psychology*, 1973, 16: 47–54.

DENENBERG, V. H. (Ed), *Education of the Infant and Young Child*. New York: Academic Press, 1970.

DIMOND, S. J., *Neuropsychology: A Textbook of Systems and Psychological Functions of the Human Brain*. London: Butterworths, 1980.

DOMAN, G., *What to do About Your Brain Injured Child*. London: Jonathan Cape, 1975.

DOXIADIS, S. (Ed), *The Child in the World of Tomorrow. A Window into the Future*. Oxford: Pergamon Press, 1979.

DWEK, C. A., Children's interpretation of evaluative feedback: The effect of social cues on learned helplessness. *Merrill-Palmer Quarterly*, 1976, 13, 275–283.

FORTIN-THERIAULT, A., Comparaison de deux méthodes d'apprentissage par conflit cognitif. Unpublished doctoral dissertation, University of Montreal, 1977.

FRESTON, C. W. and DREW, C. J. J., Verbal performance of learning disabled children as a function of input organisation. *Journal of Learning Disabilities*, 1974, 7, 424–428.

GAGNE, R. M., Contributions of learning to human development. *Psychological Review*, 1968, 75: 177–191.

GAZZANIGA, M. S. and BLAKEMORE, C., *Handbook of Psychobiology*. New York: Academic Press, 1975.

GESELL, A., ILG, F. L. and AMES, L. B., *The Child from Five to Ten*. London: Hamish Hamilton, 1973.

GLANZER, M. and CUNITZ, A. R., Two storage mechanisms in free recall. *Journal of Verbal Learning and Verbal Behaviour*, 1966, 5: 352–360.

GREEN, D. W. and SHALLICE, T., Direct visual access in reading for meaning. *Memory and Cognition*, 1976, 4: 753–758.

GUILFORD, J. P., *The Nature of Human Intelligence*. New York: McGraw-Hill, 1967.

HAGEN, J. W., Some thoughts on how children learn to remember. *Human Development*, 1973, 44: 201–204.

HAMACHEK, D. E., *Encounters With Self*. New York: Holt, Reinhart and Winston, 1978.

HAYES-ROTH, F., Uniform representations of structured patterns and an algorithm for the induction of contingency-response rules. *Information and Control*, 1977, 33 : 87–116.

HINDE, R. A. (Ed), *Non-Verbal Communication*. Cambridge University Press, 1972.

HOLT, J., *How Children Fail*. London: Penguin Press, 1965.

HOLT, J., *Escape from Childhood*. London: Penguin Press, 1974.

INHELDER, B. and PIAGET, J., *The Early Growth of Logic in the Child: Classification and Seriation*. London: Routledge and Kegan Paul, 1964.

JONES, B. N. (Ed), *Ethological Studies of Child Behaviour*. London: Cambridge University Press, 1976.

JONES, R. A., *Self-Fulfilling Prophecies. Social, Psychological and Physiological Effects on Expectancies*. Hillsdale: Lawrence Erlbaum Associates, 1977.

KEENEY, T. J., CANNIZZO and FLAVELL. Spontaneous and induced verbal rehearsal in a recall task. *Child Development*, 1967, 38, 935–966.

KIRBY, F. D. and TOLLER, H. C., Modification of preschool and isolate behaviour: A Case study. *Journal of Applied Behaviour Analysis*, 1970, 3, 309–314.

KLATZKY, R. L., *Human Memory: Structures and Process*. San Francisco, California: 1975.

KNAPP, M. L., *Non-Verbal Communication in Human Interaction*. New York: Holt, Reinhart and Winston, 1978.

KRASNER, L. and ULLMANN, L. P., *Behaviour, Influence and Personality. The Social Matrix of Human Action*. New York: Holt, Reinhart and Winston, 1973.

KRASNER, L. and ULLMANN, L., *Research in Behaviour Modification. New Developments and Implications*. New York: Holt, Reinhart and Winston, 1965.

KREITLER, H. and KREITLER, S., *Cognitive Orientation and Behaviour*. New York: Springer, 1976.

KREUTZER, M. A., et al., An interview study of children's knowledge about memory. *Monographs of the Society for Research in Child Development*, 1975, 40 (1, Serial Number 159).

LESGOLD, A. M., et. al., Pictures and young children's learning from oral prose. *Journal of Educational Psychology*, 1974, 66: 17–24.

LEVI, J. R. and ALLEN, V. L., *Cognitive Learning in Children. Theories and Strategies*. London: Academic Press, 1976.

LEWIS, D., *How to be a Gifted Parent*. London: Souvenir Press, 1979.

LEWIS, D., *The Secret Language of Your Child*. London: Souvenir Press, 1978.

MARTENIUK, R. G., *Information Processing and Motor Skills*. New York: Holt, Reinhart and Winston, 1976.

MISCHEL, W., *Personality and Assessment*. New York: John Wiley and Sons, 1968.

NEWELL, S. and SIMON, H., *Human Problem Solving*. Englewood Cliffs, N.J.: Prentice Hall, 1972.

ORNSTEIN, P. R. (1978), *Memory Development in Children*. London: Lawrence Erlbaum.

PALARDY, J. M., What teachers believe – what children achieve. *Elementary School Journal*, 1969. 370–4.

PARKER, T. B., FRESTON, C. W., and DREW, C. J., Comparison of verbal performance of normal and learning disabled children as a function of input organisation. *Journal of Learning Disabilities*, 1975, 8, 386–393.

PARSONS, J. A., The reciprocal modification of arithmetic behaviour and programmes development. In G. Semb (Ed), *Behaviour analysis and education* – 1972. Lawrence: University of Kansas, Dept. Human Dev. 1972.

PAVIO, A., *Imagery and Verbal Processes*. New York: Holt, 1971.

PERVIN, L. A., *Personality, Theory, Assessment and Research*. New York: John Wiley and Son, 1975.

PIAGET, J., *The Origin of Intelligence in the Child*. London: Routledge and Kegan Paul, 1953.

PIAGET, J. and INHELDER, B., *Memory and Intelligence*. New York: Basic Books, 1973.

POPHAM, W. J., *Educational Evaluation*. Englewood Cliffs, N.J.: Prentice-Hall, 1975.

POPPER, K. R. and ECCLES, J. C., *The Self and Its Brain. An Argument for Interactionism*. Springer International, 1977.

REESE, H. W., Models of memory and models of development. *Human Development*, 1973, 16: 397–416.

RING, B. C., Effects of input organisation on auditory short-term memory. *Journal of Learning Disabilities*, 1977, 9, 591–595.

RIST, R. C., Student social class and teacher expectations: the self-fulfilling prophecy in ghetto education. *Harvard Educational Review*, 1970, 40, 411–51.

SCHAFFER, H. R. (Ed), *Studies in Mother-Infant Interaction*. New York: Academic Press, 1977.

SCHER, J. (Ed), *Theories of the Mind*. London: Collier Macmillan, 1962.

SELIGMAN, M. E. P., *Helplessness – On Depression, Development and Death*. San Francisco: W. H. Freeman and Company, 1975.

SHORTER, E., *The Making of the Modern Family*. London: Collins, 1976.

SIEGLER, R., *Children's Thinking: What Develops?* Hillsdale, N.J.: Erlbaum, 1978.

STRAIN, P. S., COOKE, P., APOLLONI, T., *Teaching Exceptional Children*. London: Academic Press, 1976.

STRAUSS, S. and LANGER, J., Operational thought inducement. *Child Development*, 1970, 41: 163–175.

TENNEY, Y. J., The child's conception of organization and recall. *Journal of Experimental Child Psychology*, 1975, 19: 100–114.

TIZARD, B. and HARVEY, D. (Eds), *Biology of Play*. London: Heinemann Medical Books, 1977.

TORGESEN, J. K., The role of non-specific factors in the task performance of learning disabled children: A theoretical assessment. *Journal of Learning Disabilities*, 1977, 10, 27–34.

TORGESEN and GOLDMAN. Verbal rehearsal and short-term memory in reading-disabled children. *Child Development*. 1977, 48, 56–60.

GRIMM, J. A., BIJOU and PARSONS. A problem-solving model for teaching remedial arithmetic to handicapped young children. *Journal of Abnormal Child Psychology*. 1973, 1, 26–39.

TYLER, L. E., *The Psychology of Human Differences*. Englewood Cliffs: Prentice Hall, 1965.

WECHSLER, D., *Selected Papers of David Wechsler*. New York: Academic Press, 1974.

WHITE, B. L., KABAN, B. T., and ATTANUCCI, J. S., *The Origins* of *Human Competence. The Final Report of the Harvard Preschool Project.* Lexington Books, 1979.

WOOD, M. E., *Children: The Development of Personality and Behaviour.* London : Harrap, 1973.

YENDOVITSKAYA, T. V., Development of Memory. In Zaprpahets and Elhonin (Eds), *The Psychology of Preschool Children.* Cambridge, Mass. : MIT Press, 1971.

YOUNG, J. Z., *Programs of the Brain.* Oxford University Press, 1978.

Index